Women who do and women who don't join the women's movement

Women who do and women who don't join the women's movement

Edited and introduced by
Robyn Rowland

Routledge & Kegan Paul
London, Boston, Melbourne and Henley

First published in 1984
by Routledge & Kegan Paul plc
39 Store Street, London WC1E 7DD, England
9 Park Street, Boston, Mass. 02108, USA
464 St Kilda Road, Melbourne,
Victoria 3004, Australia and
Broadway House, Newtown Road,
Henley-on-Thames, Oxon RG9 1EN, England
Typeset in Baskerville 11pt by
Academic Typesetting Service, Gerrards Cross
Printed in Great Britain
by T.J. Press, Padstow

Library of Congress Cataloging in Publication Data

Women who do and women who don't join the women's
movement.
Bibliography: p.
Includes index.
1. Feminism.   2. Women – Psychology.   3. Feminists –
Case studies.   I. Rowland, Robyn.
HQ1154.W8893   1984   305.4'2   83-24502

ISBN 0-7102-0296-2

For Caroline,
and for my grandmothers,
Christina and Mary

Contents

Preface
'With or without blindfold, madam?'

I have been a feminist in action and spirit since adolescence when I first came to understand the way power operates between girls and boys when dating, and how hard it was to be 'a good girl, a proper girl' and still keep 'them' interested. It was a question of how to be desirable without being used, and no one seemed able to answer it. There was no sense of fair play about relations between the sexes at all. Fairness is to give equal validity to, equal time to, equal space to, a person or idea, and then make your decision without reducing or obliterating the other. I also railed at being told not to argue and that I, as a girl, knew nothing. I took up competitive swimming and that helped the anger as well as making me strong. I kept it up for twelve years and became the first woman at the University of New South Wales to win a swimming blue. So who said anger was unproductive!

Work has always fascinated me and continues to do so. I find that in work I can create a special relationship with myself that is challenging and exciting. Ideas are living things, flexible, flowing, or taut, depending on their mood and treatment. This is, of course, mainly the work I do 'after hours'. I work hard and enjoy it, but have always resented working three times as hard as my male colleagues for no greater rewards and lower pay.

My own articulation of what it means to be a woman in this unequal society of ours, was a gradual process. It took time and thinking and reading and arguing to develop an understanding of power and the *fact* that men as a group dominate women and have much greater control over their own lives than do women. As individuals, most men acquiesce in this system of male dominance which ensures that they are well looked after, dressed nicely, have their mothers' Christmas presents bought for them, and receive continuous emotional patching, soothing and support, without which they could not function. When denied this, much foot-stamping takes place. On the other hand, there are a few men who try to yield that dominance which is theirs purely by right of sex, and who listen and understand. For these men, their socialization towards violence and pettiness when denied their every want, is continuously fought against. But this takes the kind of emotional effort that all women make daily.

My mother told me when I was a kid that 'you can do *anything* if you try hard enough'. I said scornfully that I wouldn't be able to lift a car! My mother stared me hard in the eye and said: 'If you *really* wanted to, you could.' And she believed it – and in that moment, so did I.

My father said that debating is a skill which leads to a mastery of yourself and helps to give you a balanced view of things. He said there are many sides to an argument and you have to listen and weigh up the pros and cons. I might add that he still manages to have very strong opinions on most things! I call it obstinacy, he calls it persistence – but I bought the theory of balance.

Only my faith in women, with all their strength, their gentleness, their faults; my concern for listening to all points of view; and my tenacity and belief in doing the impossible, could have made me continue this book once it was started. There are dangers here for us all. Some feminists will be appalled that so much space has been given to the 'enemy', but may find it more difficult than they thought to condemn the women along with the ideas. Antifeminists may feel that they have misguidedly wandered into alien territory, but might find their similarities with feminists more disturbing than they anticipate. There may also be a feeling of uneasiness which it is difficult to articulate clearly, and in many ways the book is unnerving. There is also the anxiety about how it will be used, but I have no control over that. The enemies of women have always used our own words and actions against us – this will be no exception.

This is not a book meant to divide. I want to take a look at what women think the women's movement represents *now*, not back in the 1960s, and where they feel its strengths and its weaknesses lie. I want to know *why* some women can have similar experiences, yet one becomes a feminist and the other an antifeminist. What this book shows is that the 'goodies' and 'baddies' according to each 'side' are not always so clearly identifiable. And why should it be so straight-forward? Women's lives and experiences, their values and their personalities are not clear, single and so easy to under-stand.

There are opinions in this book which I fiercely agree with and there are those I would sternly condemn. But I have tried to present them all in their own light and to give validity to the experiences and opinions of all the women concerned. I have aimed for 'balance'. No woman has been 'set up': I refuse to accept the role of surrogate oppressor.

The book begins with a discussion of the women's move-ment as a social movement, and an analysis of its origins and the major issues involved in its struggle. The antifeminist 'backlash' is then discussed, and its platforms are presented. This introduction is intended to supply a social context or background to which the experiences of the contributors can be related. There follows a series of short chapters written by women who relate positively or negatively to the women's movement; and their voices bring the issues alive, creating a diverse pattern of women's interpretations of being female. In the conclusion I draw together some of the issues on which the contributors agree and disagree, and attempt an answer to the question of why women choose feminism or antifeminism.

This has been a rewarding but difficult enterprise and I have been faced with issues often side-tracked as 'too diffi-cult'. I have warm feelings for the women who are part of this book, and some have become friends. I have felt, and still feel, that I stand between two firing squads, but life and intellect are nothing if they lack challenge and the need for personal courage. More women now than ever before, feel vulnerable and encroached upon by aggressive values that fail to produce the warm, loving and caring society which the future could and should hold for us all. More women are fighting back. I share with that great writer, feminist and humanitarian Adrienne Rich, the 'dream of a common language'. I hope that after the inevitable debate over the issues here subsides, we will have reached a stronger consensus among women about the needs and rights we have, and a clearer vision of the future our daughters might demand.

Acknowledgments

In the production of a book, there are always many people who create the fabric of support so necessary for a person to write. I thank them all.

Particularly I want to thank my parents, Gwen and Norm, who gave me their love, strength, and positive attitudes; and who equipped me for my chosen tasks in the thousand ways that parents can, often without knowing and most often with little reward.

For over ten years, I was also fortunate enough to have the friendship, love and *real* emotional support that all people crave in their most intimate relationship. An unusual man, Trevor Irwin helped me to create a challenge out of obstacles and to strive always for excellence.

And to Dale Spender, whose encouragement and friendship I value so dearly, my thanks for initial discussions on the idea for this book, though I must absolve you from a part in its final form. And for being Dale: full of boundless energy, wit and humour; who makes laughter an essential part of revolution.

Finally, for their endless patience, kindness and care, thank you Judy, Bev, Janene, Ella, Natasha and Antionetta. Now *that* is a pool of real energy.

Part one
Introduction

1 The women's movement as a social movement

The modern women's movement began as early as the eighteenth century but experienced a peak of activity during the campaign for the vote for women.[1] Since the 1960s it has again experienced a resurgence in Western countries. A 'backlash' against the movement is now occurring and it too has its precedent. In the 1920s under reaction, the movement became dormant and many feminists joined the peace movement.[2] It is worth remembering, though, that it was in 1923 that the Women's Party in America succeeded in getting the Equal Rights Amendment (ERA) introduced into Congress. Now the ERA has been defeated after nearly sixty years of struggle. This book is timely then when we consider that women's groups have played a powerful role in its defeat.

A social movement has been defined as a group of people with a purpose which will bring about change and whose influence is 'spreading in opposition to the established order in which it originated' (Gerlach and Hine, 1970, p. xvi). A significant amount of power 'can be mobilised outside the power structure of a society' which can exert surprising pressure on that power structure (*ibid.*, p. 218). Both personal and social change result from social movements which, Carolyn Sherif comments, are often initiated by groups trying to deal with 'social problems that have been generated by contradictions and inequities in the ways different aspects of life are organised' (1976, p. 366).

The development of social movements passes through a number of stages. Social unrest springs from an awareness of

3

social inequality and a personal discontent. These problems are seen as social problems needing collective action, rather than as individual issues with personal solutions. This occurs during a period of strong national political activity, when governments are repressing protest.[3] A person with doubts about the existing social order is more likely to be sensitive to experiences of social injustice and will be ready to accept the need for change.[4]

Individuals then seek groups with whom to identify and communication networks are established. These encourage group formation and the recruitment of others. They develop on the basis of common problems and so their initial energy is centred on these issues and on expressing their anger and frustration. Carolyn Sherif notes that in these early stages of a movement, people are 'inwardly more united, more clear, and concentrate their tactics on what they are *against*' rather than what they are for (1976, p. 380).

As Betty Friedan indicated in 1963, during the 1960s women were experiencing 'the problem that had no name'. These were well-educated middle-class women who felt that in the process of marrying and having children they had lost part of themselves, or even their sense of self-identity.

There was at this time in Britain, America, and Canada, and a few years later in New Zealand and Australia, general social unrest in the form of a civil rights movement, a black rights movement and an anti-Vietnam movement. There is a strand of liberalism within the women's movement which stresses the rights of the individual and autonomy,[5] and this period constantly emphasised 'self'. Part of this was a reaction to the terrors of war which had sunk into the minds of people and led them to question their authorities.

Women too questioned *their* authorities who had made childbearing a burden; had made sex unsatisfying because clitoral orgasm was 'infantile'; had made them slaves to the suburban mod-con image of capitalist society in which they were the main consumers; and had used them as sex objects to sell the very products they were encouraged to buy.

Women in the civil rights movement and the New Left also became disillusioned with their roles: they were the dishwashers of the revolution. Stokely Carmichael had made his oft-quoted statement that the only position for women in the black movement was prone. In Britain, Juliet Mitchell wrote 'The Longest Revolution' for the *New Left Review* (1966) pointing out that women and the 'woman question' had been left out of their analysis and therefore their vision of the future. In Australia Zelda D'Aprano chained herself across the doors of the Commonwealth Building in Melbourne as a protest against the lack of equal pay for women. Marian Simms wrote of Zelda: 'The politics of experience had transformed her from a socialist into a feminist' (1978, p. 94). If the first wave had been motivated by the failure of the Abolitionist movement to deal fairly with women, the second wave was spurred on by disillusionment with the civil rights movements and the New Left.

But the New Left had strong networks which women utilised. Women's caucuses and professional groups were formed and women's newspapers re-emerged. A number of major organising bodies developed in each country, e.g. the National Organisation of Women (NOW) in North America in 1966; the National Women's Co-ordinating Committee (NWCC) in 1970, and the National Joint Action Campaign for Women's Equal Rights (NJACWER) in 1969 in Britain; and Women's Electoral Lobby (WEL) in 1972 in Australia. Networking linked women. It was and still is one of the most valuable contributions of the women's movement to the breaking down of women's isolation.

Carolyn Sherif has noted the need for referent groups in a new movement, with whom people can identify. The early consciousness-raising (CR) groups fulfilled this need. Women met and communicated their problems, and their 'bill of gripes'. They came to understand that social structures had defined their role for them and that others were also dissatisfied with that role. The slogan 'the personal is political' emerged, and meant, for example, that when a woman is *forced* to have sex with her husband it is a political act because it reflects the power dynamics in the relationship: wives are property to which husbands have full access. With the support of others like them, women were creating new, positive self-images.

Another important aspect of the CR groups was that women began to talk with each other. They discovered that women were interesting, stimulating and likeable. They felt a collective caring and a collective power: a belief that 'sisterhood is powerful'.

The women's movement thus re-emerged from both personal and social sources, and sought change in both areas. The basic problem was seen to be – what caused the inequalities between the sexes and how could they be changed. But groups within the movement differed in their answers to this problem and essentially two approaches to change developed: a reform of the existing structures, or an overturning of them in revolution.

2 Membership and structure of the women's movement

Like most social movements, the women's movement is not homogeneous but consists of numerous groups with different aims. Their one overriding similarity is that they seek changes in our society which give women a choice of lifestyle and help them to fulfil their potential as individuals. Feminist writers have labelled these groups according to their ideologically based approaches to social change.

Shulamith Firestone in 1972 delineated three basic groups of feminists: conservatives, politicos, and radicals. The *conservative feminists* are those concerned, in her words, with 'the more superficial symptoms of sexism' (1972, p. 39). They would be represented by NOW in North America and in Australia by WEL. These groups are structured and seek to reform the existing legal, social, political and employment situations. Since Firestone wrote her book, various governments have established departments or advisers on 'women's affairs'. Women working in these positions are often labelled 'femocrats', an ambivalent term. Whatever feelings women may have about the value of these positions, for many they do offer psychological and practical support, and often manage to change existing laws or situations which are discriminatory. Equal Opportunity Boards and anti-discrimination legislation have been created as toothless tigers, but they can often aid the individual even if they cannot change the position of women as a social class. Although many middle-class women have availed themselves of these support structures, working-class women are often too intimidated by employers and by fears of job loss to use the system.

Firestone's second group, the *'politicos'*, are basically women whose primary loyalty is to the Left or the black movement. For them, feminism is a tangent or 'secondary in the order of political priorities and must be tailored to fit into a pre-existent (male-created) political framwork' (*ibid.*, p. 41). She argued that people in the Left and black movements refused women the right 'to organise around their oppression *as they see and define it*' (p. 40, her italics). In the case of the Equal Opportunity Board, discussed above, they could argue that class was an essential and primary component in the working of such middle-class oriented committees.

The *radical feminists*, described more favourably by Firestone, are those who see 'feminist issues not only as *women's* first priority, but as central to any larger revolutionary analysis' (p. 43). They are revolutionary in their belief that change in the oppressed position of women can only emerge through a total overhaul of the social system. Radicals see men, marriage and the family as oppressors.[1]

Again the dynamic of reformist versus radical (or revolutionary) emerges. However, Jo Freeman points out that this division is misleading and simplistic and that 'it is structure and style of action rather than ideology that more accurately differentiates the various groups' (1979, p. 561).

If we consider the aspect of structure, it is clear that the *conservative* feminists working within bureaucracies or institutions are involved in hierarchical situations. They often belong to groups which are traditionally structured. But the method used by the *radical* arm of the movement was the 'rap' session or consciousness-raising (CR) group, which purportedly had no hierarchical structure. Jo Freeman sees the 'rap' group as the most valuable contribution of the women's liberation movement to social change, in that it caused personal attitudes to be questioned. She comments that 'once women have gone through such a resocialisation, their views of themselves and the world are never the same again even if they stop participating actively in the movement' (*ibid.*, p. 562). CR groups also encouraged women to learn skills they had not encountered before, like speaking out in public.

Because radical feminists believe in internal democracy within groups, the image of 'structurelessness' arose. But although unstructured groups enable women to share their experiences, they are ineffective in a direct political sense. A 'structureless' group is also a misnomer. What really occurs is a change in the *form* of the structure. An informal structure allows an individual with specific talents to achieve power by subtle means, and handicaps the less experienced woman who believes there is no structure and consequently that there are no power dynamics in the group.

In her analysis, Jo Freeman posits two ideologies within the movement which she names the Egalitarian Ethic (the sexes are equal, so the limits of imposed sex roles must be abolished), and the Liberation Ethic (not only must the limits be changed, but the contents of the roles themselves). If the first is stressed we have a women's *rights* movement, not a women's *liberation* movement. Freeman argues, however, that all groups have two theoretical concerns in common. The first is a feminist critique of society: that the sexes are basically equal and therefore observed differences between them should be carefully scrutinised. The second is the belief that women are oppressed. This oppression has two elements: *sociocultural* manifestations within the legal, economic, social and political systems; and *sociopsychological*, for example the group self-hate of women. Sexism is a particular kind of oppression and has two core concepts. First, that men are more important than women and therefore their work is more important. Second, that women are created to complement men and to assist them. Women are therefore defined *in relation to men*, and any woman who decides to live without men or outside their power and influence is labelled a 'man-hater'.

3 Issues and platforms within the movement

Because of ideological differences, varied perspectives have emerged on some issues. The major contentious issues are: abortion, sexuality, class, race, motherhood, the family and work. Of these, abortion has probably been the most difficult. As Adrienne Rich says, it is hardly the issue women would choose to 'symbolise our struggle for self-determination'; but it is one, she writes:

> which has been perhaps more mystified, more intellectualised and emotionalised than any other, and which glares out from the complex spectrum of issues surrounding women's claim to bodily - hence spiritual - integrity. (1980, p. 15)

The women's movement in general now supports the availability of abortion to all women who choose it. The drive to make abortion available initially joined the radicals and NOW in North America. Betty Friedan has commented on her concern that the issue would divide NOW, and quotes the preamble she wrote for the National Abortion Rights Action League which NOW eventually supported:

> asserting the right of the woman to control her own body and reproductive processes as her inalienable, human, civil right, not to be denied or abridged by the State, or any man (1977, p. 168).

After the Supreme Court decision in 1973 that women had

this basic right, abortion-related deaths dropped by nearly 600 per cent.[1]

Demand for safe, freely available abortion originally arose from concern over thalidomide and a rubella epidemic in the 1960s[2] and was increased by the availability of statistics on the deaths of women seeking 'backyard' help. Then it became part of the right of a woman to control her own reproduction. The stand on abortion is not in fact 'pro-abortion' but 'pro-choice'. It indicates the feminist belief that women are autonomous, independent and responsible people, and as such should be responsible for decisions affecting their lives and their bodies. It represents the right of women to be free from unwarranted governmental intrusion into their lives. It also recognises the fact that abortion is, and always has been, a method for women to control their fertility; and that if laws forbid it, women obtain it by clandestine methods endangering their lives and feeding a parasitic black market business.

The women's movement also changed women's attitudes towards their rights within sexual relationships with men. The Freudian notion of the double orgasm was dealt an almost fatal blow and women discovered they could enjoy their own sexuality. This arose out of women's freer discussion of their own bodies and how they work, and out of the availability of new and more secure forms of contraception. Women were now able to choose a partner without fear of pregnancy. *They* controlled their own fertility. With new information came an understanding that if orgasm occurred from clitoral stimulation, sexual intercourse with a male was not necessary to be 'sexual' or 'satisfied'. Lesbian groups within the movement began to speak out about their sexuality and their right to choose a female partner. Many became separatist, the political and the personal mingling to lead to a concept of society without the need to relate to men at all.

The issue of lesbianism caused (and often does still cause) divisions within the movement because many women are fearful of or have an aversion to homosexuality. For others, the meetings with and friendships between heterosexual and lesbian women has meant a broadening of personal perspectives and an introduction to a non-threatening non-male community of women.

At one period the issue of sexual identification did become

dangerously divisive. Anna Coote and Beatrix Campbell in their book *Sweet Freedom* (1982) trace the British experience which is a familiar one. The choice of lesbianism became a political act in which women were asked to hit out at men. For example, in 1979 the Leeds Revolutionary Feminists published a paper titled – 'Political Lesbianism: the case against Heterosexuality'. In this heterosexual women were described as 'collaborators with the enemy' and 'every woman who lives with or fucks a man helps to maintain the oppression of her sisters and hinders our struggle' (Coote and Campbell, 1982, p. 225). This attack depressed and alienated many heterosexual women who delayed fighting back for two reasons. First, they did not want to appear anti-homo-sexual. Second, many had husbands or lovers in relationships they wanted to continue; but *did* find a conflict in trying to wrench power from a 'social class' of 'men' while living with a member of that 'social class'.

Much of the anger generated has been resolved. But it is a conflict which the movement has had to accept as continuous and in a large part unresolvable. Writers like Adrienne Rich have done a great deal in extending the definition of sister-hood and love between women. She has created the term, the 'lesbian continuum'. This she uses to explain a range 'through each woman's life and throughout history – of woman-identified experience; not simply the fact that a woman has had a consciously desired genital sexual experience with another woman' – but meaning 'the sharing of a rich inner life, the binding against male tyranny, the giving and receiving of practical and political support (Rich, 1981).

The issue of social class has also been a contentious one. The women's movement has been labelled a middle-class movement, ignoring the problems of working-class women. Often discussions about 'women and work' are in terms of careers or middle-class jobs, but not about factory or assembly-line work. If the situation of middle-class women is compared to that of working-class women, the former are much better off. But Carolyn Sherif comments that 'relative deprivation' operates here. Women have always derived their social stand-ing and status from their fathers or husbands. Thus, in con-sidering the issue of equality, women compare 'themselves and their status with that of men at a comparative socio-economic level' and find their position unequal (1976, p. 371). In the case of both working and middle-class women, many of the dynamics of power and oppression in their relationships with men are the same.

Through the efforts of left-wing feminists the mainstream has opened up and working-class women are more vocal in and about the movement. An early instance of the impact of the movement on working-class women is evidenced in the Ford factory strike in Britain in 1968. This strike by women for equal pay had considerable success.[3] Women's groups established for working-class women are often self-help groups as opposed to CR groups, stressing a pragmatic approach to their problems. Some political thrusts by working-class women have been effective. For example, the Working Women's Charter Campaign in Australia influenced the Australian Council of Trade Unions to accept the Charter for Working Women in 1977.[4]

A number of conferences in Australia have also been attended by working-class women. Their papers are often biographically based, hopefully increasing the awareness of class difference in middle-class women. At the 1980 Women and Labour Conference in Melbourne, Thelma Prior gave a paper on 'My 45 Years in Industry' discussing her experiences as a factory worker and member of the Communist Party. Though she has serious criticisms of it, she says of the influence of the women's movement on working-class women:

> The big thing that has changed is that women are not as
> afraid as they were, and will speak out. With the support
> of the women in the women's movement, they can see
> that they are not on their own, and together, with others
> in factories or at home, we can fight and get a better
> standard of living and a better way of life for all. (1982,
> p. 132)

The class issue is important too with respect to migrant and minority group women. For example, in Australia most migrants, whether highly qualified or not, end up in lower paid working-class jobs. In a paper on Italian migrant women, Pieri, Risk and Sgro point out that Italian women had a strong women's movement in Italy and are ready to be part of an Australian women's movement if it is relevant to their struggles. They note that: '*Women at Work*, the multilingual newspaper published by the Melbourne Working Women's Centre, is well received and regularly read in the factories and offices where it is distributed, because it deals with and organises around issues that widely concern working women' (1982, p. 398).

The fourth issue is that of race. Many white women within the movement have assumed its relevance to non-white women without attempting to understand the difference in their experiences. Margaret Simons (1979) pinpoints a lack of sensitivity to the race issue in feminist writings. In Eloise Snyder's *The Study of Women* (1979), Beverly Lindsay's chapter encompasses the experiences of Black Women, Native American Women (Cheryl Metoyer), La Chicana (Noemi Lorenzana) and Asian American Women (Priscilla Ching-Chung). It is clear that 'minority' women are caught in a three-way bind: racially, sexually and economically. Often their feelings of racial solidarity have more meaning for them than identification with other (white) women.

The reluctance of minority women to be involved in the movement can originate from: a fear of dividing their own minority community; a lack of knowledge about feminism and its aims; the strong relationships of some minority groups with the church; and, among black women, the conviction that black men have been de-masculinised by white culture and it is *they* who need liberation.

Beverly Lindsay points out that many black women support some platforms of the women's movement, e.g. day-care centres, health education and adult education, and that the movement should stress the relevance of its various platforms to minority women. Pauline Terrelonge Stone argues that many black intellectuals disparage the issue of sexism because they fear it will be racially divisive, generating 'internal conflict between black males and black females' (1979, p. 583). She also attacks the concept of black matri-archy as a ploy to convince the black woman that she is only oppressed by race and not by sex, because *she* is more domi-nant than the black male. If she discusses sexism, she is adding to the emasculation of the black male. She comments:

marriage among blacks is just as much a union of unequals as it is in larger society; child rearing, domestic chores and custody of children are largely female concerns. Hence, it is erroneous to argue that the domestic patterns of white society are not replicated in the black community. The housewife model may not fit completely but it is closely approximated in the sense that black women must bear the brunt of the domestic-related chores, even when they work. (1979, pp. 578-9)

The final divisive issue involves family, motherhood and work. Radical feminists argue that because of the unequal distribution of power and the insistence that women are essentially responsible for children, we need to destroy the family and start again with a new structure. Less radical feminists have suggested changing family arrangements so that the unequal distribution of power and resources is changed, e.g. creating extended families to share the responsibilities regarding children. Whatever the perspective, most feminists agree that the standard traditional nuclear family had developed to a point where it enslaved women. It took away their power as a single independent individual (symbolised by their name change), restricted their ability to earn in the economy, and therefore made them dependent on men, like minors. It made the enjoyment and fulfilment of their lives dependent upon the moods and goodwill of a husband. Part of the marriage game involved the skill of choosing a 'good catch' - a man who had high status in the community and allowed you access to his resources on a fairly equitable basis. This exchange system in marriage, in which the women gave service both sexually and emotionally while rearing the children, and the man supplied food, shelter and financial support, came to be seen by many feminists as a form of prostitution.

It also emerged that in fact many women did not receive their due in the exchange, and that the 'services' performed by women were devalued. This was primarily for four reasons: they were domestic duties which even in the job market have low status; they were unpaid in a society which values paid labour; they were repetitive and not productive; and they were carried out mainly by women, who are socially less valued than men and therefore bring the value of the job into disrepute. In addition, the homemaker was found to be socially isolated, often able to talk only to small children during the day, and creating a self-definition which was negative and low in self-esteem. Stress was also put on husbands who had to supply all intellectual, emotional and social needs for their wives at the end of the day (see Myrdal and Klein, 1956).

The problem was that many feminists were living in a family unit and had also experienced its positive aspects. This produced tension and conflict within feminists themselves about their role in their own families and has led to divisions in the movement over solutions to the problems of family life. Anna Coote and Beatrix Campbell comment:

> Of course, it would be easier to develop a clear political analysis of family life if it were altogether a bad thing . . . but . . . there *are* ways in which the family can be a source of care, affection, strength and security. (1982, p. 101)

One of the major solutions to the domination and oppression of women in the family has been to encourage women to work in the workforce, thus decreasing their dependence. The platforms demanding, e.g. child-care, maternity leave and job sharing, arose because of the perceived rights of women (married or otherwise) to work in a job *and* to have children, if they choose to.

Feminists have also questioned the need of women to mother at all, and criticised the concept of the 'maternal instinct'. Some argue that it is a socially constructed 'instinct', while others that it is a female need which has been defined negatively by a male-dominated culture. For many, the choice not to have children has become a reality for the first time.

This is a brief presentation of the major platforms and issues of contention in the women's movement. The aim was not to argue the validity of these perspectives, nor to support positions with data readily available elsewhere, but to give a context and background of experience from which the pro-movement women in this book will be writing.

4 Antifeminists and the backlash

It is inevitable that a reaction or backlash should arise against a movement which is struggling for wide social change and having success in some areas. These successes could actually alter existing social structures. Furthermore, people are being asked to reconceptualise what being female and being male really mean, which is according to Judith Bardwick (1979) a threatening situation for many. The reaction to the movement is both a reaction to change of any kind, and a reaction to specific changes intended by feminists. Antifeminism is therefore a 'backlash', 'an attitude of opposition to change rather than a movement' (Heberle, 1951, p. 50).

It is also not without precedent. For example, in the mid-1920s a backlash to the movement occurred in which a variety of women's groups participated. Fears of what women would do with their vote spurred it on. Feminists had so narrowly pursued the vote, that they were left open to attack on issues of social and economic change, on which there was no consensus. Tactics in these attacks were similar to those of the current backlash, e.g. the red-baiting smear. Barbara Deckard notes an instance in America in 1924 when ex-Senator Weeks, who had been defeated by women's votes, 'produced a chart showing that all liberal women's groups were part of a "spider web" directed from Moscow!' (1979, p. 305).

There are social reasons why antifeminism appears now. In general, recession makes people insecure about the future and more likely to act in a conservative manner. In times of economic stress, people become more self-orientated materially, in the sense of wanting to ensure that *their* standard of living and set of values are not under threat. When youth unemployment rises it is easier to see the cause as a women's movement which insisted on 'changing things', than as the social and economic structure itself.

In addition, it could be argued that social structures in Western capitalist societies can cope well with a limited push for change which may be readily co-opted, but if the push begins to force real and lasting changes in the system it becomes a danger and needs to be crushed. Toch comments that in terms of social order the danger of a social movement can be counteracted in two ways:

> The first is to deal with the problem situations that give rise to social movements. . . . The second is to destroy the social movement. In most instances, the second alternative is far less expensive. (1966, p. 277)

The current conservative backlash is as much an attack on *all* changes brought about by the social movements of the 1960s, including black rights and gay rights, as it is on the women's liberation movement. In this sense there are a number of 'anti' groups which are in loose coalition, most often referred to as the New Right. Carolyn Sherif (1976) makes the observation that conservative pressure groups 'seldom appear as "anti-women" but as "pro" some value or institution that some women in the movement would be reluctant to attack, such as the Church, family, or even the economic and mental well-being of young males' (p. 384). These groups also present themselves as the previously 'silent majority' who are struggling to be heard over an articulate minority who have the ear of the press. Thus the pro-family women claim to represent 'the homemakers' of society, who on the whole do not support the women's liberation movement.

5 Who are the antifeminists?

Rosalind Pollack Petchesky (1981) claims that the New Right has gained ideological legitimacy through its focus on reproductive and sexual issues. It has thus appealed to various church groups and pro-family groups because of its self-identification as a coalition fighting to keep society 'moral'. Seymour Lipsett and Earl Raab write that backlash movements 'require an aggressively moralistic stance and will find it somewhere. There needs to be invoked some system of good and evil which transcends the political or social process and freezes it' (1970, p. 117). All the groups in the New Right have a strong moral stance: they represent a set of values which are good and decent and need defence against licentious, selfish and promiscuous people. The stress on issues like sexuality reinforces this position. Alan Crawford (1980) sees the rise of the New Right as also motivated by 'status frustration' which takes place when people see their prestige threatened by social inferiors.

The most clearly articulated discussions of the New Right have come from America. It is here that the backlash has been most organised and most successful. One reason for this is that it had a target at which to aim and around which to consolidate. That target was the defeat of the ERA, which has been attained. A second goal was the presidential elections. But fragmentation over specific issues is already surfacing.[1] Many anti-abortionists or pro-lifers are *not* pro-militarisation and pro-nuclear, which members of other New Right groups are.

The rise of the New Right in America provides a model

many backlash groups in other countries would like to emulate. Groups within the coalition represent, e.g. the Moral
Majority, Pro-Life, Pro-Family, Eagle Forum, Fundamentalist and other church groups, and the Right-To-Life associations. Their joint forums create an antifeminist, anti-social
welfare backlash. They claim a moral right to defend the
traditions of America, which include the 'self-made man',
the traditional family, and the right to a lack of interference
from the state in the lives of individuals.

They have used a networking system similar in style to
that of the women's movement. Their networks were gleaned
from organised religion and the right-to-life movement, which
gave them a nationally and locally established mass constitu-
ency.

Most of the organisations in the Right are led by men.
Sean Morton Downy is chairman of the Life Amendment
Political Action Committee; Richard Vigueri is chief fund-
raiser of the New Right; Paul Weyrich is head of the Committee for the Survival of a Free Congress; and Jerry Falwell
is head of Moral Majority. Zillah Eisenstein notes that these
men, along with George Gilder, an economist and consultant,
argue that to revitalise the American economy, 'policy
makers must aim to re-establish the dominance of the traditional white patriarchal family' (1982, p. 568).

The most prominent women leaders are Phyllis Schlafly
of Eagle Forum, Midge Decter, and Anita Bryant (before her
divorce). There have always been prominent women in antifeminist organisations.[2] They are necessary to ensure that
conservatives cannot be accused of being anti-women and
they give validity to the argument that 'women themselves
oppose women's liberation'. Because of the predominance of
men in the antifeminist backlash however, there is always the
strong contention that women are being used as 'stooges' to
repeat the antifeminist and sexist propaganda of right-wing
men.

Within the New Right there is a coalition of three basic
groupings: business groups threatened by changes in the
capitalist system; groups joined through moral issues and
traditional values; and groups fighting specific issues like
abortion. There are within this coalition, possible divisions
over differing ideologies. The New Right opposes politicians

who are liberal on issues like welfare, the environment and defense spending. But the right-to-life coalition attempts to appeal to 'humanist' people, who would support civil rights and welfare benefits. The 'pro-life feminists' and the growing 'left' of this coalition also support welfare and oppose nuclear power. To win the abortion issue, the right-to-life must maintain its humanist position, which the New Right may threaten.

Church groups are also objecting to the methods and values espoused by Moral Majority. In a 1976 editorial, the liberal Catholic journal *Commonweal* warned the bishops that they may become 'The conservative so-called "pro-life" (and perhaps anti-busing, anti-"welfare chislers", pro-arms race, pro-CIA) candidates . . . and the Church will have been had.'[3] Judith Bardwick (1979) also contends that anti-abortionists are only 'incidentally anti-feminist' because their 'antagonism to abortion is based on a moral principle and not on anti-feminism per se' (p. 17).

6 Motivations of the antifeminists

On the individual level, why do people become part of a backlash? If many women were inspired to join the women's movement in the 1960s and demand liberation, how is it that some *did not*? There are, of course, women too tired, too oppressed and too concerned with the survival of themselves and their children to have time to search for self-fulfilment. There are those who do not come into contact with the ideas of equality and liberation. But what about those who assertively *reject* the women's movement? What is different about these antifeminist women which leads them to denounce the moves for equality?

First, as indicated above, the backlash is not a 'women's' backlash: both men and women are involved. Of course, there are men who support feminism too. Many of them live with feminist wives and daughters, and try to empathise with, and understand, the experience of oppression as it is for women. But they do not attempt to *lead* the women's movement and do not presume to speak for women.

Men who are involved in the antifeminist groups often fear equality and a loss of power. Economic and political control are challenged by feminists, as are the rights of men to retain male preserves of any kind. The traditional power and privileges of manhood have been to have power over *some* men and over *all* women, and changes brought about by the women's movement have changed that dimension to a large extent. Some men agree to an equal sharing of power, but most do not, particularly when it relates to their own family.

There are two further groups of antifeminist men. The

first is conservative, idealising women and the traditional role. They see a true womanly fulfilment in the wife and mother role. The second group is antagonistic to women in general, is cynical about their abilities to fill *any* role and think they are suited to household labour, which they themselves devalue.[1]

The women who are antifeminist fall into two groups. The first are those who resist any change, fearful that it will aggravate a situation rather than improve it. Furthermore, when social roles change rapidly, women who are in a traditional situation may become anxious about their identity and role in life. Women in this group often perceive the women's movement to be devaluing the work done by the traditional wife and mother. They may find the job creative and satisfactory and feel they are being told their lives have been wasted.

The second group are those who are ideologically opposed to the women's movement. These fall again into three subgroups: the Specific Issues Antagonists, the Professional Traditional Women, and the Queen Bees. Specific Issues Antagonists are those who might oppose one or two aspects of the women's movement's platforms on ideological grounds. So, for example, they might be pro-child-care, equal opportunity and so on, but oppose abortion. Or they might oppose child-care, while believing in equal pay for women who work.

The Professional Traditional Woman is she who has reared children and worked in the home, and found it comfortable. She has done well within the traditional role for women. Having achieved this through her own initiatives, she then proceeds to professionalise her position by becoming a 'symbolic housewife'. That is, she is not so much one who actually stays within the realms of home, but one who speaks at official gatherings and travels frequently, delivering talks on the values of home life and home labour.

The third group are the Queen Bees, discussed by Graham Staines, Carol Tavris and Toby Jayaratne.[2] These are women who have achieved success within the system or the 'man's world', while often also raising a family. They have both *'professional* success (a high-status job with good pay) and *social* success (popularity with men, attractiveness, a good marriage)' (p. 55). Their antifeminism stems from a number of possible sources. They may be motivated by self-interest. Having been co-opted into a male system, they find it necessary to 'keep in' with the powers that be, identify with that power, and refer to other women as 'them'.

Queen Bees often do not want competition for their jobs and so attempt to keep other women *out* of the workforce. They have an 'individualism' philosophy, knowing that they achieved success because of their own efforts, and assuming, therefore, that any woman can. The Queen Bee ignores the argument that women are socialised to fulfil the female role, insisting that women make choices about their lives. She therefore opposes the concept of collective action.

So within the antifeminist groups there are women totally opposed to women's liberation, those who are opposed to only some of its platforms, and those who feel threatened and insecure by the changes proposed. There are also, of course, women who are indifferent or neutral on the topic, often because they feel they have never experienced discrimination and cannot understand what the fuss is about. Eloise Snyder (1979) points out that some antagonism may come from women who are unable to identify with the distorted picture of the movement delivered to them through the media's eye.

7 Platforms of the antifeminists

Because antifeminism is a *reaction* to the women's movement, its initial major energies have revolved around discrediting the movement's leaders and ideology. The women's movement is simplistically reduced, its major issues are presented as hard and fast and then attacked. The first mode of attack involves undermining the self-identity of women in the movement by personal derision. Snyder comments that 'such tactics as depicting movement activists as being ugly, man-hating, castrating bitches who were passed over in marriage, and should be at home performing household tasks' (p. 21) have been used against both the current and past women's movements.

Participants are labelled lesbians or communists or socialists, encouraging women who are not in those groups to be sidetracked into defending themselves. There are, of course, homosexual and communist women in the movement, just as there are heterosexuals and conservative politicians. By labelling feminists as 'lesbian' the antifeminists hope to bring into dispute the 'womanliness' and therefore 'desirability' of feminists. The strategy has doubtful impact, however, on women who are recreating their friendship and liking for other women, while breaking their dependence on men for their self-esteem. But it has helped to create the popular image of the 'ugly' feminist, which may have dissuaded some women from naming themselves as 'feminists'.

The second method of attack is to discredit the platforms of the movement. This is often done in cynical, ironic or vitriolic tones. Stassinopoulos writes:

Liberation is an ever-shifting horizon, a total ideology
that can never fulfil its promises. It acts as a temporary
palliative for its true believers by generalising their specific
problems into universal grievances. It has the therapeutic
quality of providing emotionally-charged rituals of solidarity in hatred – it is the amphetamine of its believers.
(1973, p. 159)

In response to the feminist call for choices to be made
available to women, Midge Decter comments that women
have too much choice at present which is causing unnecessary
anxiety:

Women are for the time being caught in a transition in
which they feel themselves too little shaped by society,
its demands on them too indefinite, their own demands on
themselves (or lack of them) far too operative, and they
cannot even get their consciousness organised. (1973,
p. 52)

There are three basic ideological differences between
feminists and antifeminists. First, a basic concern of feminists
is to eliminate sexism, but antifeminists feel there is no
sexism operating. They reject the theory of male oppression
as a paranoid fear among feminists. Some antifeminists stress
that they want 'emancipation' rather than 'liberation'. The
need to be emancipated is not related to 'oppression', but to
a devaluing of the female role, brought about by 'women's
libbers'.[1] Stassinopoulos has argued for emancipation rather
than liberation, because it 'recognises the innate differences
between men and women that disqualify women from certain
jobs such as combat roles in the army' (1973, p. 115). She
sees a need for 'equal status for distinctly female roles'
(p. 15).

George Gilder (1973), on the other hand, accepts that
there is a system which perpetuates difference between the
sexes, but he perceives this to be positive. He says there are
devices and conventions which society has developed to
ensure 'that women perform their indispensable work'
(p. 247). One of these is 'the system the feminists call sexism,

which in fact is based on the exaltation of women, acknowledgement of the supremacy of domestic values, and the necessity of inducing men to support them in civilised society' (p. 247).

The need to 'induce' men arises because they would otherwise not feel obliged to support wives and children. In fact, antifeminists warn that the ERA would give men the legal right to refuse to pay alimony or to support their families, based on the belief that 'men are deviant in the sense that many of the qualities admired in them are also ones that society has to regard with disapproval' (Stassinopoulos, 1973, p. 136).

The second ideological difference involves whether sex differences are innate or socially conditioned. Feminists stress social conditioning. They use cross-cultural studies (e.g. Mead's work),[2] psychological and sociological research, to support their position that socialising agents like the family, the church, schools and other social institutions determine the development of the individual. This allows for change *within* the individual and attacks the concept that there is such a thing as 'natural behaviour'. Antifeminists, in contrast, place overwhelming importance on innate biological sex differences, using research on differences within the brain, sex differences in children, and some anthropological studies (e.g. Tiger's work)[3] to support their claims. The role of women is thus preordained by biology and nature, and anyone differing from their allotted role is deviant. So Decter can comment that women's liberation demands 'nothing less than the radical alteration of nature itself' (1973, p. 175). This belief forms the basis of their stand on many issues like motherhood, which is natural and necessary for the fulfilment of women. It also leads them to oppose the elimination of sexism in schools on the grounds that the differences between the sexes should not be interfered with.

The third ideological difference between feminists and antifeminists is in their understanding of women's experiences. Feminists see women as part of a social group experiencing a shared oppression. Antifeminists see the individual woman as responsible for her situation and her life. Phyllis Schlafly comments that 'thanks to the women's liberation movement, [women] no longer see their predicament in terms of

personal problems to be confronted and solved' (1977, p. 9).
Her concept of the positive woman follows this philosophy:
that a positive mental outlook will overcome most problems.
She calls it 'the power of the positive woman', and has
modelled her book on her own life.

The issues debated by the antifeminists are in direct reaction to those of the women's movement. Abortion, sexuality,
motherhood, the family and workforce women, are of prime
concern to them. Class and race issues, however, do not
appear to be central for the antifeminists though religion is
important.

The pro-family backlash has been in response to calls for
changes in family structure and to the value placed by the
women's movement on 'working' (workforce) women. It
is tied into the value placed on women's traditional role by
the antifeminists, particularly the motherhood role. Decter
has commented that 'in the critique of motherhood lies the
very nub of the revolution this movement means to make'
(1973, p. 175).

To antifeminists the family is essential to the well-being of
society. It enables a woman and a man to fulfil their natural
roles and provides a secure place in which to bring up children. George Gilder argues (in *Wealth and Poverty*) that
disruption of family life disrupts the economy. Men need to
direct their energy towards the economy and they can only
do so when spurred on by family duty.

The family should also be autonomous, self-sufficient and
independent of state influence and welfare packages. This
issue of what Petchesky calls 'privatisation' emphasises the
private sphere once more and the right to do with one's
family as one will. The women's movement has made 'private' issues political in the last twenty years. It is now the
business of society if women and children are bashed by
husbands or fathers or if a woman is raped; and the issue of
sex education in schools implies at once that it is the duty of
society to educate its children to avoid unwanted pregnancy,
while at the same time acknowledging that teenagers participate in sexual activity against the moral values of their
parents' generation. Thus, 'feminism calls forth all those
unspoken "personal" relations and renames them as political
questions, questions of power and social determination'

(Petchesky, 1981, p. 223). But the antifeminists argue that this is unwarranted interference by the state.

Attacks on the family by feminists are also perceived as attacks on motherhood and on being female. A great deal of the literature espouses the noble role of motherhood and the eternal and strong bonds between mother and child. It also stresses that women must be self-sacrificing and unselfish, and must work to ensure a successful marriage. The 'positive woman' needs to 'appreciate and admire her husband' because a 'woman's chief emotional need is active (i.e. to love), and a man's prime emotional need is passive (i.e. to be appreciated or admired)' (Schlafly, 1977, p. 54).

The corollary to this natural place of mother and child-bearer in the family is that workforce participation is a 'costly luxury of choice' (Decter, 1973, p. 49) for a married woman. Neither her husband nor her children will appreciate the lack of attention which ensues if she 'works'. No husband need share household chores when it is not his job and his wife has chosen to add to hers.

Within the pro-family stance there runs a strong 'protective' philosophy. The family is the sphere in which children and women are 'protected'. The ERA has been attacked as aiming to remove the 'right of protection' and 'right of support' which wives deserve from husbands. Crawford (1980, p. 149) has commented that 'New Right women do not want equality but preferential treatment which Schlafly calls "rights".'

The pro-choice stand on abortion by feminists is opposed by antifeminists. Because of their pro-life and pro-family philosophy, they cannot accept the right of a woman to destroy potential life. They argue that children could be adopted if unwanted. Morality is strongly invoked to support their stand that the foetus is a child and that the mother kills her baby. The issue is thus not one of fertility control but a form of infanticide.

An alternative view is often presented in the statement of male antifeminists. They tend to see abortion as robbing them of their rights to ownership of the foetus. Tying family, morality and sexuality together, Wilke, the first male national president of the National Right to Life Committee, wrote regarding feminists and Planned Parenthood groups:

It is they who are doing violence to our beloved nation by
their systematic undermining of the basic unit of our
society, the family. They do violence by their so-called
sex education which is encouraging sexual promiscuity in
our children leading to more and more abortions. They do
violence to us by driving wedges, barriers, and suspicion
between teenagers and parents. They do violence to
marriage by helping to remove the right of the husband to
protect the life of the child he has fathered in his wife's
womb.[4]

This statement moves the issue away from the rights of the
child, stressing the rights of the father. Feminists certainly
would not agree with the stand that men should decide a
woman's right to reproductive control, and antifeminists
stress only the rights of the foetus/child.

Phyllis Schlafly attacks the new morality, pointing out
that it is the woman who ends up suffering under the new
egalitarianism. She discusses the innate differences between
the sexes when it comes to sex, commenting that:

women are simply not the equal of men. The sexual drive
of men is much stronger than that of women. . . . The
other side of the coin is that it is easier for women to
control their sexual appetites. A Positive Woman cannot
defeat a man in a wrestling or boxing match, but she can
motivate him, inspire him, encourage him, teach him,
restrain him, reward him, and have power over him that he
can never achieve over her with all his muscle. (1977,
p. 17)

The motivation behind women's sexuality is a maternal one
and the pleasure she receives from her husband's satisfaction.
Antifeminists indicate that sexuality is not necessarily
enjoyed for its own sake and orgasm is not necessary. Decter
writes:

And her pleasure in sex is not found in, or determined by,
explosive release – but rather in the general erotic atmosphere; in the engagement of her fantasies; in the enhance-
ment of her experience and sense of self, in the power to

elicit affirmations of her worth and desirability, in the excitement of *giving* pleasure. . . . Sometimes . . . she will delight in the sensation that sex is a pestilential swamp in which she is helplessly emired; sometimes, that it is the simplest of all human contacts. (her italics) (1973, p. 90)

Within this perspective there is no room for homosexuality. Lesbian women are pathologically deviant or motivated to be lesbian because they cannot form relationships with men. Their relationships are unnatural because they do not lead to a fulfilment of the maternal and family requirements. Schlafly considers it outrageous that feminists believe 'that homosexuals and lesbians should have just as much right to teach in the schools and to adopt children as anyone else', behaviour which she finds 'offensive to the religious and moral values of parents and taxpayers' (1977, p. 25).

The issue of religion is raised frequently. The basic support for most of these 'moral' stands is that God has ordained them. Schlafly points out, for example, that the female body with its 'baby-producing organs was not designed by a conspiracy of men but by the Divine Architect of the human race' (1977, p. 12). The antifeminist positions on family, sexuality and motherhood are frequently supported by appropriate biblical quotes.

The backlash also carries its own brand of extremism. This has appeared in two forms. The first is represented by Esther Vilar (1972) in her book *The Manipulated Man*, which is anti-woman and misogynist. Vilar sees the choices facing women as working like a man or becoming a 'dimwitted, parasitic luxury item' (p. 19). Most women, she claims, have chosen to be 'prostitutes', 'or to put it another way, they have planned a future for themselves which consists of choosing a man and letting him do all the work. In return for his support, they are prepared to let him make use of their vagina at certain given moments' (p. 14).

Women have manipulated men totally: they are 'trained and conditioned by women, not unlike the way Pavlov conditioned his dogs, into becoming their slaves' (dustcover). The emancipated woman is 'just as stupid as the others' and women's liberation failed because women fought their allies, men, while they should have been fighting housewives (p. 160).

A second and more sophisticated version of this extremism appears in Helen Andelin's *Fascinating Womanhood* (1965) and Marabel Morgan's *The Total Woman* (1974). These books are supported by courses for women, and the main aim of both is to reassure women that the 'old rules' are the way to happiness. But these rules are clarified for them in an absurd way. Women are told that subservience to their husbands will get them what they want and keep him happy at the same time. They are encouraged to play dumb, be childish and deferential, but be submissive and seductive at the same time, appearing at the door to welcome him home in nothing but black stockings and an apron, or adorned in leopard skins.

8 Aims of this book

This book explores the experiences and personal statements of pro- and anti-movement women. It is an attempt to understand how and why it is that some women choose feminism and some reject it. As a feminist myself, I felt baffled by the strength of feeling expressed by antifeminist women and felt I could not really understand *why* this emerged and how two groups of women could be so apparently different on issues of such importance to them both. I feel that women divided are women isolated, alone and powerless. This book aimed to get feminists and antifeminists to clarify their position in relation to the women's movement now, and to relate it to their personal lives and experiences. During this process I have kept in mind Adrienne Rich's comments:

> But it is pointless to write off the antifeminist woman as
> brainwashed, or self-hating, or the like. I believe that
> feminism must imply an imaginative identification with all
> women . . . and that the feminist must, because she can,
> extend this act of the imagination as far as possible.
> (1980, p. 71)

9 The contributors and their work

Selecting contributors for any book is difficult. For this book I tried to include an equal number of women who 'do' and 'don't'. I also tried to get a representative group with respect to age, class, marital status, sexual preference, children or no children, and race. I could not, of course, achieve this ideal state, but the list came close. One strong regret I have is that I did not have space for a more varied representation from young women.

Using the above groupings as my guide, I talked and wrote to many women collecting suggestions for contributors. Women were approached who refused, some never answered, and some, like those approached in the Country Women's Association, felt insecure about committing themselves on paper (women from country areas are not adequately represented). Some women were unable to write because of their concerns about jeopardising their jobs or their lifestyle, and many were just too busy. I used the international networks available from both feminists and antifeminists. The extent of both surprised and impressed me. Contributors come from Britain, Australia, New Zealand, Canada and North America. There are black, migrant, lesbian, heterosexual and religious women involved. Some have children, others do not; some are married, others are single. Their ages range from 17 to 75 years young.

Each contributor was told the expected form of the book. I also explained to each author who I was and the fact that I had taught women's studies and sex role psychology for six years. The book was described as 'about women, written by women who speak their own story', presenting 'a variety of perspectives on the current women's movement and why some women choose to align themselves with it and others choose not to'. Contributors were asked to investigate their own experiences in relation to feminism and the women's movement, and to consider the following points:

1 Do you draw a distinction between being a feminist and being part of a women's movement? What is your relationship to them?
2 How have you come in contact with the ideas of equality and liberation?
3 Why did you become/choose not to become a feminist? Was it an event, or series of events, or have you always felt this way?
4 What is your current involvement with women?
5 What were the experiences which shaped your current beliefs about women?
6 Is there a tension between your allegiances? Have you resolved this tension and if so how?
7 How do you feel about women (in general and in the particular)? Have you always felt this way or did your feelings about women develop and change?
8 How do you feel about men? Is there a difference between men in a generalised sense and the particular individual man? Have these feelings changed and developed through your life?
9 What has been your experience of conflict with other women? Why does it arise? How do you cope or deal with it?
10 How do you feel about yourself? What are the things you value in your life?
11 Are you satisfied with the current position of women?

It was only after reading some early chapters that I saw a bias within the outline. Concentrating on the backlash as 'reaction', I have neglected to ask the pro-movement women for their attitudes to anti-movement women.

The next section of this book contains, then, the experiences, feelings and thoughts of a group of women who relate in a positive or antagonistic way to the women's liberation movement.

Notes

1 The women's movement as a social movement

1 D. Spender, *Women of Ideas and What Men Have Done to Them*, London, Routledge & Kegan Paul, 1982.
2 See B. Deckard, *The Women's Movement: Political, Socio Economic and Psychological Issues.* 2nd edn, New York, Harper & Row, 1979; and O. Banks, *Faces of Feminism*, Oxford, Martin Robertson, 1981.
3 D. Snyder and C. Tilly, 'Hardship and collective violence in France, 1830–1950', *American Sociological Review*, 1972, 37, pp. 520-32.
4 H. Toch, *The Social Psychology of Social Movements*, London, Methuen, 1966.
5 Z. Eisenstein, *The Radical Future of Liberal Feminism*, New York, Longman, 1981.

2 Membership and structure of the women's movement

1 Banks, *op. cit.*

3 Issues and platforms within the movement

1 B. Friedan, *It Changed My Life. Writings in the Women's Movement*, New York, Dell, 1977, p. 169.
2 Banks, *op. cit.*
3 A. Coote and B. Campbell, *Sweet Freedom. The Struggle for Women's Liberation*, London, Picador, 1982.
4 See K. Hargreaves, *Women at Work*, Ringwood, Australia, Penguin, 1982.

5 Who are the antifeminists?

1 R.P. Petchesky, 'Antiabortion, antifeminism, and the rise of the New Right', *Feminist Studies*, 1981, 7 (2), pp. 206-46.

2   See Banks, *op. cit.*
3   R.P. Petchesky, Editorial, *Commonweal* (2 January 1976). Quoted in Petchesky, *op. cit.*

6   Motivations of the antifeminists

1   See J. Bardwick, *In Transition. How Feminism, Sexual Liberation and the Search for Self-Fulfillment Have Altered America*, New York, Holt, Rinehart & Winston, 1979.
2   G. Staines, G. Tavris and T. Jayaratne, 'The Queen Bee Syndrome', *Psychology Today*, 1974, 7, pp. 55–60.

7   Platforms of the antifeminists

1   'Women's lib' and 'Women's libber' are derogatory terms for women's liberationists. See Rich (1981).
2   For example: M. Mead, *Sex and Temperament in Three Primitive Societies*, New York, William Morrow, 1935, or chapters in M.Z. Rosaldo and L. Lamphere (eds), *Woman, Culture and Society*, California, Stanford University Press, 1974.
3   L. Tiger, *Men in Groups*, New York 1969, and L. Tiger and J. Shepner, *Women in the Kibbutz*, New York, Harcourt Brace Jovanovich, 1975.
4   J.C. Wilke, Memorandum, National Right to Life Council, 21 February 1978. Petchesky (1981).

Part two
Feminists and antifeminists

Mary Stott

Aged 75, Mary Stott is widowed with an adult daughter and two grand-daughters aged 17 and 13. She is British, and a member of the Fawcett Society, the National Council of Women, and the Women's Action Group. A journalist throughout her life, she retired in 1972 from the Guardian, *though she still writes occasionally for the* Guardian *and for various books, and is involved in broadcasting. She has also written three books, two of which are:* Forgetting's No Excuse *(Faber & Faber), and* Organization Woman *(Heinemann).*

It is mortifying not to be able to answer the question 'How did you become a feminist?' There should have been some blinding flash of illumination, or some exacting, time-taking process of analysis. There wasn't. This feminist, like Topsy, 'just growed' – in an egalitarian family where equal status and opportunity seemed both logical and morally right. My mother did not call herself a feminist – indeed, she had been anti-suffragette – but her whole lifestyle was a rebuttal of the 'second sex' concept.

She was an elementary school teacher when my father met her. So was he, but he was also the founder and editor of a local weekly newspaper for which he persuaded my mother to write. In due course she became a full-time journalist, and she never stopped writing women's columns for local newspapers until she died, aged only 57. Both parents were

politically active and took part in a wide range of organisations: Father's mainly music and amateur theatre, Mother's
women's associations for social welfare. Mother was a natural
leader both at home and in public. You might say that in any
organisation Mother would tend to be the chairman, the
'front woman'; Father the secretary, the back room boy. . . .
A reversal of the roles the sexes are expected to fit themselves into.

So it never crossed my mind that my destiny was marriage,
children, cooking and cleaning. It never occurred to me to
regard men as superior to women. But neither had I any
reason to regard men as women's natural enemies, the oppressors of our sex. My father not only dearly loved my mother,
he fully recognised her abilities, and came to value my
potential also. He once said to me, smiling affectionately,
'For years I have been "Mrs Waddington's husband". Now it
looks as if I shall have to get used to being "Miss Waddington's father".' In due course I met and married a man whose
attitude towards me was exactly the same. It simply never
entered his mind that I should stay at home, providing his
meals, having his slippers ready by the fire and mending his
socks.

When we married I handed him half the wedding licence
fee, saying, 'You are not buying me for seven shillings and
sixpence.' It was a jokey gesture, but did symbolise our truly
equal partnership. My husband used to say, 'You are the head
of the household.' I used to reply, 'No you are.' It simply
meant that we both respected the other's importance in
decision-making, from where our child should go to school to
what sort of wallpaper we should like for the dining room.

Having had it easy, as you might say, with a supportive
father and a supportive husband, I might have been expected
to become one of those silly women who see no need for
equal pay and equal opportunity legislation. It was not so,
and never likely to be. I can remember myself as a young
reporter of about 19 nerving myself to rebel against being
the 'tea lady'. 'Why does it always have to be me?' I said.
The reporters sent me a Round Robin, signed by all and
adorned with a seal from a beer bottle, but I would not
budge. We must take it in turns or there would be no tea.

By the time I was 21 there was a much more significant

landmark in my feminist progress. In 1928 the British Parliament granted the vote to women on exactly the same terms as men. (Previously, from 1918 onwards, only women aged 30 or over who were married or householders could vote.) At the General Election of May 1929, aged 21 years 10 months, I cast my first vote, wearing a scarlet frock to indicate my political allegiance. I was deeply conscious that this was an important moment in history. So were a good many other female first-time electors, despite the fact that the popular press called us 'flapper voters', with the implication that we wouldn't have a clue about the political issues of the day. ('Flapper' was as derisory a term in the 1920s as 'libber' became in the 1970s.)

It seems important to me to state emphatically that there was not a great yawning gulf between the women's movement typified by the militant suffragettes in the decade before the First World War and the women's liberation movement, which dates from about 1966 in America. There were still plenty of ardent feminists around in the 1920s who influenced me in my growing-up years. Ray Strachey wrote her landmark book, *The Cause*, in 1928, which I still have always to hand. Vera Brittain and Winifred Holtby were writing feminist articles for the women's page of the *Manchester Guardian*. (The only reason I could bring myself to return to editing a women's journal or women's pages after a brief escape into hard news, was that I knew how influential and constructive a feminist page in this internationally famous Liberal newspaper could be.) Viscountess Rhondda was editing the strongly feminist weekly review *Time and Tide*. Britain had her first woman Cabinet Minister, Margaret Bondfield. Virginia Woolf had not only written a trenchant attack on the different educational opportunities and standards for men and women, *A Room of One's Own*, but a powerful foreword for a book of letters on *Life as We Have Known It* collected by her friend Margaret Llewelyn Davies from members of the campaigning working-class organisation, the Women's Co-operative Guild, of which she was general secretary.

I myself later edited the co-operative movement's *Woman's Outlook* and women's pages of the Co-operative Guild, and knew at first hand about the struggles for equal pay, for the removal of the marriage bar, equality in divorce and custody of children. There are many rebellious young feminists who scorn parliamentary processes, but only political pressure by organised women has rescued, and still can rescue, some women from grievous suffering. The law of the land used to deprive a woman of her nationality if she married a 'foreigner'. It used to refuse you the right to divorce a deserting husband except in the country of *his* domicile – which in the case of a woman whom an uncle of mine wished to marry, was Australia. How could she follow him, or trace him, to the other side of the world?

In 1926 I joined one of the very few trade unions which had negotiated 'equal pay' terms from its inception in 1907, the National Union of Journalists. In those days and for many more years, it was quite common to see advertisements in political and educational journals for paid jobs, such as headmaster for a boys' school and headmistress for a girls' school, where the advertised salary for the man was at least half as much again as the advertised salary for the woman.

I said earlier that I had always 'had it easy' in my family life. Not always in my working life, though. During the Second World War the editor of the *Co-operative News* moved on to another job and as his tacit deputy I was the fairly obvious potential successor. But no – the Board of Directors decided to bring in a man from one of our provincial offices because it might be difficult for a woman to meet, on level terms, the important men of the Co-operative Wholesale Society and Co-operative Union. This naturally made me anxious to move out, and I was fortunate to find a job as a news sub-editor on the *Manchester Evening News*, experienced sub-editors being in short supply towards the end of the war which had taken most men of fighting age into the services. This was what I had wanted to do for years. To me then, editing women's pages and journals was a female ghetto. After the initial nervousness, I was as happy as I have ever been in a newspaper office. Women engineers, surgeons and barristers may understand the extra zing of satisfaction that comes from doing well a job previously always done by men, and which popular opinion holds *can* only be done by men. I went up the line; I always helped the 'new boys' to find their feet. Eventually I became deputy-deputy chief sub-editor, but only for a few weeks. I was told that my name had been dropped from the duty list not because I had failed on the job, but because 'We have to safeguard succession, Mary, and the successor has to be a man.'

Do any of my young friends wonder that the very heart and core of my feminist conviction is a passionate belief that there should be no legal or social barrier to any woman, or any girl, doing what it is in her to do? Why should choir schools recruit only boys, because it is believed that as the composers of previous centuries wrote for boys' voices in their sacred cantatas, only boys' voices are suitable for this or any other kind of sacred music? Why should girls continue to be allowed to assume that mathematics is a subject beyond their brainpower, when as long ago as 1890 Philippa Fawcett, one of the early students at Newnham, and daughter of the great suffrage leader, Millicent Garrett Fawcett, was placed above the Senior Wrangler in the Cambridge mathematical Tripos – which meant that she had one of the best mathematical brains in Europe? Why should women be recruited in such humiliatingly small numbers to public bodies, quangos, commissions of inquiry, and so on, because men think that *their* qualifications are so much more impressive and important? (The British Prime Minister, in 1982, giving the first Dame Margery Corbett Ashby Memorial Lecture, said 'The reason I can make decisions at remarkable speed is because I have run a household.' Not one national newspaper reported this immensely important statement.)

As I said, I have suffered from the prejudice of blinkered men in my newspaper career. But this has not left me with a hostility to men. They were all children of their times, as we are. That newspaper editor who smashed to pieces my career as a news sub-editor had, I believe, both affection and admiration for me. Twenty years after, he wrote to the *Guardian's* managing director complimenting him on the awards the paper had won, including one for the women's page. I can't resist quoting from that letter, because it validates my claim to have been an efficient sub, and also because it illustrates how ludicrous are those tradition-validated blinkers.

Mary wanted to sub hard news in a tough man's world and there was nothing came tougher than the *Manchester*

Evening News subs' room. I threw the stool, the bucket
and the lot at her, made her a splash sub and she loved it
. . . she thrived on it all. . . . She wasn't going to permit
any frail womanly foibles on any account, so it is all the
more appropriate that when today she receives the
honours for 'Woman's Guardian', she should start a series
on Women's Liberation. She is well qualified. I reckon she
started it – in the *Manchester Evening News* subs' room.

I don't doubt that some of my women friends would
regard this panegyric as sickening hypocrisy. I don't. I think
that men need a lot more educating than women, and that we
have to help this process. I am by no means unsympathetic to
lesbians. All my life I have found my closest friends and most
faithful supporters among women, rather than men – apart
from my husband, father and brothers. But I do not see why
a preference for your own sex should lead you into hatred of
the other sex.

I understand why battered women's refuges and women's
centres exclude men. I support the idea that consciousness-
raising groups and specialist women's groups like Women in
Media, Women in the Civil Service, Women in Manual Trades,
the City Women's Network, and so on, need to get together
on their own, both to establish a common viewpoint and to
support one another in their professional and public life. I
take an active part in the drive to get more women into
public life. But I could never participate in a project – such
as the Women's City idea in London – which rules out
men's presence totally and utterly, from the very beginning.
We have often used the slogan 'Women are people'. Men
are people too.

Men are our fathers, brothers, sons; our lovers, husbands
and friends, as well as our employers and employees. They
are the fathers of our children as well as, sometimes, our
gaolers. Without the fertilisation of the female ovaries by the
male sperm, the human race would come to an end. I am not
unwilling to accept the idea of artificial insemination, but to
regard men as purely the providers of seed to fertilise our
wombs strikes me as being as monstrous as to regard people
with black skins as domestic, agricultural and industrial
menials.

Now in my mid-seventies, I intend to go on until the end of the road campaigning for equal opportunities, equal status and equal recognition for women. When you are old you come to realise that the differences between men and women are much less than you thought when you were young, and were mainly concerned with the child-conceiving and rearing function which comes to an end for women in their early fifties. My life as an elderly widow differs very little from the life of a man on his own. The majority of our sex differences are cultural rather than innate. I long for my two beloved grand-daughters to grow up into a society which gives them, in the fullest possible sense, the right to choose what their life shall be.

Teddi Holt

Teddi Holt is a white American, living in Georgia, aged thirty-two, with three sons. She is national president of 'Mothers on the March' and is writing a book, The New Woman. *Teddi has been a full-time homemaker for ten of her thirteen years of married life, previous to which she was a salesperson and secretary.*

I became aware of the goals of the women's liberation movement in my nation about five years ago. I first responded to this movement after receiving information dealing with the International Women's Year (IWY) Conference which was held in my state. Until that time, I had only considered the women's movement as a 'passing fad' involving women who did not want to be treated like ladies but exactly the same as men - doing men's work such as working on the roads and putting up telephone wires. I was much too involved with my home and church to care whether other women liked 'special treatment'. But after meeting with ladies much like myself, I was made aware that there was much more at stake and began lecturing and debating pertinent women's issues across my state.

I am pleased that God blessed me with the privilege of being a woman. I have never been envious of the role of men but have had respect for both sexes. There's no doubt that there has been discrimination against women, but that is past history, just as discrimination against blacks is past history in the US.

Believing that God's word is true when it says, 'I can do all things through Christ', I am firmly convinced that I, or any other woman, could run for president for we women are intelligent, very exciting, and very, very necessary. Probably the fact that I have three sisters and a mother with whom I have very close non-competitive relationships, has caused me to feel good about myself and other women. Also, we all have a close relationship with our father who never showed any of us partiality.

The battle between PRO-ERA (Equal Rights Amendment) and STOP-ERA forces is my first experience with controversy and conflict. Many women have been outraged by my pro-family/pro-life stand. Under different circumstances these women might be my friends, because they do not truly believe in the goals of the feminists. However, there are also women who know their goals and are dedicated to achieving them.

The National Organisation for Women (NOW) had produced a pamphlet consisting of a summary of resolutions and policies they wished to see incorporated into our Constitution and our state laws. In the pamphlet, *Revolution: Tomorrow is Now*, three resolutions disturbed me. First, NOW's primary goal was to pass the Equal Rights Amendment (ERA) without amendment. Second, it included as a secondary goal - 'right to abortion on demand'. And third. it supported 'a woman's right to . . . Express her own sexuality and to choose her lifestyle. . . . NOW acknowledges the oppression of lesbians as a legitimate concern of feminism' (p. 20).

Such goals were foreign to me. I could not imagine any woman with my background having such goals, because they did not hold to traditional values and/or Judeo-Christian ethics on which the Constitution and our laws are based. I decided that I would study the subject from both points of view. I found that this was not a male versus female issue but a female versus female issue - both sides consisting of very dedicated supporters.

Since the legislative history of a law or an amendment is the best way for a citizen to find out just what the passage of such a law/amendment might mean, I studied the legislative history of the ERA. It was obvious to me that ERA was certainly not a protection of women's rights. In fact, it would remove many protections and exemptions that were specifically placed in our laws, recognising the fact that our Creator had most certainly created us male and female: two separate, very different, equally important human beings.

The US Constitution is not a sexist document, as the feminists would have us believe. It is 'sex neutral' because it speaks to persons and citizens. Every right guaranteed to men in our Constitution is also guaranteed to me, because *I am a person and a citizen.* They also said that women could not get credit and therefore own property. However, due to the Federal Equal Credit Opportunity Act of 1975, I most certainly can. Another claim they made was that women are not paid the same as men. According to Title VII of the Civil Rights Act 1964, 'discrimination in employment based on sex is prohibited', and 'all discrimination in hiring, firing, wages and other conditions of employment are unlawful'.

Realising that the claims of the feminists were not grounded in truth, and that all privileges and protections guaranteed men under the Constitution were also guaranteed to me, I decided to find out just who was behind this so-called 'liberation movement'. Betty Friedan, the 'mother' of the feminist movement in my country, wrote a book called *It Changed My Life* (1976)[1] in which she discusses feminism with Simone de Beauvoir, a famous French feminist. De Beauvoir said:

> No woman should be authorized to stay at home to raise her children. . . . Women should not have that choice, precisely because if there is such a choice, too many women will make that one. . . . In my opinion, as long as the family and the myth of the family and the myth of maternity and the maternal instinct are not destroyed, women will still be oppressed. (p. 312)

I became very concerned that such anti-family/anti-mother-hood statements should be in the book of a woman who claimed that she wanted to help women. As a Christian, I believe that Jehovah God, my Creator, created man 'in His own image . . . male and female created He them' (Genesis 1:27). When God joined man and woman, they became the first 'home'. Man plus woman (plus children) equals the 'home' and family.

Another book, published by McGraw Hill, called *Feminist Frameworks* (1978)[2] states:

> no group other than the Feminists has publicly taken a stand against marriage. (p. 240)

> many in the women's liberation movement saw the nuclear family as the chief evil that had to be combatted in order to be liberated. (p. 233)

Just what were we women to be liberated from? These women were calling for liberation from the things women like me love most – our husbands, our children, our homes. My cry became: 'God, liberate us from the Liberators!'

As I continued my research, debating and lecturing against ERA at every opportunity, a new movement began across our nation called the children's rights movement. I began to hear about IYC (International Year of the Child) conferences being held in each state after which a National IYC conference would be held. Interestingly, in the book *It Changed My Life* by Betty Friedan, she referred to what she called the old-time communist women's group, the Women's International Democratic Federation (WIDF), who introduced a resolution to the United Nations in 1969, declaring 1975 as International Women's Year and 1979 as International Year of the Child. The United Nations also wrote up a Declaration of the Rights of the Child, and assigned implementation of the IYC to UNICEF. In other words, the International Year of the Child (IYC) and International Women's Year (IWY) formed two branches of the same tree, with the same philosophy, same world leaders, same goals, and so on.

On 7 August 1978 a diagram appeared in the *U.S. News and World Report*, which showed the Women's International Democratic Federation as a communist front, with Moscow Communist Party Headquarters at the centre of the diagram. This information caused me concern, because I had connected the IWY and the IYC with the WIDF, which was called a communist organisation by Betty Friedan and the *U.S. News and World Report*.

As a 'free citizen of the US', I felt threatened. Not only was the women's movement begun by communist and socialist leadership, but these same people were now saying that our children needed to be 'socialised' and used the socialist countries as the best examples of the principles of the Declaration of the Rights of the Child. The Union of Soviet Socialist Republics (USSR) most definitely leads the world in the so-called 'emancipation of women' because somewhere between 75 and 90 per cent of all women there work.

In an article in WIDF's magazine *Women of the Whole World*, called 'Women and Work', February 1979, I read some distressing statements made by women who attended a regional seminar in Budapest, Hungary, 14–17 November 1978, dealing with the situations of working women around the world. Mirgam Vire-Touminen, General Secretary of WIDF, said:

> More and more *women* are coming out of the narrow
> family circle and *going into production*, into political,
> economic, and cultural life, and becoming a powerful
> factor in the development of the whole society . . . *an*
> *inevitable process demanded by the general world-wide*
> *trend production forces.* (My emphasis)

I could hardly believe that these people believe that work makes us human and that women working was an inevitable process. The achievements of the socialist countries were stressed. If these women got their way, homemakers world-wide would be forced to leave their children and homes in order to meet their *obligations* as 'workers'.

As a homemaker and Christian mother, I believe that children are 'a heritage of the Lord' (Psalms 127:3). I believe it is my responsibility to care for and teach my children and to lead them into 'all righteousness'. The philosophy of these men and women is that mothers need to be liberated from their children and children need to be liberated from their parents. It is quite clear to me that we are not fighting people: 'We wrestle not against flesh and blood but against principalities, against powers, against the rules of the darkness of this world, against spiritual wickedness in high places'

(Ephesians 6:12). It is Satan who stands behind these two
movements in our nation, and he seeks to destroy the 'Home',
God's First Institution. Since the beginning of the women's
movement in the early 1970s, divorce has doubled, and even
tripled in some places, across the US. Since the 'Children's
Movement Rebellion', many children have left their homes,
seeking independence before they could cope with adult
problems – many ending up addicted to drugs and alcohol;
many living with the opposite sex outside of marriage; many
selling themselves as heterosexual and/or homosexual prostitutes; and many ending their problems through suicide.

In March 1980, three other homemakers and myself sat
down at a kitchen table, discussing the attack on our homes.
We prayed in one accord. That day we established a non-
profit corporation called Mothers on the March (MOM).
Our purpose was and still is, to preserve and strengthen the
home, teaching mothers who the enemy of the home is and
how to fight him.

About six months after MOM began, I read a letter from
Eleanor Smeal, the President of NOW, to the leadership of
the White House Conference on Families (WHCF) defining
family as: 'People who . . . have established a lasting relationship involving, living, loving and working together for their
individual and mutual benefit.' She also called for the:

> end to custody judgements that deny gay parents their
> children . . . enactment of civil rights laws at the local,
> state, and federal level which provide lesbians and gay men
> with the same protections as others . . . the government
> can aid individuals . . . by mandating complete private and
> public health insurance coverage for reproductive health
> services including abortion, sterilization . . . amniocen-
> tesis, and genetic counselling.

Attached to this letter was a memo from the National Gay
Task Force calling for a 'revision of all governmental and
private sector policies so that "family benefits" are conferred
equally upon all units of two or more persons which function
as . . . self-defined families'.

Had President Carter remained another term, we would
have surely seen full implementation of these resolutions by

now. However, in 1980, Ronald Reagan became our president – PRAISE THE LORD! Along with the election of a conservative, pro-life (life defined as beginning at conception), pro-family (family defined as those related by blood, marriage or adoption), Christian (believer in the life and resurrection of Jesus Christ) president, we also elected a conservative, pro-life/pro-family Senate.

As Mothers On the March, we stand firmly in favour of all legislation that protects the life of the unborn baby, for example, the Hyde and Hatch amendments and the Helms Bill. We also firmly favour the teaching of all scientific fact dealing with 'creation' and when life begins, and we stand firmly opposed to teaching theory and opinion as fact. We believe that this has contributed to the ignorance of the children of our nation, and to their lack of respect for life. Such teaching deprives children of a balanced education. We are in favour of teaching children that crime is crime and that children should not be criminals. Therefore, though we do not speak to the issue of homosexuality within the privacy of a person's home, we stand firmly opposed to textbooks and classroom materials referring to homosexuality as a 'preferred lifestyle' or 'sexual preference' when it is a criminal offence in most states.

We believe that the mothers of this and other nations, must stand up for the protection of our homes and our children. In no way are we extremists, unless we be guilty of extreme devotion to our husbands, our children, and our homes. It is our sincere belief that if we do not unite against the threats to the home, if we retire to the convenience and security of our houses and do not speak out, then it will not be long until we, the 'keepers at home' (Titus 2:5) will not have a home to keep!

Our creed states:

I AM MOTHER . . . The Creator of this universe chose me to be His instrument to bring all future human beings into His world. . . . Lying dormant in me, to arise when needed to protect my young, is the fierceness of God Himself. I AM MOTHER. The world should hope that it never hears me roar, for if I do,
I WILL SHAKE THE FOUNDATIONS OF THE EARTH!

Notes

1 B. Friedan, *It Changed My Life. Writings from the Women's Liberation Movement*, New York, Random House, 1976.
2 A.M. Jaggar, *Feminist Frameworks. Alternative Theoretical Accounts of the Relations Between Women and Men*, New York, McGraw Hill, 1978.

Ann Curthoys

Ann Curthoys is an Australian aged thirty-six, married with a seven year old son. She has a Bachelor of Arts (Honours), Diploma of Education and Doctorate, and lectures in Australian history, social history of women and ethnic relations at the New South Wales Institute of Technology. She has published articles in Refractory Girl, Arena *and* Politics, *a chapter in* Australian Women: Feminist Perspectives *edited by Grieve and Grimshaw (Oxford University Press, 1981) and has co-edited* Women at Work *(ASSLH, Canberra, 1975) with Eade and Spearitt. She was on the organising collective for the First Women and Labour Conference (Sydney, 1978); participated in the Women's Employment Rights Campaign and co-ordinated the Women's Studies Courses at the Australian National University 1976–77.*

Born in Sydney at the end of the Second World War, I was a 'red diaper' baby. My parents are both Australians of British descent, and were members of the Australian Communist Party, which was then at the height of its influence in Australia. My mother was actively concerned with 'women's equality', especially in the Union of Australian Women, within a communist framework of theory and activity. My father was an Australian communist academic. During my student days at the University of Sydney I was actively involved in student left-wing politics: in the Campaign for Nuclear Disarmament and the Labour Club, later in movements opposing racist policies and practices towards Australian Aborigines, and

Australia's involvement in the Vietnam War. In relation to the feminism that was to come later, key influences then were not only from my mother but also from my reading of the works of Betty Friedan and Simone de Beauvoir. But I never discussed this reading with anyone, and indeed regarded 'women's issues' as, in political terms, trivial, boring, and somewhat embarrassing.

It was while I was studying for my doctorate on racism in Australian history that I first encountered women's liberation. In December 1969, while marching in a Vietnam war protest demonstration in Sydney, I was confronted by women giving out leaflets urging women to join a recently formed women's liberation group. How trivial and diversionary, I thought, in a march opposing a wholesale destruction of the Vietnamese people. Yet a month later, when I learnt of a women's liberation meeting to be held at a Left meeting place, I went. Several women spoke about the need to see sexual oppression as a real and living force affecting all of us. One woman spoke about how we as women sought the approval of men, and devalued each other. This made a great impression on me, for I recognised it as true of myself. Something, as other feminist accounts of this sort of experience have put it, had 'clicked'.

I regularly attended women's liberation meetings in Sydney, and gradually, from discussion and reading of the mainly American literature, absorbed the feminist perspective - women are oppressed as women, are given the worst jobs, are economically dependent on men, are denied abortions, are sexually objectified and generally devalued. For many of us there, our experiences with New Left men, surely the most aggressively sexist breed alive, made our commitment to women's liberation deep and strong. Sisterhood must be powerful, or we must remain individual victims of sexist ideology. In 1971 I became involved in the production of Sydney's first women's liberation newspaper *Mejane*, and married, my concession to women's liberation being that I did not change my name.

Around 1973-4 the term 'women's liberation' was gradually dropped, and replaced by 'feminism' and the 'women's movement'. I was never too pleased by this, for 'feminism' seemed devoid of socialist politics, while 'women's liberation'

referred to a whole set of socialist perspectives. But in time
I adopted the new terms and called myself a feminist.

Through the mid-1970s I was involved in having a baby,
finishing my doctoral thesis, and then acting as a co-ordinator
for two years of the women's studies courses at the Australian
National University in Canberra. My intellectual concerns
were increasingly with the study of women and work. I
returned to Sydney, to take up my present position as a
lecturer, and to be involved in the editing of a feminist
journal, *Refractory Girl* (the title taken from an early
nineteenth century Australian convict women's song).

What, then, do I think feminism is about? Feminism is not
one single ideology or movement. The varieties of feminism
are held together only by a common commitment to seeking
some kind of better life for women as women. For me,
feminism is about both a political and a personal assertion of
the ideal of sexual equality, and about working for the achievement of that ideal. But not all feminists would accept this
notion, many rejecting any ideal of equality or any hope of a
sexually egalitarian world. For such feminists, men are the
enemy, and the task of feminism is rather one of creating
women–identified women, of 'getting men out of our heads'.
Even within those strands of feminism that do subscribe to
the ideal of sexual equality, there are differences between
those who concentrate on immediate political and industrial
changes, those who focus on achieving psychological and
ideological change, and those who ally the struggle for
sexual equality with the struggle for socialism.

The chief values of feminism for me are these. First, it
provides a means of gaining insight into those psychological
processes embedded in family experiences and sexist ideology
generally, whereby we are all constructed as 'masculine' or
'feminine', and are psychologically limited (and if female,
guilt-ridden and dependent) as a result. Second, my brand of
feminism denies the basically biologically determinist argument that women's childbearing functions necessarily determine for them a confinement of tasks of child-caring and
housework. It argues that child-caring and indeed all other
human activities, should be shared between men and women.
Third, feminism points to the institutional bulwarks of sexual
inequality – in the family, in the workplace, in cultural life,

and in politics. Feminism argues that apparent choices are institutionally framed.

For these reasons, I must continue to call myself a feminist. But I am increasingly critical of some of the directions recent feminism seems to be taking. I have begun to think that many feminists *are* anti-male in a crude sense, *are* simply seeking their own advancement *vis-à-vis* middle-class men, *have* abandoned socialist ideals and organisations, and *are* out of touch with or unsympathetic to the very real problems of working-class people, both female and male. Living with two males and no females as I do, I find discussions in some feminist groups about whether men are 'the enemy' utterly absurd. Not having rejected men at a personal, emotional and sexual level, I find those developments within feminist theory which depend on such a rejection uncongenial. I find many recent feminist characterisations of men to be bordering on the racist, to be, in fact, a reversion to the biological determinism we once so fiercely rejected.

This return to biological determinism leads to a rejection of the ideal of men and women sharing child-caring, on the grounds that men are evil incarnate, and children should therefore be reared by women only. In some versions it leads to a moral prescription against having children at all. The earlier interest in the processes of the construction of people as 'masculine' and 'feminine' comes to be replaced by a position which sees men as the all-powerful definers of patriarchy, and *women* as the socially constructed, the objects, the other. Women's task thus becomes one of recovering their 'stolen energies' from the all-powerful, the subject, the one – men. 'Patriarchy' becomes an all-embracing term, and with its use, or over-use, comes the abandonment of the task of *explanation* of sexual inequality and difference altogether.

Feminism is now under renewed attack from the forces of the Right, the new moral conservatism. These forces combine a highly individualistic and extreme laissez-faire ideology in relation to the State, with a defence of the patriarchal (in the old power-of-the-father sense) family, of female economic dependence, of female-only privatised child-caring, or sexist ideology generally, and specifically a denial of the right to full reproductive control. Their ascendancy reminds us that the recent gains have been hard-won, and are easily lost.

In this context one becomes wary of being too critical of current feminist theory and practice. But it's all the more important in this new embattled context for feminists to reappraise their own priorities, ideology, and strategies. There are two key issues here: first, the question of socialism and the relation of feminism to it; second, the question of the family, child-care, and children.

Feminists need to recognise more than many of them do that their concerns are not the only concerns of great importance. Also important are: the increasing possibility of nuclear war, the destructiveness and gross inequality produced by capitalism, the reassertion and strengthening of a truly socialist movement, and the ending of racism (especially in Australia as it affects Aborigines). Recognition must enable feminists to see that some women can be underprivileged *as women* but very privileged indeed if they are well-off financially, politically powerful, or if they do not belong to a dispossessed minority. The notion of 'women's oppression' tends to obscure the reality of those cases of female privilege and male underprivilege arising from class or ethnic group.

Yet if feminism, through its notion of 'women's oppression', tends to obscure a class analysis and a socialist politics, there are two ways in which its political effects are more positive. One is that many middle-class women, through their active involvement in feminism, have been brought face to face with the harsh realities of many working-class women's lives, with the effects of living in a society where child-caring renders women economically dependent on men whose own wages are low and insecure, where material poverty lays the basis for tense and violent family situations.

The other way in which feminism affects class relationships in a positive way lies in its influence on some working-class women, especially those active or becoming active in their trade unions or in other kinds of workplace action. Feminist demands for abortion, child-care, and equal pay have a lot of support amongst working-class women, but what does not have their support, on the whole, is the feminist rejection of the family, and its apparent rejection of mothering.

Feminists often attack 'the family' while anti-feminists claim to defend it. In my view this is a simplistic division, for one can be a feminist and yet defend the family as a residential and emotional unit, or an anti-feminist and advocate policies which undermine it. It's about time feminists began sweeping the ground from under the feet of the Right – not by defending 'the family' *per se*, but by defending those values which it is held to represent – long-term relationships, emotional commitment, kinship ties, and especially the importance of the close bonding which occurs between parents and children. We need to sever the connection so many feminists assume between, on the one hand, a critique of the present structure of the family, with its economic dependence for women, association of daily child-care with women rather than with men and women equally, its psycho-pathology and privatisation, and, on the other, a rejection of family life altogether, of the co-residence and emotional ties between parents and their children.

We need to say more strongly than we have that having children should be a positive experience, and even under present conditions has strong positive elements. While feminism has successfully and rightly attacked the ideology that women should and must have children, and has eloquently defended women's right to make other choices, it needs also to assert equally successfully the right of all women to have children without the financial stress, economic dependence double burden or confinement to child-caring only, which children in this society so often entail.

This means taking seriously the deep needs in adults that children satisfy, the rights of children as individuals, and the importance of developing residential and work patterns that take both of these considerations fully into account. It means advocating policies and practices which ensure for children the following: stable home environments, links with the world beyond the home *via* child-care centres and schooling and community activities, parents who have links with the world outside the home, and equal responsibility taken by men and women. It means insisting that such things will never be available to all children equally as long as we have an exploitative, inegalitarian capitalist system. And it means a re-evaluation of feminism's emphasis on individual self-expression and independence, and a facing of the fact that on the other side of the equation are those key concerns of security, commitment, and continuity. We just have to get the balance right.

In the long run being female *does* matter, trying to write a gender-conscious class analysis of Australian society *does* seem worth doing. And I'll keep contributing, if asked, to books like this one, for all those thirteen years experience are still there, the issues do matter. But next time around I don't think I'll see myself as part of an oppressed group, and I won't submerge those larger issues of war, exploitation, and poverty. I see the choices facing me now not as arising only from my being female, but also from my being relatively privileged in a crazy and inegalitarian world.

Bobbi Sykes

*Bobbi Sykes is a black Australian from North Queensland.
Her job is Education Liaison Officer for Aboriginal Health in
the New South Wales Health Commission, though she is
currently on leave for study purposes. She has a Master's
Degree in Education from Harvard University (1981) and
is currently a Doctoral student in the Harvard Graduate
School of Education. Bobbi is founder/editor of* AIM, *a
black community newspaper, and has co-authored* Black
Power in Australia *with Senator Neville Bonner. She is
author of the biography* Mumshirl *and a book of poems,*
Love Poems and Other Revolutionary Actions.

A question often raised in conversation with white women is
why there are so few black women involved in the women's
movement. This is no local phenomenon limited only to
Australia, but a little-understood statement being made by
black women globally. But by necessity, this discussion will
be limited to the Australian *urban* situation.

I personally have never been involved in the women's
movement, although I have been in contact with sections of
that movement since these women have control of a range of
resources which is not available in the black community.
I am not sure if this means that I patronize the women's
movement, or whether the women's movement patronizes
me, but on more than one occasion, we have had mutually
beneficial exchanges.

These exchanges, however (and I hope that I do not offend

any of these women), have not been in any way a meeting of equals. Always, the white women are in the position of 'helper' and I am in the position of the 'helped'. The exchange is lop-sided. White women give me access to their resources, whether that is the opportunity to address their numbers at meetings, financial resources, access to their printing presses, or their distribution avenues, and I give them information from outside their sphere, as well as, on many occasions, the opportunity to feel charitable and/or 'liberal'.

Some readers will resent my stating these things like this, but it is possible to test their validity. If your first reaction was 'Well, how are whites *supposed* to help?' – then it is obvious that you identify with the helper role. If you think me ungrateful, that too identifies the emotion that I am supposed to feel as the helped.

It matters little whether this inequality is intended. The power relationship that exists between the white community and the black community exists also in the relationship between white women and black women. The options available in this situation are that when black women and white women approach each other, they can *pretend* that the power relationship doesn't exist, or they can attempt to deal with it within the relationship. While the latter is possibly the healthiest solution, it is also the most difficult, and further-more, dealing with it is not a once-only event but an ongoing process because the power relationship always continues to exist.

Black women, sensitive to the feeling of embarrassment which always being the inferior party in the helper/helped dyad creates, stay away from the women's movement and, *in general*, away from relationships with white women either individually or in groups. This emotional level avoidance of the women's movement is quite apart from the fact that the goals of the women's movement are also often in direct con-flict with measures deemed necessary for the survival of the black community.

Political level avoidance also operates and became most obvious following an issue that directly affected most black women on the personal level. The women's movement was lobbying and crusading for easy access to legal abortion. Forced and coerced abortions and sterilizations, however, were commonly practised on the black community to such an extent that, feeling that community survival was threatened, black women wanted even stricter controls over these procedures. Easier access, we felt, would merely create greater opportunity for abuse against black women. If under the then-existing stringent legislation we were not protected, under more relaxed legislation there would virtually be open hunting season.

These concerns of the black community did not daunt the women's movement. Relentlessly it pursued its own objective, forcing debates in Parliament and publishing widely the stance of elected official representatives on the issues, in their effort to bring about changes. Few black women were heard on the subject, and those whose voices did surface were in opposition to relaxed abortion legislation.

In response to a newspaper article which appeared, a male interviewer organized a prominent white movement woman to debate the subject with me on television. Unfortunately, the woman used the opportunity to scream at me that I wasn't the right sort of black, and that I didn't have a dozen children and live in the creek-bed at Alice Springs. I had been asked by Mumshirl (Shirley Smith) to represent her opinion as she had recently publicly opposed relaxed abortion legislation. That I, representing an opinion of the black community, brazenly dared to confront and oppose an option of the white community, was sufficient to crack the veneer over the movement woman's racism, and through that crack spewed forth the most virulent and racist comments that I had heard publicly for some time. The interviewer closed off the program immediately, threw a chair across the set, and walked out - so it is not my intention here to say that all white people are to the same degree racist. However, the woman is a well-known mouthpiece for a sizeable segment of the middle-class section of the women's movement. This example occurred publicly and on live television and can therefore be verified. Privately, many similar events occur constantly.

It is from these types of different and conflicting goals at the political level, which occasionally manifest themselves on a personal level, that black women can be seen to practice politically motivated avoidance of the women's movement.

Black women realize that black community priorities will not become priorities of the white women's movement, even when something as important as attempted genocide threatens the existence of the black community.

In general, the black community views the struggle of the women's movement according to the diagram below.

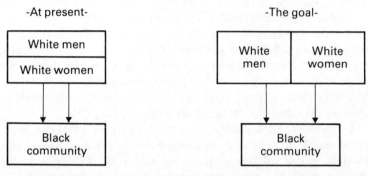

Power diagram

The struggle of the women's movement can be seen to be a struggle for power and control. This struggle is between white men and white women.

The problems of black women are occasionally referred to in the rhetoric of the women's movement and, even more rarely, black women are recruited to the women's movement. Both references to, and recruitment of, black women are not for the purpose of seeking solutions to problems in the black community, but rather to dress up the argument of the women's movement as it seeks more power and control for white women. The basic premise is that this struggle will bring about a more equal distribution of power between the white sexes, but not that the power and control should fall out of the hands of the white community. Somehow, black women are supposed to believe that the trickle down theory will operate – some fragments of power and control will trickle down into the hands of black women.

This premise fails to recognize that the sexual/power dichotomy that exists in the white community is not replicated in the black community. Indeed, neither the sexual nor the pseudo-power relationships that exist in the black community are within its own control. But let's examine this more closely.

First, let us agree that the black community lives in *de facto* segregation. The 1967 Referendum supposedly dispensed with legislative segregation when it accorded blacks citizenship, but there are noteworthy exceptions to this.[1] in all states, by any statistical measure, whether economic, health, crime, standard of living, of education, blacks are separate from the white community. In all cases blacks are far less well-off. In criminal statistics, blacks rank highly, not because of greater criminality, but because of less justice. The black community is also emotionally and socially separate and, in many cases, geographically separate. Any comprehensive appraisal of the situation must conclude that the black community is therefore segregated.

The historical process of dispossession, colonization, decimation, and incarceration was designed specifically to wrest power and control of land and life from the black indigenous people. There are few who would deny this history, but many who deny the contemporary manifestations of it, and the need for justice and retribution.

Because of this loss of power, the black community is not self-determinative, but must react to forces outside of itself in every area of its existence. The decisions regarding the community as a whole, such as where it should live, whether it should be traditional/Europeanized, literate/illiterate, healthy/unhealthy, productive/unproductive, employed/unemployed, have been made and are being made *outside* the black community. Forces acting on the black community dictate that one in four black males will be dead by the age thirty, and two of the remaining three will be incarcerated or caught up in the justice system.[2] This means that outside forces dictate that at least three out of every four black women will sleep alone, will bring up children without the benefit of black paternal presence, and will have no black male with whom to share their lives. It also therefore means that modes of child-raising, welfare existence, quality and quantity of food, and quality and quantity of life, are being determined from outside the community.

An *illusion* of power and control exists, and that illusion places non-existent power in the hands of black women. Very few black women would deny that it is only an illusion, though for some the illusion is necessary for them to continue their vital work.

The premise behind the power diagram showing the goals of the women's movement fails to take into account the real-life situation of the black community. Any movement in our community can only attract our attention if its operating model has built into it a means for the black community to gain *real* power and control. More specifically, they must be available not only to black women but particularly to black men. As these are not the goals of the women's movement, the women's movement is obviously wasted effort for black women.

White women, and particularly movement women, will decry this general analysis and its conclusions. 'But *women*', they will say, 'are without power and control, and are oppressed in the white community too.' However, now we are talking about a matter of degree. White women merely have less power and control than white men. I do not doubt that some white women experience this state acutely, but in comparison to both black women and black men white women are extremely powerful and have control over many resources. In every area of education and professional achievement, white women have succeeded, whether we wish to talk about medicine, law, architecture, or corporate affairs. Their numbers are smaller than their male counterparts – but do you see any blacks in there at all? A tiny handful of black law graduates, still numbering about six nationally, are the only real exceptions.

White women's participation in the fabric of the white controlling group can hardly be questioned. White women own land, and stand to inherit land – land of which the black community has been dispossessed. White women have gained from every massacre of black people, whether directly or indirectly. White women eat at the table of, and sleep in the bed of, the white males whom they would like to have blacks believe are the sole oppressors of blacks.

My discussions with other blacks who have received educational qualifications leads me to the conclusion that at no level are blacks permitted to participate in the wider society. Outside the black community organizations and government departments especially established to take care of the concerns of the black community, blacks are rarely employed. Even within this capacity, extremely few blacks hold administrative positions, most being employed as community workers. The New South Wales Health Commission, for example, has no blacks employed outside the Aboriginal Health Section.

Black lawyers are seen only defending black cases, as though they had taken some special course in law that solely and especially equipped them to do this. Black clerks seem only to be able to add up black figures. Black bureaucrats only work in black departments. If readers doubt the validity of these assertions, check it out! In comparison, white women, when they advance through the ranks, are not employed only in positions in relation to other women. They more generally participate in the wider community.

Black women, despite their sexual oppression, are correct in their belief that oppression is greater on the question of race, that along race lines white women participate with white men in creating this oppression, and that the division of the black community along sex lines can only weaken our already unenviable position and may, in fact, spell doom to all of our black people.

Notes

1 Noteworthy exceptions include – (a) compulsory voting for whites but non-compulsory 'right to vote' for Aborigines in Federal election process; (b) negative, prohibitive and discriminatory State legislation existing particularly in Queensland and Western Australia.

2 B. Sykes, 'Killing Me Softly', *Australian Penthouse*, May/June 1980, pp. 84-5.

Juliet Mitchell

Juliet Mitchell was born in New Zealand but moved when very young to England where she has lived since. Previously a lecturer in English, she is now a psychoanalyst. At forty-one she is married with a four year old daughter. Well known as an activist in the early years of the women's liberation movement in England, she has published a number of books and articles: 'Women: the Longest Revolution' in New Left Review *(1966, vol. 40);* Woman's Estate *(1971);* Psychoanalysis and Feminism *(1974) and* The Rights and Wrongs of Women *(editor with Ann Oakley, 1976).*

The following chapter was taken from an interview with Juliet Mitchell which I taped while she was a Visiting Scholar at Deakin University. The questions follow the outline given to all contributors.

RR What do you perceive feminism and the women's movement to be?

JM There are two strands to any women's protest movement; both strands are concerned with social change. I would not regard any women's demonstrations, any women's advocacy of anything that *didn't* lead to social change as part of a women's movement. Of the two strands, feminism and the women's liberation movement itself come about historically when women became aware of themselves as a socially distinct group and they fight, protest, and organise on behalf of women *as a group*. But even when feminism is not being articulated as a social and political movement, women still fight and protest from the positions that they're in as women, and this is the second strand. So we have a history of women staging bread riots, women fighting for better social conditions for their children, fighting for better pay and so on. They are not thinking of themselves as women as a 'social group', but are thinking of themselves as people in a position of being exploited or oppressed unduly. At the moment of a women's liberation movement, at the moment of feminism, the two strands come together. The first one, the feminists thinking of women as a social group, tend to be middle-class, tend to be educated, tend to be thinking about women as a category: 'women'. The other protest, which is extremely important and strong and has been neglected from most historical accounts, is that women, because they are in the lower echelons, in the lowest paid jobs of society, and because they are hit worse by abuses of social welfare, protest from where they are without thinking of themselves as a social group 'women'. Any women's movement I think needs to be aware of those two traditions.

RR Would you then see feminists as a specific middle-class group?

JM I wouldn't say they're *necessarily* middle-class. I think there's a tendency for the middle-class women to *articulate* the notion of the social category 'women' and that group's oppression.

RR So if you consider what are called the 'conservative' women's groups who say that they are part of the women's liberation movement, would you say that they are women's liberationists?

JM No, definitely not. I would make a two-fold definition of women's liberation. One aspect is that you articulate your demands in terms of a social group 'women'. Second, that your demands are for change. A conservative women's group by definition is against change. It's in favour of preserving the *status quo* and of preventing changes that have begun to be made to the position of women.

RR What if they are fighting to keep women in the home, but to have that role valued more?

JM   I'd want to ask questions about what they meant by women in the home, and which women they are trying to keep in the home. When they want the home re-valued, what sort of home do they want revalued? Do they really mean that they are going to try and sup-port single mothers to stay at home? Are they pro-women, so that women in oppressed minorities, and migrant women can stay at home? If so, where are they going to get the cheap workforce that they probably depend on to support their own class position?

RR   Some antifeminist groups say that feminists have de-valued the role of mother and are forcing women into the workforce.

JM   These groups offer the well-known reactionary program from a particular social class perspective. Women have been in the workforce for hundreds of years. They have been both mothers and factory workers, mine workers and so on, through economic necessity. It's only a cer-tain small section of the middle classes that haven't. These women in that small sector want their own posi-tions validated, they don't want 'motherhood' as such validated. Although it is a familiar charge, it is not correct to accuse the women's liberation movement of neglecting the importance of motherhood and child-bearing. From its outset it has fought to improve the conditions of motherhood. Motherhood is always highly regarded in our society in theory, but the conditions in which most women have to realise the ideal are often atrocious. Reactionary women are probably employing other women to help them look after their children. What happens to those women as mothers? It is similar to the eighteenth and nineteenth century when wet nurses were used. Motherhood was valued enormously if you were in a middle- or upper middle-class position. The mother who was a wet nurse would usually have to let her own children die so that she could nurse the children of the upper-class woman. So it's not mother-hood, it's a certain social class of motherhood, that is valued. In fact, the ideology of motherhood is com-pletely class-based.

RR   In terms of what you were saying about women's

liberation and feminism, would you call yourself a feminist?

JM The two terms are now used synonymously and in that sense, 'yes'. But that was not so in the late 1970s in Britain. Then, my definition of women's liberation as opposed to feminism was that those of us who called ourselves liberationists when we came into the movement didn't think that the *primary* oppression was necessarily the oppression of women, that there are other oppressions, class exploitations, and so on, that were equally important. I still think that. I think all societies differentiate between the sexes and differentiate to women's disadvantage, and therefore it is a major oppression. But I don't think there are no other oppressions or even that woman's is always the most important oppression. You can't miss out on a class analysis and an analysis on race lines as well.

RR If, for example, black women are very anti-women's movement they often say there is no need for it. Their greatest oppression is by whites, and that includes white women as well as white men.

JM Yes, that is possible. It's only perhaps when they're freed from white oppression that they will have time to see that there's also male/female oppression within their society. They're victims of racial oppression which dominates over the sexual oppression, and that would be true of many groups. But I think one has to be careful not to take that too far and simply say that because their dominant oppression is one of suffering from imperialism or colonialism or racism that sexual oppression isn't going on as well. If you neglect sexism then you can get into positions like the one Franz Fanon advocated in the Algerian War: that women only needed to be liberated from the French colonialists. In fact, to have an Algerian identity you must also have a traditional Islamic concept of womanhood within society that is very negative for women. There has to be a struggle for women's equality at the same time as there is a struggle against an imperialist power or a struggle against racism. If there isn't, first of all your struggle against racism is going to be very partial, and, second, if you win that struggle you're going to be left with an appalling heritage of sexism. Struggle against sexism has to be a part of every revolutionary struggle, and vice versa: if we're in the women's movement and we're struggling against sexism, we have also to struggle against class exploitation and against racism as it affects women within the women's movement.

RR How did you first come in contact with the ideas of equality and liberation?

JM My personal experience is that I was working with a Marxist group of men at the beginning of the 1960s, and people were becoming increasingly interested in third world revolutions. I became interested in the position of women as almost a 'third world' category within capitalist society; but 'woman' was a non-subject. When I talked to my revolutionary friends about the position of women I was told you couldn't separate the question from a class analysis: women didn't exist as a social group and hence they weren't exploited as such. I finally wrote an article for the Marxist magazine I was working on which was called 'The Longest Revolution'. It addressed the question: what are the structures within which women can locate their oppression? That was taken up by an emergent women's movement in the States. At that point the women's movement really took off and I became very active at a grass-roots level of organisation. I spend hundreds of hours with other women licking envelopes and organising women's groups.

RR Were these consciousness-raising groups?

JM Some were consciousness-raising groups, some were study groups, some were groups on specific topics like, 'You and Your Family'. I worked in one group where we studied what I called home work – that's people who take work from factories and do it at home. In the area in which we were living we realised that this was extra exploitation: women were paid way below an acceptable minimum wage because they were not unionised. When you calculated that they paid all their overheads, they were sometimes getting as little as a shilling an hour. This was happening particularly to

black West Indian women or Pakistani women who were
working at home. The factories had no overheads. They
just supplied the materials to the women. We did a
survey on the conditions of these women. But other
groups would be consciousness-raising. In one we did
some work on the nature of the family. So for several
years I did a lot of practical political work. Meanwhile
I was trying to look at the question of how does sexual
differentiation come about? What is sex difference?
We have to become human as men and women within
a culture. And that's where I got into psychoanalysis as
a possibly useful theory for trying to understand the
construction of women as a category 'woman' – as a
social construct distinct from the obvious biological
differences between the sexes and distinct from the
obvious sociological notions of conditioning.

RR Would you say that the differences between the sexes
have biological origins or are socially conditioned?

JM I would put the stress on neither social conditions nor
biology. I feel that all societies are built around a
fundamental construction of men and women as socially
different. This construction will use biological differences, and will be implemented by social conditioning.
But it's not reducible to either, so that 'woman' is a
social construct and so is 'femininity'. A man can feel
feminine, a woman can feel masculine. So biology
doesn't give you your psychological socially constructed
identity.

RR You were working with Marxist men and you became
aware that there was no concept of women as a group
within their thinking. What was it that made you realise
that?

JM I'd say that it's a combination of personal experience
and an historical moment. I'd been co-educated as a
child in the sort of environment where it really was
expected that girls and boys would do the same thing.
It was a progressive co-educational school. It wasn't
strongly differentiated along sexist lines. I'd grown up
without my own father, and with my mother always
working. In a sort of pre-women's movement way my
mother had feminist consciousness. She was very pro-

women, a very independent sort of woman. After school, I went to a very privileged, 'women on pedestals' sort of university, Oxford, where women were one in twelve of the student population. At Oxford it was an ambiguous status. You were told you were rare, being a woman at Oxford, but that you weren't extraordinary in the way men were. So educationally I moved from an atypical equality to an atypical position of privilege. It was a very odd sort of situation but one which, in a sense, you didn't really realise you were in. I didn't really understand clearly that women were in a particularly differentiated position until I had my first job as a university lecturer. I was twenty-one and I was in an established English Literature department. Literature was the subject dominated by women students, yet I was the first woman they'd ever appointed. That sort of privilege finally made me wonder. I looked through the educational history of women. As girls we were doing fine up till roughly age eleven and then we just slithered downhill so that there were far less women doing well at sixteen, even less doing well educationally at eighteen, and even less doing well at post-graduate level. They just weren't there at all at post-graduate levels of university appointments. Then in the Marxist group I was the only woman on the board of twelve. Where were the other women? I had grown up with other women who had expected to do well. I was brought up in an ideologically privileged environment, believing in the possibility of individual choice. This is nonsense for most people.

RR   What do you think of the issue of individual choice: that women can change their lives if they want to?

JM   It's rubbish. It's class limited. I had some choice because I came from a particular social group where there were some possibilities. But even within that group it was quite difficult to exercise choice and to do differently.

I think the other thing about privilege was how one lost out in relation to other women. The early days of the women's movement were a fantastic rediscovery for most women of other women; of friendships and liking, and disliking. We formed relationships that had been missed out on because most women in my generation primarily related to men. The first time one spoke in an all-women group, one didn't feel one was speaking at first, and then it became really freeing and amazing. I think that really was it. To change one's relationship to women and therefore, of course, to men too. It's a real gain of the women's movement that women will take each other seriously and talk to each other.

RR What about your current involvement with women and with the women's movement?

JM It's rather informal. I attend conferences and participate but am not involved at basic organisational levels any more. My basic involvement is that I'm still interested above all in the question of 'what are women?'

RR And your work itself has moved, hasn't it, more into your own discipline?

JM Yes. I wrote *Psychoanalysis and Feminism* because I was interested in whether we could use psychoanalysis as a theory that would help us understand the construction of the social difference between the sexes. After I had finished writing it I was still very interested in psychoanalysis and trained as a psychoanalyst. I work part-time as a psychoanalyst and the rest of the time I write on women. In analysis I don't only work with women. I think when you're an analyst you're listening to what the person brings you and that's what you hear and that's what you work with, so I don't set out with any self-conscious feminist intention.

RR Women who are married and have a child, like you do, can experience conflict in terms of the women's movement, men and motherhood. Have you got any feelings about those? About being heterosexual?

JM There was a point in the women's movement when one really was denounced for being heterosexual. One can still be denounced for living in a conventional family situation as I certainly do. I haven't always done so. It's relatively recent in my case. I think there are conflicts there certainly. I just feel I've always lived with conflicts. I think it's not a major conflict in my life, probably because I got married and had a child really quite late. I had my daughter when I was thirty-seven. I think that if you have a child when you're younger there is conflict about what you want to do, whereas I'd done quite a lot. I'd studied, worked, travelled, lived alone, lived with other people. I wanted to marry my husband, I wanted a child at that point and I adored having her. I still adore having her. It doesn't mean that there are no pressures. It doesn't mean that there are no conflicts. There certainly are. Social conditions and men's and women's attitudes do not make it at all easy to continue with one's work and have a family.

RR   If what Betty Friedan's now saying is, 'Look we're so exhausted and so tired because we've been liberated. Let's go back to where we were', that's not a solution?

JM   That's not what feminism is about. First of all, I don't think we have been liberated, but let us, for argument's sake, say that we have. So what. Nobody guaranteed that was going to make you feel happier, it means you are liberated from certain conditions of exploitation and oppression. 'Liberation' is simply a pre-condition for greater fulfilment. That's all it is. When a country is liberated, it has overthrown a state of oppression and exploitation but then its problems as a liberated country commence. Women have not been liberated; when we have it will not be time to give up, but to go on with the struggle. Conditions for some women are being improved but always in a very vulnerable way. Our gains can always be lost, because the basic structure of sexual differentiation and its consequences has not been altered. When changes are made it's always in a way that they don't actually affect the structure of the system, and when the system is stressed they can be eliminated easily.

RR   What about men?

JM   Well essentially we construct our societies along that division, 'men/women'. Men in that sense hold the dominant position. But many don't relate to that category 'men'. I don't think a lot of men feel that they've got much power to give up. For the individual man it's a question of feeling yourself to be yourself: 'If I go home and do all the washing up and the child care, then I'm not a man, and what am I if I'm not a man?' Our social definition of being a man is not to be a woman, and that becomes equated with not doing the tasks that women do. Men are not going to feel secure. In times of basic change people feel insecure. In a sense a women's movement does provide security for women because they've got other women doing it. Men being asked to change have to do so on their own; there's no reference group for them.

RR Why do you think conflict with other women within the women's movement occurs?

JM Just as I don't think liberation and freedom from oppression are necessarily happiness, I don't think that women are automatically nice. In our society I think we have absorbed part of the ideology that women as such are nice. Once we're trying to question the ideology we're questioning that definition of women. We're no nicer than anyone else and we can have fights. People like their own way; they like their own opinions. Women have grown up having to be seductive to men, nice to men. They may then behave more decently to men at some level and probably in a rather superficial way, than they do to women. Women have been oriented to see themselves in relation to and relating to men. They compete with other women for men, and some of that's bound to carry on into the women's movement where women may be still competing, though not for men. We have splits along issues such as sexuality because we differ as to the explanations for the causes of women's oppression. In that sense the movement is bound to be diverse and multifarious while we're working at understanding the causes of women's oppression.

RR You've talked about the fact that women have to keep struggling. Is that really the answer: that it is a continuous struggle?

JM Yes, otherwise absolutely every reform gained is the victim of economic pressures and the ideological reaction of a dominant social group, such as 'the right to life'. Because of money, social class, and so on, such ideology can become dominant again and women can lose all the social gains, all the 'miniature' social gains, that have been made.

Gwendolyn Landolt

Gwendolyn Landolt is a Canadian lawyer, a member of the Children's Aid Society, the Canadian Institute of Law and Medicine and legal counsel for the Toronto Right to Life Association. She is married with two girls and three boys ranging in age from sixteen to seven years. She has written many submissions for government, the latest being a brief to the Parliamentary Committee on the Constitution (1981). Gwen has written a number of articles for journals and has contributed a chapter to the book Death Before Birth, *edited by Synan and Kramer (Griffith Publishing Co., 1974).*

I was always a feminist in the sense that I have always thought that women are as intelligent and capable as men and are entitled to the same legal, political and social rights as men. This belief gave me the confidence to study law and enabled me to graduate from the University of British Columbia, Faculty of Law, in 1958, prior to the recent feminist wave which 'legitimized' women in the legal profession.

The first few weeks in law school were traumatic in that there were only four women in a class of 110 students. We were regarded by some of the male students with considerable suspicion. I remember an earnest young man asking me one day in genuine puzzlement – 'Why would a nice girl like you study law?' His comment was a revelation to me, as up to then I had not thought that girls, 'nice' or otherwise, should not be there. More importantly, his comments revealed to me for the first time the anxiety obviously felt by some males at the presence of women in the profession. I also learned a very important fact which experience as a practising lawyer subsequently confirmed – namely that a man's reaction to women lawyers was directly related to his own sense of masculinity. If he was sure of himself and his masculinity, then he was not threatened, and treated women as colleagues and equals. If he was unsure, then he was uncomfortable, and tended to downplay women as intellectual and professional equals. In the 1950s and 1960s he would express this adverse reaction openly, but in the enlightened 1980s, although he may still *think* the same, rarely would he openly express this for fear of being regarded as reactionary. However, in spite of pressures to the contrary, I could not see any reason why I should submerge and hide my interests and abilities simply because of what others thought or society dictated.

Perhaps, too, it was just that I had no idea that I was supposed to have been oppressed and had no 'right' to enter a male profession. My feelings at that time been best expressed by the American author-historian and two-time Pullitzer prize winner, Barbara Tuchman, in a speech she gave to her alumni at Radcliffe College in 1975 when she stated:

I had no idea that growing up female in America was a position of slavery. Not that I was always happy; I often was very unhappy even miserable. But I always thought that that was due to personal failings. I didn't know that to be a woman was really a very terrible fate. In fact, I thought we had an advantage. I thought that the capacity to create life, to create another life, which was what the Bible gave to God and Nature gave to women, gave us a superiority over men. I don't know why; I just grew up with that idea. I thought it was fine to be a woman. As you can see, I was ignorant.

Because of my interest in law and politics, I was naturally interested in the legal and political rights of women. I remember burning with indignation, when I came across instances of past injustices to women. I appreciated the efforts of the pioneer feminist women in Canada, such as Nelli McClung, who won the right to vote for women in the province of Manitoba in 1916, and Emily Murphy, who was the first woman police magistrate appointed in the British Empire. Both Nelli McClung and Emily Murphy were involved in the famous 'person' case which led to the Privy Council declaring that women in Canada were, in fact, legal persons and, therefore, were eligible to be appointed to the Canadian Senate. Had I been born at the time these women were striving for their goals, I would most certainly have been an active supporter and ally in their efforts.

After my call to the British Columbia Bar, I practised law for seven years, enjoying my independence and challenging work. However, in my late twenties I began to feel that something was missing in my life. For all my smartly furnished apartment, travel, fashionable clothes, and an active social life, I began to feel that surely there was something more to life. To be a lawyer was an achievement, but at the same time it was not completely satisfying in that a part of myself wanted something more.

I began to realize that there was another side to my nature to which previously I had not paid much attention, namely my feminine or maternal side. I realized that I was not only an intellectual and professional being but also a woman, quite distinct and different from the male lawyers with whom I associated. I began to understand that women, although equal to men in intellectual capacity and ability, were none the less born with a difference – the difference being the powerful maternal instinct. Some women never develop this instinct to any extent, some deliberately suppress it, but *all* women are born with it to a lesser or greater degree.

It was not surprising that I subsequently married and am now the mother of five children. I found that being a wife and mother was a very creative and rewarding experience and more fulfilling than the practice of law alone. It seemed to me that anyone could be a lawyer, but I was the only one who could be the mother of my children and who could pass along the values and philosophy which I believed would prepare them for their future life.

I found my role of wife and mother so all-encompassing and busy that I concentrated full time on it, and for several years gave up my legal career without regret. I probably would have continued thus except for a development on the

Canadian political scene which had a profound effect on my life, and my attitude and relationship toward the feminists and the women's movement (which at that time were synonymous to me). At this time, the abortion law in Canada was widened, which has resulted in over 100,000 deaths from abortion each year. I made no deliberate attempt to become involved in the issue at first. But I saw a feminist on the national Canadian Broadcasting Corporation television network, claiming 'a right to her own body' and a 'right to abortion'. In law school I had learned that an unborn child could inherit property and could be the subject of a trust, and suddenly someone was telling us that the unborn child had no rights and could be disposed of simply because it was inconvenient and unwanted. Nonsense! I was incensed over this disregard for the rights of the unborn child as I had previously been over the disregard for the rights of women. I felt that the comments of the feminists with regard to abortion could not go unchallenged.

Almost immediately I founded and became the first president of the Toronto Right to Life Association and was one of the founders of the political arm of the pro-life movement in Canada. I also subsequently became National President of the educational arm. I presently serve as legal counsel for the political arm, Campaign Life, as well as for the Toronto Right to Life Association.

It became necessary for me directly and openly to oppose the feminists for two reasons. It quickly became apparent that the militant feminists would not accept or tolerate any expression of opposition to, or criticism of, any of their decisions. For anyone to do so, was to be labelled 'reactionary' and mindless. This intolerance on the part of the feminists came as a surprise to me, as my experience up to then had been mostly with men, whom I found to be relatively more tolerant of differences of opinion. Secondly, and most importantly, I did not want to be part of an organization or movement which ignored the fundamental principle of a right to life at all, without discrimination. It seemed to me nothing short of hypocrisy on the part of the feminists to object to the oppression of their own rights but at the same time to demand the right not only to suppress but actively to destroy the rights of another human life that was inconvenient to them.

The inclusion of abortion in the feminists' platform led directly to a split in the women's movement. Thousands of women like myself, although firmly believing in the legal and political equality of women, could not accept the killing of unborn children as a valid solution to an unplanned pregnancy. The feminists were thus denied the support, intelligence, energy and resourcefulness of many thousands of women, and the women's movement in Canada became then, and still is, badly fragmented.

Abortion was to be the great equalizer which would make women equal to men. They would no longer be subject to the tyranny of the womb which allegedly impaired their ability to compete with men. However, I believe that the feminists have fallen into a male trap. They are attempting to adapt women to a wombless male society instead of adapting society to meet the needs of women. Women *do* have maternal instinct, they *do* have wombs and they *do* get pregnant, and society must meet these needs.

This push for equality for women on male terms is based on the mistaken concept that the differences between male and female are not caused by nature, but rather, are caused by the stereotyping of children from birth by society. In order to alleviate this alleged stereotyping, the present-day feminists have gone to great lengths to 're-educate' the younger generation. For example, our children's reading material has been carefully sanitized. My young son's Grade 1 reader has scrupulously neutered all the people in it. The children have been given genderless names ('Pat' and 'Jan') and the stories are replete with 'successful' women – the working mother, the female doctor and school principal, who are all carefully attired in genderless clothes and with masculine hair styles.

This denial of the maternal side of woman's nature and the attempt to adapt women to male standards is not new in history. For example, it was fashionable for well-to-do French women of the seventeenth and eighteenth centuries to send their children to the country to be cared for and nursed by a stranger immediately after birth and they scarcely had any contact with the child from then on. These women were conditioned to think by their society that what they did with their children was unimportant and that their intellectual activities were all-important. Many of the children did grow up to become well-adjusted adults because they often got the mothering, the attention and security, from the women who raised them. Unfortunately, in present-day Canada, because of feminist pressures, it has now become fashionable or 'conventional wisdom' that women should be fulfilled on male terms by way of a career or, at least, an occupation outside the home, and the role of mother and homemaker has become badly denigrated. Women who stay in the home are regarded as being wasted. Unfortunately, the majority of women, just like men, are sadly unable or unwilling to think independently on this issue, and to determine what is best for themselves as well as for their family. They seem all too prepared to merely go along with what 'society' dictates regardless of the consequences. Unfortunately too, for society, far too many children as a result of this are not getting the necessary love, security and mothering. According to one of the Toronto Children's Aid Societies on which I serve as a board member, the number of children entering into the agency's care because the parents are 'unable to cope' or because of 'parent-child conflict' increases alarmingly each year.

Unfortunately, more and more women today are being obliged to enter the workforce, not because they necessarily yearn to make decisions in the boardrooms of the nation, but more often out of sheer necessity to pay the mortgage or to buy winter boots for the children. Again, where are the feminists who should be agitating for women to have a real choice as to whether they go to work or stay at home? They should be demanding increased government grants to alleviate the financial pressures on families.

This would also allow women some independence economically as they would not then be totally dependent on their husbands financially – a sensitive issue with many women who remain at home. Ultimately, government grants to mothers at home would be much cheaper than the alternative of more government-established day care centres, and the ever-increasing number of emotionally damaged children. The family unit is a building block upon which society rests – and its preservation must take priority in any government policy.

A decent mother's allowance would enable many women to stay in the home and raise their children. Why should a stranger be paid to raise your child when you can do it better yourself? In most cases no one can take the place of the mother. Yet the feminists, who demand loudly that women have a choice, do not really want that choice but rather want women to be obliged to enter into the workforce, on male terms.

This is not to say that women who work full-time, whether by necessity or choice, do not make good mothers; of course most do. It is just harder – a whole lot harder, and usually at an enormous personal cost to the women, both physically and emotionally. A career should not take precedence over motherhood and family life. This was the position taken by the early Canadian feminists who saw motherhood as the highest achievement of their sex. As Nellie McClung stated: 'Every normal woman desires children.' They agreed that a woman's primary role was that of wife and mother, and they saw her public responsibility to society as an extension of this role. Not surprisingly, the feminists in Canada have remained very quiet about this aspect of their forebears' platform. It may be sixty years later – society may have changed – but the nature of women has not.

Until the feminists come to terms with reality and attempt to adapt society to meet the real needs of women; until they widen their vision to include the needs and interests of all members of society, men, women, and children, born and unborn – then I cannot support them.

Jocelynne Scutt

Jocelynne Scutt is a Barrister-at-Law, currently Associate to a High Court Judge in Australia. She is single and at thirty-four has six degrees and diplomas in the legal field from the Universities of Western Australia, Sydney, Michigan (Ann Arbor) and Cambridge (UK). She is on many committees relevant to women's affairs and belongs to a number of women's groups, for example: Feminist Legal Action Group, Women's Electoral Lobby, Steering Committee Women's Refuge Evaluation Committee (N.S.W.), New South Wales Women's Advisory Council to the Premier (1978–81), Chairperson, Australian Capital Territory Advisory Committee to the Australian Broadcasting Commission. Jocelynne has written and delivered numerous papers on issues relating to women and the law, is co-editor of Women and Crime *(Allen & Unwin, 1981) and author of* Even in the Best of Homes: Violence in the Family *(Penguin, 1983).*

I am a lawyer, feminist, women's liberationist. I am single, with no children – not because I do not like companionship or children, but because my commitment to feminism and my career exclude any thought of marriage or childbearing. Fortunately for me, I have friends, including a sister, who have children whom I like – and who like me.

The women's liberation movement is, to me, reflected aptly in the slogan 'Sisterhood is Powerful' and, when in a cynical frame of mind, in its more recent formulation, 'Sisterhood is Powerful . . . It Can Kill!' I am not a blind acceptor of any fairytale that women are always, everywhere, 'good' to one another, but I sincerely believe every one of us is trying as hard as she can to alter a world that is unkind to women. I am willing to work to alter the present world structure through what some might call 'reformist' means – for example, by law reform. Some think that by reforming laws, protest is contained, making the oppressed more likely to take their oppression kindly. I do not. I believe that reform of laws makes the oppressed more ready to protest at discrimination, at powerlessness, and to demand – eventually to take – power over ourselves. The 'second' path is the gaining of autonomy, which is what revolution means to me. In taking these approaches, I endorse the Manifesto of the New York radical feminist group, the Redstockings:

> Women are an oppressed class. . . . We are exploited. . . . Our prescribed behaviour is enforced by threat of physical violence.
>   Because we have lived so intimately with our oppressors, in isolation from each other, we have been kept from seeing our personal suffering as a political condition. This creates the illusion that a woman's relationship with her man is a matter of interplay between two unique personalities, and can be worked out individually.
>   In reality, every such relationship is a *class* relationship, and the conflicts between individual men and women are political conflicts that can only be solved collectively. We regard our personal experience, and our feelings about that experience, as the basis for an analysis of our common situation . . . We will not ask what is 'revolutionary' or 'reformist', only what is good for women.[1]

I cannot think of a time when I did not know, with absolute certainty, that women have every right to do anything that men have the right to do. As a child I can recall feeling rage at not being included in a boys' touring cricket team – not because I could play cricket (I couldn't – that part of my socialisation into a female stereotype was quite secure), but because I was being excluded, as a female, from a particular group because they were boys and I was not. This was in a small country primary school, where a touring cricket team was not made up of cricket whizzes, but simply of male students. The senior class had just enough boys to make thirteen, plus standbys and the obligatory supporter or two to stand on the sidelines; all boys were included, all girls excluded.

Neither my father nor my mother tried to persuade me that I should conform to a so-called female role. Rather, the message I received was that women, like men, grow up to have careers. At the same time they might meet a knight on a white charger, but this would be a bonus, not the answer to life. At thirteen, during a rugged debate with my maternal grandmother, she told me I should be a lawyer to put my ability to argue to good use. It was the force of my grandmother's belief in my right to take on a profession mostly inhabited by men that resulted in my entering the field. Marriage did not go with it.

Women in my family had a far greater impact upon my growth as a feminist than did men – although the latter (particularly my father) were not irrelevant. Maude Helen Needham, my maternal grandmother, was a delegate to the first Labor Women's Conference in Western Australia in the early part of this century. Reared as the beautiful Maude, eldest of three daughters and four sons, pampered by an admiring mother and father, trained in the art of being a nineteenth-century lady, she later became a businesswoman and owned (and drove) one of the first motor cars in Western Australia. On my father's side, Frances Elizabeth Davies spent time in India as a child where she was socialised by her father, an army Colonel, into being somewhat cold, but strong. My mother married at twenty-eight. She continued her career until six years after the birth of my elder sister Robin and myself, when our sister Felicity was born. She was an intellectual woman who wrote plays, short stories and novels – but dared not put them to the test of a critical publisher's eye. Her timidity in some situations was incongruously matched by a bravery that led us all off on a holiday (when my father was away on business) to Busselton, a seaside town in Western Australia, without having made any plans for accommodation or return travel, and never having been there before. We ended up at the local police station where the sergeant was aghast at the sight of a young-looking woman (she aged well!), a toddler and four year old in tow, asking for a cell to be made available for an overnight stay. Luckily, he found us a beachside house in Busselton!

The Law Faculty at the University of Western Australia was designed to crush any young woman who entered it into a straitjacket of conformity. The ethos propelled me further in my vision of women being entitled to do anything, and prejudice preventing them from doing it. Certainly at this time there were two types of woman firmly depicted in my head: those women who did things, were not cowed by so-called masculine superiority, and who denied that all women were valuable only as social companions, appendages, or embroidery on the arm of a man; and those women who were only social companions, appendages, or embroidery on the arm of a man. There were four women in my year, and about ten women in the entire Law School. In the first year there were sixty men. All staff, apart from one tutor, were men. Apart from female friends in other faculties, I came into contact with women only when they came, together with male law students, to various Law School shows. They concentrated more upon being simpering or sexy than upon talking politics or law or sociology. Later, when I joined the women's liberation movement, I recognised how unjust I had been to those women, and how society had deliberately forced me into a position where I had divided women into those who, like myself, wanted intellectual stimulation and humour from men or women, and those who, like they, desired only to catch a man.

When I was in the United States, at a private university in Texas, where southern belles engaged in strong debate about social, political and economic issues when they talked with other women, but reverted to the ante-bellum type when a man appeared on the scene, I realised that the women I had known at the University of Western Australia were not bereft of intelligence or of conversation. They had pretended to be so, terrified of being cleverer than the elitist young men who were studying the law, and who would (in conventional terms) make such wonderful husbands, with houses in the 'right' suburbs, partnerships in the 'right' firms.

At the University of Michigan, Ann Arbor, in 1973 the women's liberation movement had taken a firm hold. The university had been in the forefront of demonstrations and student activism against the war in Vietnam, and many women students had been involved as leaders and supporters. One professor, Virginia Blomer Nordby, had developed a women and the law course and was in the midst of drafting the now renowned Michigan sexual assault law. She was active in organising with students and women in the National Organisation of Women (NOW) and other feminist groups. In the United States I found women who articulated their concerns about the oppression of women and our relegation to the lower echelons of paid employment. The Women Law Students' Association held regular meetings tackling sexism within the Law School. They organised delegations to the Dean to demand the eradication of sexist language. When there was a suggestion that women and the law was not a 'proper subject' for law schools, they lobbied members of the Faculty as well as the Dean and received a firm assurance that the subject would remain on the curriculum – although the professor responsible was never granted tenure. During 1973–4 I researched the law relating to rape in marriage as a project outside my strict university credits, as part of a rape law reform project then underway. For credits, my major thesis dealt with discrimination against women in criminal law from an Australian and United States' perspective.

In July 1974 I left America for England – and was shocked at the apparent lack of awareness about the women's liberation movement of the women I met at the University of Cambridge. At this time, I even began thinking perhaps I was mad for believing what I had believed all my life and what had been reinforced so well in the United States. Was it incorrect to recognise that discrimination against women existed? I came upon women at the university who thought they were there, the whole 15 per cent of them, because they were somehow undeniably more brilliant than their sisters. They accepted (at least outwardly) that less women than men should be at Cambridge. At the time some women in England were active – the *Sex Discrimination Act* was passed in 1975, and in 1974–5 a number of the all-male colleges at Cambridge went co-ed. Recent histories of the British women's movement testify to women's activism and to raging ideological debates taking place in some parts of England and Scotland.[2] Somehow, at Cambridge we were isolated from the dashing assertion that was the North American women's liberation movement. If a woman overthrew her 'traditional' role, it was somehow because she was 'special', more hardy, more intellectually gifted . . . or had more money or more breeding than the rest.

In West Germany in 1975–6 the support and strength of the feminist movement was obvious. Women demonstrated in hordes against a ruling by their constitutional court limiting the circumstances under which they might seek an abortion. At the Max-Planck Institute, I continued my study on rape laws. The years I spent analysing rape laws from a feminist perspective taught me that male chauvinism does not stop at the borders of Australia, the United States or England. It lies in attitudes and behaviours that have built up the legal systems of the Western world, whether Scandinavian, European, or Anglo-Saxon. I returned to Australia determined to work collectively with other women to change the laws relating to rape in the short term, and to help the long-term effort of altering our entire socio-economic, legal and political system so that women would no longer be forced into second class citizenship, or be relegated to the status of property to be raped, beaten and tossed aside, or locked up in the Australian equivalent of the Englishman's castle. I joined the Women's Electoral Lobby to work for changes to the laws that might advance women to a position where we would make laws to suit our needs rather than those of the other 49 per cent of the population.

Today, my commitment remains to women and the women's liberation movement. In my private life that commitment does not mean that I cannot have friendships with men. Contrary to the often stated view that feminists are 'man haters', I believe that the problem for the women's liberation movement is that we care about men too much. That is, we care about all humanity irrespective of gender. All my time is spent doing something about the oppression women suffer (an oppression which is ultimately to the detriment of men, also), and I would never accept any argument that we should be only concerned about 'people', not 'women'. (By 'people', those putting the argument invariably mean 'men'.) However, what makes fighting for the rights of women and against women's exploitation so difficult is that the world I want at the end of it is a world peopled by women and men, living as equals. If I wanted a world without men, the fight would be far more simple: get rid of all the men. What is important for women who care about men is that it renders us incapable of sufficient brutality to end male-female exploitation immediately, by severing relations. In my sexual friendships, for example, I do care about men. I continue to hope that through personal intimacy it may be possible to build an egalitarian, caring, non-oppressive way of relating to those who are presently the exploiters, thus eradicating that exploitation. Yet if one has just seen a film about rape, or attended a conference on violence against women, it is impossible to relate to men in a responsive way, even if they are relatively less chauvinistic than the mainstream male. The force with which women's subjugation is brought home makes it impossible calmly to communicate with a representative of the group that enforces that subjugation. This is why, apart from every other reason, like independence, my career, my time, my own humanity, I would never begin a long-term relationship with any man friend. The price to be paid – loss of identity, of the right to be solitary, to be alone, to be uncommitted, to be one's own woman – would be too high. It would mean surrender of self.

In my professional life I am involved in legal work that often does not directly relate to the rights of women, but into which I inject feminist philosophy. A great deal of my work involves writing analyses of laws that have been inimical to the interests of women; these articles are published in so-called legitimate journals. To be airing feminist views in such journals, so that conventional lawyers cannot ignore them (or find it more difficult to do so) is worthwhile. They are flags for feminists ploughing through conventional areas of law and criminology, that they are not alone.

Other actions can be more direct. With the push to reform rape laws in Australia and most particularly in New South Wales, to me the most important aspect was that of education. I was able, as a member of the New South Wales' Women's Advisory Council with the backing of government, to travel around the state to country towns talking with women from various backgrounds about the problem of rape laws and the proposals to make those laws less unfair to women. This experience was valuable to me, too, making me aware of the energy existing amongst women in the country and letting me know how strongly women were together on the need to change attitudes towards violence against women, and more important, to stop it.

The rape law reform experience was also important from a negative viewpoint: it taught me that not all women have similar commitments to women; and that although we believe we are all part of the feminist movement, we are not immune to being duped by male power plays. I had believed that all women with a commitment to feminism would be able to work together for positive ends. From 1978 to 1981 I learned that this is not so. Sometimes when women have a commitment to the movement and to the bureaucracy, there is a conflict of interest that can lead to a partial deadening of their ability to see that what women in the liberation movement want, at grass roots level, is more important than what male bureaucrats or male members of government want. There is no point in women attempting to make women's issues legitimate in the eyes of the bureaucracy, for women's issues are by definition incapable of being legitimated according to masculine standards. That is why they are hived off as separate 'issues'. In the fight for rape law reform, some women allowed themselves to be used to temper feminist demands. The saddest thing about this was that those at the head of the government were prepared to go as far as women in the community wanted. Some women in the bureaucracy and in advisory positions cut down the demands of women in the community on the ground that government would never tolerate them. This meant that the government was never tested, and New South Wales ended with a rape law reform not as far advanced (nor in accordance with feminist principles) as it should have been and could have been. It is not bad – but not bloody good enough!

The conflict arises because there are men in powerful positions and women in powerless positions. The women who seem to have power in the masculine sense of the word, have no power. They are subject to the control of the men running the government and the bureaucracy. They have no real freedom to decide, no autonomy. Any oppressed group 'naturally' criticises and conflicts with members within the group rather than with those outside who are the oppressors . . . at least, some of the time. The miracle is that within the women's movement there is as *little* negative conflict as there is. Despite being driven by outside forces to class amongst ourselves, the achievements of the movement cannot be denied.

The women's liberation movement is centuries old. Throughout that time attempts have been made to put us down, but those attempts have been futile. Women now are firm in talking about our rights, in demanding equal time with men, equal rights with men, and equal power. Each one of us suffers from a lack of self-esteem, yet we stay upright, demanding. This is not, however, to deny the strength of the forces against what we want. The women's liberation movement works from rundown offices or houses, with an occasional electric typewriter to type up press releases and newsletters that are copied on bad quality paper on burnt out roneo machines. The patriarchy operates from skyscrapers, with the latest in office machinery, and with slaves to type the press releases, do the shit-work, make the tea. That we continue in the feminist movement is a tribute to the power and the strength of all women. Although the achievements are not sufficient, in the end we have to believe we are advancing. To believe otherwise would be a denial of women's whole existence.

Notes

1 Quoted in Anna Coote and Beatrix Campbell, *Sweet Freedom – The Struggle for Women's Liberation*, London, Pan Books, 1982, p. 15.
2 See, for example, Coote and Campbell, *op. cit.*

Nance Cotter

Nance Cotter is an active member of the Women's Action Alliance. Australian, aged 55, she has been married for thirty years and has seven daughters and two sons ranging in age from 29 to 15 years. Prior to marriage she was a typist and stenographer. Through her association with WAA she has presented many papers on Parenthood and Family Life, The Role of Women in Today's World, and Financial Support for Families. Nance has always believed in fostering the advancement of women, feeling that the well-educated, confident woman is a better mother. She therefore advocates the best possible education for girls.

I am a human being, a woman, a third generation Australian on one side and second generation on the other, in good health, and rational for the most part. I have nine children, seven daughters and two sons, and that no doubt will class me as rampantly heterosexual.

I am a feminist through and through. I always have been and always will be. When the fanfare of women's liberation sounded in 1975, I had to ask myself some questions. There were wrongs to be righted and discrimination to be eliminated, but from what were I and others like me to be liberated? It seemed we were to be freed from the oppression of the family. The work of the home was denigrated simply because it was the work of women and not paid for. Now to be equal and fulfilled I ought to join the paid workforce. No matter that those who were telling me this had very well paid jobs –

they still insisted that fulfilment took place on the assembly line. So women in their droves forsook the hearth and became low paid menial workers to be free and equal and the same as men.

If there's one thing I cherish, it is the fact that I am different from men, that I have a feminine outlook, a feminine approach to life. *Vive la différence*!

The extreme women's movement and its offshoots clamoured for full-time child-care so that women could be freed from that task. What struck me very forcibly was that there was no real concern for children and no recognition of the child-care done in the home. If work was done in the home it was an oppression; if it was done in the marketplace, it had value.

Since my marriage I had been observing the reactions of children. The first year we offered holiday accommodation to two part Aboriginal brothers from an orphanage, who then became regular visitors to our home. My experience with them taught me a lot about the child who had been deprived of a one to one relationship and about the real needs of children. My observations were further expanded, not only with the rearing of my own family, but by filling in during emergencies for three different families who had lost a mother through death. All I had experienced made this demand for child-care facilities sound a bit phoney. Women's liberation wasn't concerned for the children, only for freeing mothers from caring for them.

A further question struck me – who was going to pay for all these facilities? Naturally it would be the taxpayer; people like us who believed in the best care for children and who were destined to become the new poor in the community – the single income family.

It would have been naive of me to believe that 1975 was a spontaneous outburst from women straining their bonds of slavery and oppression to breaking point. In fact, this widely circulated view of women as an oppressed class, who needed to be liberated, was something I could not accept. It simply wasn't true, certainly not for the women I knew. My own mother had worked hard to rear her family, but she was not oppressed. No doubt she often wished things were better (don't we all), but she had a lively and earthy sense of hum-

our, a lovely singing voice and her interest in the politics of
the day was remarkable.

My paternal grandmother was born in Australia in 1851 and
knew the hardships of early life here. She lived to the age of
92, having borne thirteen children in the then wilderness
of the little township of Rye on Port Phillip Bay (Victoria)
but she was not oppressed. She too was an enthusiastic,
intelligent woman interested in all that was happening. She
knew that the work she was doing was the most important
work done anywhere and her optimism and strength were
passed on to her nine daughters and four sons.

These women certainly influenced my own thinking and
perceptions of life; after all, that is one of the values of
family life. They were feminists who really believed in
women as women and not pseudo men, and for all the
hardship they endured, they had no wish to become like
men, whom they regarded as slightly inferior.

Before 1975 the softening up process had started. Socialist feminist groups were actively campaigning to:

> fight the oppression of all women both supporting demo-
> cratic reforms and measures to break down the material
> barriers to equality thrown up by the family. To do so
> requires measures and institutions to make household
> duties a collective social responsibility and free women
> from the burdens of forced motherhood, such as free
> abortion on demand, free 24 hour child care facilities,
> socially provided collective laundries and other services
> and the extension of freedom of children from parental
> authority and dependence. (p. 94)[1]

Much of this is happening now, but even in 1975 it was not
difficult to sift the real aims of the women's liberation
movement.

What was I going to do? I could say 'that's life', but the
implications were going to affect women everywhere. I had
seven daughters; what was their future? The liberationists
were claiming to be speaking for all women, well, they were
not speaking for me. There had to be a balance to the extreme
women's movement.

I met with friends and we were joined by younger women

from tertiary institutions who were turned off by the women's liberation activities on campus. They wanted equality with men, but they did not want to be pseudo-men. As individuals, we were not going to achieve much, but as a group there was a lot we could do. In April 1975, we publicly launched our organisation – Women's Action Alliance (WAA) – and drew a crowd of 1200 women. This *was* spontaneous and gave us the courage and incentive to go on.

WAA threw itself wholeheartedly into the fray. A Constitution was drawn up and policy formulated covering all issues relating to women. Immediately, we were accused of wanting to chain women to the home, but that has never been our objective. I have most certainly never been chained to the kitchen sink, in fact I don't even do the washing up, and we don't own a dishwasher.

WAA stands for equal opportunity and believes that all careers should be available to both men and women, but we also believe that men and women are different, physically and psychologically, and that there will always be a preponderance of males in some professions and of females in others, if they are given choice. More and more, this difference is being attested to by scientific data and no matter what the liberationists do, they cannot change that. What they can do, however, is confuse young people about their role and ultimately cause great unhappiness.

It has become plain to me that the people who are pushing this philosophy have very well paid careers, so of course they want everything geared to their own situation. They are not concerned that most women who work outside the home do low paid jobs for eight hours and then catch up on the work in the home.

I believe that we must allow women the right to choose whether they will work outside the home, or be full-time workers in the home and the community. They must be allowed to care for their families without financial penalty and government and social policy must be directed towards this end. It is useless to talk of liberation and equality when so many women are economic conscripts, who simply must work outside the home because the family income is insufficient. The unpaid work in the home has been estimated at between 30 and 40 per cent of the gross domestic product.

It is time these figures were taken into account. Unfortunately we live in a society which does not recognise work which is not paid. Financial recognition of the work done in the home would raise the status of all women. Freedom of choice must surely be the basis of liberation, but I do not hear any liberationists upholding the right of women to choose the role of wife and homemaker. Their attitude is 'Right, let her do that if she wants, but let her starve while she's doing it.'

If all women had the confidence to speak their real thoughts, there would be a groundswell of support for family life. Unfortunately, those who shouted the loudest were heard. Women who were busy building families had neither the time nor the money to go to conferences. I believe that these women will be heard especially if they learn the value of organising.

We are now half way through what has been termed the Decade of Women, and we find that some of the leading protagonists for women's liberation are doing an about-face. Betty Friedan was a pacesetter in 1963 when she wrote the book *The Feminine Mystique*. In her new book *The Second Stage* (1981), she says: 'The true potential of women's power can be realised only by transcending the false polarization between feminism and the family. It is an abstract polarization that doesn't exist in real life' (p. 218). What a pity that so much heartbreak and destruction was wrought by people who had such little foresight. Small worry for those like Betty Friedan – she made good money out of the first book and will no doubt make good money out of the second.

My eldest son is married and has three little daughters; my younger son has been married eighteen months and he and his wife are expecting a baby – perhaps it will be a girl. My eldest daughter is a teacher; my second daughter is an occupational therapist who works with handicapped children. My third daughter is a dental therapist working in a school clinic and a fourth daughter will start teaching this year. Two younger daughters are in tertiary colleges and my youngest daughter is still at school but hopes to do nursing. We are in fact almost a feminine community but we do care about all people, men, women and children. I could be accused of steering my daughters into female occupations. These occupations were their own choices and to be realistic, I would say that there is far more satisfaction and reward in their jobs than that of my son who is an engineer. You may be wondering what kind of an income was needed to educate all those children. Believe me, it is earned by one member of the family, my husband, and it is a moderate income. We do, however, live moderately - we are not consumer-oriented - what big family is? Large families are, in fact, the best ecologists.

I have concentrated on the family, because I believe it to be the crux of the debate. The future of society lies with the family functioning as an effective unit in society. I believe in that future, and that belief separates me dramatically from the radical feminists. I am an emancipationist, but I am a whole lifetime of reality away from women's liberation.

Finally, it is worth quoting Betty Friedan from her new book, because she has been through the whole program (1981, p. 229):

> Family is not just a buzz word for reactionaries; for women as for men, it is the symbol of that last area where one had any hope of control over one's destiny, of meeting one's most basic human needs, of nourishing that core of personhood threatened now by vast impersonal institutions and uncontrollable corporate and Government bureaucracies. Against these menaces, the family may be crucial for survival as it used to be against the untamed wilderness and raging elements, and the old, simple kinds of despotism.

Those words have a rare beauty.

Notes

1 'Towards a Communist Women's Movement' from the Natural Women's Conference on Feminism and Socialism, Melbourne, October 1974. Distributed by the Women's Conference Committee, 50 Little La Trobe Street, Melbourne (Words Press), pp. 91-5.

Claire French

*Claire French is fifty-eight, with two sons and a daughter.
She was born in Bavaria and migrated to Australia after the
Second World War. She has had a variety of jobs from grape-
picker, to Secretary to the French Consulate, university tutor
in German, and now a tutor in Women's Studies. She received
her Master's degree in 1969. A feminist, Claire now studies
women's history, Jungian psychology, religion and sexuality
and the mythology of goddesses, all of which she has written
on.*

I was born shortly after the First World War in the Bavarian
Woods. My mother was the eldest daughter of a factory-
worker who knew himself to be the bastard of a Bohemian
count. His mother was a legendary 'Mother Courage' figure
of poor background. In her prime Old Kathrina had borne
and raised twenty sons and one daughter, all sired by various
upper middle-class worthies – and she made no secret about
the paternity of her children.

As my grandfather grew up he lost no time in seducing the
local jeweller's daughter, thus forcing his way into the
respectable business class as a first step to achieving social
acceptance. With his wife's dowry he bought a pub and a
grocery, where he kept his wife and daughters gainfully
employed without ever paying them a penny in wages.
When his wife bore him the third girl he publicly accused
her of adultery and took mistresses whom he paid from his
wife's earnings.

After a traumatic struggle my mother managed to escape into marriage. But the ecstasy she had expected was short-lived. My father, an artist, was a man with all the charm Austrians are famous for, yet there was little substance behind his suave veneer. By the time I was born – yet another unwanted first daughter – my mother knew she had made a big mistake. Rejecting divorce as the worst of social disgraces, both my mother and my maternal grandmother died young, their great and loving hearts broken by their men and the brutal patriarchal marriage code.

Apart from this unhappy family background my earliest impressions were of the sufferings of women: the workers' wives waiting outside grandfather's pub on Friday nights to rescue some of their husbands' earnings so that they could feed their children; those hollow-cheeked, under-nourished children, who often entered life with broken limbs because their mothers had been beaten up during pregnancy; those terrible stories of family beatings, incest rapes and passion crimes, with which our neighbourhood was rife.

I loved the factory women. Beautiful, strong and proud, they managed to hide their agonies behind an infectious laughter. 'Swamp-flowers' the middle-class people called them, and whether they lived within or without the bourgeois moral code, their lives were doomed from the beginning. Once married, they would rise at five o'clock in the morning to get their menfolk and children ready for the day, sharing a wood-stove, a toilet and a water-tap which was frozen in winter, with half a dozen other families. At seven, when it was still pitch dark during the winter months, the factory siren would howl and they had to clock on for work. I can still see them hurrying over icy roads lined by bare rowan trees glittering with frost – dark faceless figures, taking long strides beside their men and carrying their babies wrapped up against the cold. Oh yes, German factory owners did have crêches back in the 1920s, as they could ill afford to lose the potential of the women workers. And the women knew their worth. I remember some of them who, after ten hours in the factory and several more hours cooking and cleaning, would still find the energy to go to a WEA class or run up a frock for their daughter. There was tacit agreement amongst them that they had to be stronger than their mates if life was to continue.

At age six I helped my mother to do the washing. Standing on a footstool and rubbing the clothes on the washing board over a wooden tub I can still hear her admonitions. 'Don't get wet, my dear,' she would say. 'Girls who wet their aprons will get drunkards for husbands.' A drunkard for a husband was the final horror, the great secret fear of every young girl. 'He's not that bad. He's never beaten me yet', was the best these women could say in favor of their menfolk.

As the living hell of a woman's life unfolded before me I made a solemn vow never to get married. One day I asked my grandfather, who was something of a bushlawyer: 'Is there a law that girls must get married?' 'No law required,' he laughed, 'since they are all itching to rush into it.' That could not be true. There were nuns and deaconesses in our town, and Fräulein Meyer, our hunchback seamstress, was a spinster. I approached my mother. She was reluctant to discuss the subject, but finally confessed her secret hopes for me. 'It is a wonderful thing to become a mother – and you need a husband for that. But if a marriage turns out bad a girl should have the chance to fall back on a job.' I must have looked astonished, because she immediately corrected herself. 'No, I don't mean a factory job. I mean a good job: a teacher, or a nurse or a secretary. But to get a good job you need a good education.' That sounded all right. I liked school and I didn't mind studying. Yet Mother was not satisfied. 'If I see to it that you get a good education, don't imagine you'll be rid of housework. You'll have to learn every aspect of housekeeping. No daughter of mine is going to be a bluestocking.' I knew what she meant. There were a few intellectual women in town and they were the butt of the local wits. It was assumed that their homes were crawling with vermin and that they didn't know how to boil an egg.

So, against massive resistance from the men in the family, I became the only girl of my class and vintage who was allowed a liberal education in our little town. It consisted of four years in a convent school and five years in a state high school operating under Nazi directives. The outcome of this unorthodox schooling was schizophrenic, particu-

larly as far as my sexuality was concerned. In the convent
school we were not allowed mirrors in our dormitories.
Even whilst brushing my hair I was admonished not to take
too much care of it. 'A girl's tresses are the ropes by which
the devil pulls young men into hellfire.'

In the German schools of the Nazi era the accent in girls'
education was on motherhood, on the bearing of sons and
the solace of heroes, according to Nietzsche. There wasn't
an ounce of rebel in me. Yet diligently as I tried to absorb
Christian principles, humanistic values and political slogans,
there was but one basic truth that penetrated my unfolding
consciousness with the clarity of inspired revelation. It was
the fact that Hitler and the Pope, pastor, priest, and party-
leader were all agreed upon one universal law – and that was
the subjection of women.

A woman was born to be subordinated to the will of man,
for the gratification of his desire. 'Above all, let woman learn
to serve.' This quotation out of Goethe's *Iphigenia* was
repeated to us endlessly by the teachers of the old humanistic school. The younger teachers knew an even better
one: 'Thou goest to women? Remember thy whip', out of
Nietzsche's *Zarathustra*.

Life in post-war Germany became even more nightmarish.
If during the war we had been able to ward off the attentions
of our own troops by taking refuge behind the bourgeois
code of premarital chastity, the victorious Allies, like victors
everywhere, went for us womenfolk as their rightful share of
the booty. The world will never know the full horror that
was the lot of the women who came under the 'liberating'
care of the Soviet Army. The Americans, while less vindictive, cheerfully produced newspaper articles about the
human studfarms of the SS and expected everyone of us to
be a willing broodmare at the drop of a Camel carton. The
British, bless them, enjoyed the reputation of giving us the
fairest treatment of all our respective liberators. I lived
during these war and post-war years in a state of complete
sexual amnesia. Helplessly, I felt an icy tide of white hatred
surging within me. It was hatred against men and their
martial ambitions; hatred for that moloch State which
ground the youth of the world into blood and gore; hatred
for the State machinery which held us all helpless hostages;

and hatred above all for those praised virile virtues which
exhibit competition, aggression, nationalism and intolerance.

It was hard to suffer the humiliations reserved for the
women of the losing side. We were branded for life, just as
our leaders had branded the Jews in the concentration camps.
The concept of collective guilt was now brought to bear on
us full force. No matter how much we had tried to resist the
forces of unbalanced virility, we had refused to die with the
victims, and we had to pay dearly for our survival. The
judgment of the world and our own conscience accused us
of the most hideous crimes – because we had not raised
our voices in protest. We knew that such a protest would
have meant death for us at the time, as indeed it did for some
heroic sisters, such as Sophie Scholl of Munich who had
organized the students' uprising of the White Rose movement. For years to come we lived in a state of psychic
shock.

How had it all been possible? How could a great and
decent nation like the Germans disgrace themselves so
utterly? Why was the world so unfair to women? The answer
was: *The abysmal subjection of women in Germany and the
overvaluation of masculine values were but two different
symptoms of the same soul-sickness.* The same inner weakness that makes a man a bully, a family tyrant, a petulant
fanatic in religion, in politics or in racial strife were psychological traits which, given the right conditions, could reach
epidemic proportions and the outcome would be the Klu
Klux Klan, apartheid or Auschwitz. It is not the strong man
who is secure in his values and in his social role who falls
prey to these perversions, but the weak man, who feels
obliged to put on a show and to 'prove himself'. I suddenly
realized that women had no part in the bonding frenzy of
national fanaticism. When during the war the radio blared
out the German news of victory and the high enemy casual-
ties, my mother used to say: 'They are all some mother's
son. For every one of those killed a woman has suffered.'

I survived five years after the war in Germany, and finally
escaped to Australia, though some close to me starved to
death. I met Jack in a construction camp in the Kiewa
Valley, one of those forsaken places which are very much a
man's world. In spite of his veneer of beerswilling mateship

I sensed at once that he was not a patriarch. Once he asked me what made me tick and in a fit of grim resentment I said that I was determined to hang on to life with tooth and nail, if it killed me. 'You'll do me', he said. And that was that.

There were problems and hardships galore, but gradually I became a normal woman again and the hatred and bitterness subsided. Jack built us a house with his own hands. He also made me a mother. I can't say I made him a father, because he had been a father all along. He had been a father to me when he had found me in the bush, soulsick and miserable, and his rough kindness had made me feel better. He cares little about the finer things of life, but he cares about life itself. We have achieved happiness by allowing each other a maximum of freedom.

What about my relationship with my sisters? And how do I relate to other men in this time of transition?

When the feminist movement began to gather momentum during the 1960s one thing became clear: just like men with political ideas, so women too were easily polarized into a Left and a Right, a radical revolutionary and a staunchly conservative stand. It is the way our system works and therefore to be expected.

The left-wing *avant garde* spoke a language I had never learnt to speak: the clear, cold, loveless dialectics of Marx and Hegel. In a study on the sociology of the family Ursula Erler exposes both the Marxian and the Calvinistic ethic of productive work as completely neglecting the most important work of women: the labour to give birth and the labour to socialize our children.[1] The result is women's unbearable double burden in Communist countries and her economic insecurity in the West.

On the other end of the gamut we find the 'colonized woman', the socialite who has never cooked or washed or cleaned for her family, yet ironically wants to help her less fortunate sisters. The social stratification among women is there, just like among men, and the co-ordinates of the system go right through our hearts.

Under these conditions the flight into spirituality seemed the only way out – but there again the doors were barred by institutionalized Christianity. Like Mary Daly, I discovered the subtleties of women's repression in the Church. Elise Boulding, Professor of Sociology at the University of Colorado,[2] maintains that at the end of the Classical era, when the Old World collapsed, it was the networking of the Christian women which had made possible the break-through of Christianity. Those were the times when Christianity was young and women believed the words of Paul in his letter to the Galatians: 'In Christ there is neither Jew nor gentile, neither freeman nor slave, neither male nor female . . .'. In the centuries to come the Church Fathers saw to it that those early promises never did come to fruition. As far as women were concerned, their efforts for a new, free humanity suffered a never-ending betrayal.

How do men fit into this ongoing quiet revolution? In her book *The Goddess and her Hero*[3] the German author Göttner-Abendroth proposes a new concept of manhood. She calls it the 'Matriarchal Man'. What she means is the thoroughly humane man who is himself firmly grounded in the mysteries of life and reveres them, just as he reveres woman as giving the greater share of her life to life's continuation. This kind of man has always been with us. His lovable, warm, kindhearted charm never fails to win us. Far away from all machismo and *virilità* we see in him our ideal father, brother, friend and lover. He knows his own worth and will never misuse woman to prove himself. But like the New Woman, the New Man needs to be proclaimed, and from the two a new humanity shall be born.

At the threshold of old age, I am committed to research and teaching in the hope of making some contribution, however small, towards a new society without aggression and without sexual discrimination.

Notes

1 Ursula Erler, *Zerstörung und Selbstzerstörung der Frau* (Destruction and Selfdestruction of Woman) Stuttgart, Seewald Verlag, 1977.
2 Elise Boulding, 'Women in Community', publ. in *Earth's Answers*, New York, Lindisfarne/Harper & Row, 1977, pp. 60ff.
3 Heide Göttner-Abendroth, *Die Göttin und ihr Heros* (The Goddess and her Hero), Munich, Verlag Frauenoffensive, 1980.

Eve Fesl

Eve Fesl (Gabi Gabi Tribe) is an Australian Aborigine, married, with no children. She has had a varied employment history and is currently Director of the Aboriginal Research Centre at Monash University and is studying for her Master's degree.

I want to state at the outset that I firstly view myself as an environmentalist, secondly as an Aborigine, then as a woman. I believe in the ideal of equality of opportunity for both sexes and that in order for either men or women to achieve their full potential they need the support of each other. My success in sport, academia and the workforce is due in part to the support of my father, brother and husband, as well as the female members of my family. Through their help I now have an important position which I enjoy, despite long hours and a commitment that extends into my personal and social life, for with each project completed goes a sense of achievement – a step forward for Aborigines.

In my work I appreciate the help and advice of male and female members of staff but in employing non-Aboriginal males I always discuss with them their attitudes to taking directions from a female. So far racism has played a more significant role in staff relations than has sexism – one has to be careful of non-Aborigines who after a short time on staff are perceived by their friends and then themselves as being 'experts' on Aboriginal culture and who very quickly begin to resent your Aboriginal authority over them.

How the early anthropologists have misrepresented us! That's why we keep getting asked why we don't join the feminist or women's movement. The first answer to such a question is that we don't need to form or join a women's group – we already have a sisterhood of our own.

The second point is that as an oppressive agent of women in our society, sexism runs but second to Australian racism, which we have imposed upon us not only by white men but by white women. We, along with our men, after 150 years of British occupation of our land are still fighting this – there is no room for a sexist division in our society. If one were to measure oppression, on one side of the scale we would see white women being greater oppressors of black women than black men have ever been.

Although I fully support the ideal of the feminist movement that there shall be no discrimination on the basis of sex, I was personally 'put off' the actual practices of feminism when I first attended a gathering of women involved in the movement. The incident which I found distasteful was a very nasty verbal reaction to a young man who had come along to lend his support, followed by an almost unanimous decision to tell him to leave the meeting. How insensitive and cruel I thought that group was, even to a supporter from their own people.

As an Aborigine I felt more in sympathy with the young white man than I did with my 'potential sisters', so I decided not to join the group. Of course, I realise all groups aren't like this, but when I considered how my people had been treated over the past 150 years, the amount of racism that still exists towards us, and this act of intolerance, I decided that my time could probably be more positively spent elsewhere.

To get back to our first point, however, let us take a look at what was meant in the first place by the term 'sisterhood'. Early anthropologists, who were almost entirely male members of a male-dominated society, interviewed only Aboriginal males, and therefore had no input into their research and subsequent writings about the roles of Aboriginal women in their society. In fact had they been more aware of their own sexism and ethnocentrism, they may have attempted to see Aboriginal society not in a comparative manner, but as something new and vitally different.

It has since been established that women in Aboriginal tribal society were, in most regions, the main providers of the food, and therefore the 'breadwinners' of the family. In effect, the men of the tribe were dependent upon the women for their food and provision of shelter. This was in complete contrast to the European society where females were, and mostly still are, dependent upon the males. Our women were economically independent and if they chose, or necessity demanded it, could exist quite comfortably without husbands.

Aboriginal women also had their own secret and sacred life (from which men were barred), had their own rituals and at times their own special language. The men respected and still respect these separate roles of women in Aboriginal tribal society. Conversely, in European society the spiritual and sacred realm was/is solely in the control of men and one would be surprised to ever see a female holding a position equal to that of the Pope.

Aboriginal men, who had more time for religious ritual, held their own ceremonies from which women were barred, and also were seen to play a larger part in religious life, but one must not forget that the women had complete autonomy in a religious sphere which men were not permitted to enter.

On a recent trip to a tribal area a group of us, both male and female, were walking through the countryside when it was said that ahead was a women's sacred cave with women's paintings therein. Immediately the men took another path and said they would meet us further among the valley. There was no question that men would sneak around or attempt to enter the domain of the women, nor did derogatory remarks or sniggers follow – a demonstration of the deep respect with which women's rights are held.

Because our women worked together and shared rituals together we have a strong female bond. In urban society as well as tribal, we sing and dance together for ceremonies, this being a normal part of Aboriginal women's role. These experiences shared between women form us into a disciplined and cohesive group.

Another factor which is instrumental in forming this sisterhood is the extended kinship system and the responsibility of reciprocity: one is obliged to help one's kin. This rule has meant the survival of Aboriginal people throughout the days when attempts at genocide and cultural disruption could have resulted in complete annihilation of our race. This obligation still exists and sustains Aboriginal families in cities, towns and other areas of Australia.

An instance of this was seen amongst my staff a year ago when simultaneously we employed a non-Aboriginal woman who was a sole-supporting mother with two children and an Aboriginal woman in the same situation. Before and after work the non-Aboriginal woman had to take her children to a crêche (although she had a family in Melbourne) and then rush off each night to pick them up – if she were late she would be charged extra money at the crêche. On the other hand, however, the Aboriginal woman had sisters, mothers, cousins and aunts, all of whom took it in turns to look after the children and, if she was required to work or wanted to go away for the weekend, there was always someone with whom she could leave the children. She, on the other hand would assist the family in other ways due to her ability to earn extra income.

Despite what early anthropologists wrote about women in our society, we have always had a voice in the decisions affecting our communities. Men, more frequently than women, *announce* the decisions but there is trouble if these decisions are made without consultation with the women's groups. Also, women have always been inheritors of land.

An example of the respect held for women is that under the law of most Aboriginal tribes, rape was punishable by death, but the imposed British law soon watered this down to reflect its own attitude to women, i.e. rape is regarded as a minor offence rather than a major crime.

It was just as well that our women were strong in their own society, for after the invasion of Australia by the British, Aboriginal men were often taken away to work or were killed or imprisoned. All responsibility for the family was then left to the women, who because of their sex were not so feared and were allowed to enter the dominant society to a greater extent, albeit as slaves. Today, while our own men are still unable to obtain employment, the task of bread-winning and of running the home falls upon women. Again, in such cases Aboriginal women are able to turn to their 'sisters' for help in coping.

Many Aboriginal women have confidence in themselves as people, and are playing a public role in wider Australia on behalf of their people. They also have the support of their men in these roles differing again from their less fortunate non-Aboriginal counterparts. Both Aboriginal men and women support each other when either aspires to roles in the wider community. Pride in the other's achievement is more prevalent than in the white society, where jealousy or a feeling of being 'threatened' seems to be more the norm – perhaps this is due to the sub-ordinate/super-ordinate roles which the majority of both sexes accept in that society.

In the period since the British landed in this country it appears that Aboriginal women proportionally have made greater 'progress' into the non-Aboriginal alien public arena than white women themselves have. When one considers the tremendous obstacles they have had to overcome, one must ask the question 'what enabled them to do it?' Certainly there would be no simple answer, but 'confidence in oneself' must be an essential ingredient.

Aboriginal women are evident in political areas. Four out of four Aboriginal representatives on the two major national advisory bodies to the federal government are women. Women also hold important positions as directors and managers both inside and outside Aboriginal organisations. Non-Aboriginal women, on the other hand, are just emerging into the public arena. This seems to indicate that women who have not faced sexism from their men have had distinct advantages over others in respect to self-esteem. Many problems have been caused by the imposition of the mores of the male-dominated British Australian society on to Aboriginal women. An indirect one, cited by Bell and Ditton,[1] concerns the payment of unemployment benefits to male members of the family. Aboriginal women say this undermines their economic role as providers – that cheques should be split or paid directly to the women, who have always been responsible for looking after the family. The women say that control of the family is being put into the hands of men, who are not used to providing for it. Another occurred in land rights issues, where initially women's ownership of land was ignored.

One aspect that sets our women's groups apart from most non-Aboriginal women's groups is that we work along with, and stand as partners beside, our men – we do not as a whole oppose men *per se*. (It seems to some of us that in Euro-Australian women's groups there is often an element of man-hatred.) This, of course, does not mean that if a decision that affects us is made without consultation, we will not oppose the man or men who made that decision.

We also *like* working with women, a fact that perhaps can be attributed to an aspect of tribal life of which many people are unaware. In tribal life Aboriginal women, unlike European women, are the sought-after spouses in the marriage game. That is, when an Aboriginal female is born her birth is welcomed, as it is a means of political and social alliances through the tribal groups and inter-tribality. When she marries she confirms the structures arranged at her birth. Men compete for her as a bride. She does not have to pretty herself up from babyhood or be taught 'we must dress you up nicely to make you a pretty girl so one day you will find a husband'. She does not have to compete with her sisters for a man. On the other hand, European women from childhood have been taught they must prepare themselves to be attractive, to outdo other women, as a saleable item in a race to 'catch' a husband.

Outsiders should not interfere in Aboriginal matters. I cite a case in which outsiders interfered with a social arrangement which they viewed in ignorance, coloured by their own cultural biases; a case which received publicity and condemnation from non-Aborigines (whose statistics show their marriage rules are not ideal).

A young Aboriginal woman had been promised under tribal law to a certain man and for years prior to the marriage both families had met social and political obligations associated with the arrangement. When the time came for the marriage to take place the girl was persuaded to run away. The matter would have been settled eventually to the satisfaction of all concerned, had not the non-Aboriginal media and outsiders who knew nothing of Aboriginal social norms stepped in with reports fantasising what would happen to the bride and expressing how they, the good white people, would

save her from the assumed barbarity of her Aboriginal relations (who loved her) and other tribespeople. An unconfirmed
report says the young woman was last heard of living in a
de facto relationship with a non-Aborigine – if he leaves her
she will be in dire straits, particularly if she is pregnant or
has a child.

It would be unfortunate if, as racist attitudes changed and
Aboriginal men eventually were accepted as equals by white
males, they adopted some attitudes of the white men, including sexist attitudes based on dominancy and subordination.
Given, however, the extent of racism towards Aborigines
which still exists in Australia it will be a long time before we
will have to confront this sexist problem. By then hopefully,
it will no longer exist.

To conclude, although many Aboriginal women emerge as
strong and confident there are quite a number who have not
been able to cope – who have been raped and battered, and
have become the victims of non-Aboriginal Australians as
well as alcoholic Aboriginal husbands. The report below, in
a daily newspaper, tells how they fared when they wanted to
use a women's shelter:

The bashed wives of Alice Springs come in two colours –
black and white – and their paths cross at the women's
refuge in Bath Street. But nothing seems to be ideal when
it comes to black and white in Alice Springs. The women's
refuge has been turned into a battleground over who
should have the right to shelter there. On Sunday, it was
occupied and barricaded by 13 'Concerned Women' who
claimed the two houses on behalf of all the battered wives
lucky enough to be born white.[2]

Notes

1 D. Bell and P. Ditton, *Law: The Old and the New*, Canberra,
   Aboriginal History, 1980.
2 *Age*, Melbourne, 27 March 1980.

Ngahuia Te Awekotuku

Ngahuia Te Awekotuku had titled her section 'Maori and Lesbian: My View' and she expands on these two strong elements in her experience. At thirty-three she lives, with her two cats (Pingao and Shiro), in Aotearoa (New Zealand). She is 'serene and settled in multi-racial monogamy, with my sapphic muse'. A researcher and writer by preference, she nevertheless lectures in the Continuing Education Centre at Waikato University. She belongs to the Te Whenua Women's Collective and Mana Wahine Maori. Among her many papers are 'Lesbian/Separatist: Some thoughts for Maori Women' and 'Maori Women and The Environment' (New Zealand Environment, Autumn, 1982).

Ngahuia Te Awekotuku describes herself thus – Came aboard this planet with Aries rising, a Taurus sun, and the moon in mercurial Gemini, thirty-three years ago. Raised in many different households, Maori fashion I enjoyed the feather-down soft cuddles of a doting, gentle Kuia (grandmother), graced by the warm safety of a tribal environment. I was fortunate in having a school teacher aunt, whose attentive ministrations and private needs had me reading at four years old: precocious and alien.

School. I loved it, particularly as I grew older, and the cosy security of early childhood years fell away to the temerities of death, illness, violence, and change. The classroom became my safe place, especially the convent of intermediate school. Wonderful, fierce, strong nuns politicized me radically,

116

nourishing me with stories of the IRA, the horrors of Auschwitz and the Klan, the heroism of Violette Szabo, female
freedom fighter. And my fearless, stroppy mother, at home.
Then off I went to high school, to be expelled for insolence,
perversion, and numerous escapades, at the end of my first
year.

Delinquency soon bored me. All my wild mates got pregnant - god! Loathing that option, which the world was
convinced was my fate, I settled down, started my retreat
into study-books, writing, fantasy and politics. These have
persisted, as I gathered degrees - a challenging, often sour
harvest - along the way. BA and MA (Hons.) in English
literature; a recently completed Doctorate in social sciences.

The Doctorate is important for my people; a study of the
social and cultural impact of tourism on my tribal community. In many ways it is a gift to them, to our descen-
dants, for it records the stories, memoirs, anecdotes and
reminiscences of many who have since gone on. And although
I wrote the pieces in between, the story itself, the actual,
substantive and substantial fabric, was woven by the people,
by Te Arawa, my tribe.

I have spent four years in the Hawaiian Islands, cherishing
each balmy moment, and on the North American continent,
aghast; then around the various states of the Pacific, wondering.

Briefly, some basic facts about myself that won't change.
I love women, cats and ducks. Actually, I love animals. Make
myself run a little, swim a lot. Share my life with a superbly
strong and wise woman. Have an insatiable appetite for fantasy science fiction, particularly feminist. Enjoy eating, and
Mozart, Vivaldi and Grace Jones. Adore, need, cherish the
ocean, Hine Moana, her savagery and calm, her enveloping,
enlightening beauty. Her smell. And I dream crazy creative
dreams.

> Whaia ki te iti kahurangi
> Me tuohu koe, he maunga teitei.

> Seek after your innermost wishes;
> and bend only to the highest mountain.

This is a proverb of my people, the Maori of Aotearoa:
New Zealand, where the White Man came, imposing his God,
wielding his technology, indulging his avarice and greed.
Generations later, resilient and resourceful, we reconstruct
and regenerate, drawing some knowledge from within ourselves, and celebrating our language once condemned. Land,
culture, language – all threatened, now emerging with new
meanings and form. Particularly for women, because as the
refurbished tradition develops, a potent and ironic misogyny
appears. Cluttered beneath the superficial structure of
Maori-tanga – a generalized Maori-ness – are concepts, roles
and notions that put woman down, reinterpret her story, and
shove her into a latterday Judeo-Christian line. Following
what the missionaries taught – the debasement of woman as
unclean; the elevation of God the Father, God as Man.

And woman suffers, while the warrior snarls within her.
I am one such woman.

Maori – lesbian – feminist. Born into a colonized tribal
patriarchy in the thermal districts of Aotearoa, I discovered
my lesbianism relatively early, although I certainly did not
survive the stormy years of late adolescence a maiden intact.
Years of study at university fashioned a cosmopolitan exter-
ior, and the galloping madness of antipodean hippiedom and
antiwar actions soon sharpened my political edge, making
me aware and verbal in the white, middle-class world. Particularly on issues I felt affected me directly: class, and deeper
still, colour. Despite a lightish skin – my parents' delight –
and an educated accent, I was still visibly, boldly, Maori.
Nothing could ever change that – it was/is permanent, wonderful, and as inexorable as my femaleness.

Working with flatmates, other female members of our
ghetto student activist community, I often pondered how we
were still chained to the stove or sink, still mute when the
actions, excitement, indulgences of that late 1960s early
1970s world were decided. Any opinions offered by women
were shrugged off, blown away as so much froth atop the
ubiquitous beer mugs of that period. And as a lesbian –
'like that' – I had even less validity. Apart from being Maori,
good god! I wasn't even a *real* woman!

Our day did come, the first gentle ripples that precede a rising tide. *Notes from the Second Year* arrived at the local political bookshop. And never was a volume so cherished: articulating our grievances, exposing our pains, releasing us from our own doubt and self-denial. Suddenly, we women realized, like the valiant Viet Cong, like the blacks, like the working class, we were an oppressed people, a voiceless, hushed, unseen majority – with the right to demand equality. Over the summer of 1971–2, it did the rounds of radical households. By March, a women's liberation group was mustering in Auckland, including the readers of that book, and many other politically involved but exploited women. Most of us felt we'd had an utter gutsful of the macho radical left or hippie 'gentle' men. Ideologically, I felt I'd finally come home, despite being a Maori, despite being a butch role-playing lesbian, despite being a dozen conflicting, different, contradictory selves.

Throughout my life, I have never doubted that women are stronger, braver and more resourceful – regardless of men's rules, men's games, and men's petty triumphs. My role models – of the fierce women fighters, shamans and poets of Maori legend and myth; of the resilient, courageous women of my own extended family – demonstrate this to me. For as much as colonial and contemporary ethnography and tribal record attempt to annihilate the relevance and radiance of their achievements, it is my responsibility to them, as their inheritor, to ensure their stories are not lost in a mawkishly romantic muddle of male-translated history.

The movement in Aotearoa – the contemporary feminist wave of the last dozen years or so – had predictably bewildering beginnings. Issues were relatively tame; men were often active group members; we focused on equal opportunity in education and employment, child-care, and the end of sex role stereotyping. We aimed for the end of the oppression of *all* women, whatever their own credo, perspective, or accountability. We had loads of fun in comic actions, commanded extraordinary media space, and indulged in shrilly competitive bickering while engulfed in massive ideological confusion. Other women noticed us, joined, argued, mobilized. They became aware, became involved, became excited by the reality of feminist revolution. And over the years, the movement gathered momentum.

For me, feminism means working as much as one can to
end the oppression of women; to break our dependence on
men, and to subvert, challenge, and ultimately destroy those
bastions of male power that enslave us. Strategy may vary.
So may commitment. The feminism I ascribe for myself is in
many ways markedly different from that of my friends. Yet
our intention is basically the same. Being a woman-oriented
woman whose lifestyle is as much as possible - socially,
politically, sexually - focused on women, I attempt to define
a clear line for myself by as complete and uncompromised a
commitment to women as I can possibly sustain.

Yet inevitably, the line shifts, for being a fourth world
woman I must also function within the vividly determined
tribal world of female and male, and function effectively. My
ethnicity sharpens my focus brutally, essentially, because
racism is an integral part of cross-cultural relationships in
post-colonial Aotearoa. We strive to acknowledge and exter-
minate those attitudes through countless hours and days and
weeks of gutsearing workshops, sobbing confrontations, and
exorcizing guilt. Yet so many pakeha,[1] including feminists,
remain safely locked into the inertia of not looking, not seeing, but still 'wanting so much to help, to understand.'

The disease must be dealt with, though I feel that racism is
the responsibility of the racist - and *they*, not I, should work
it out. Nevertheless, I count women, initially, as my allies,
because I believe sexism to be the primary offence against
humanity, whatever terse prioritizing the other issues may
engender. However, some thinkers may refute that any one
issue or struggle is more loaded than another. Until women
are free to choose, to chance, to challenge, to change, *no one*
is truly free. And the planet is deprived of half its creative
potential.

As a Maori lesbian, I am often compelled to consider the
colliding urgencies of my life. I have risked the brand of
'house nigger', for I will defend the middle-class white rape
victim before the disadvantaged and deprived brown rapist
- for his act violates *all* women, and welds the manacles of
sexist oppression more fixedly than ever. I move within many
worlds, yet share the confidence and security of my community of tribal women, and a branching global network of lesbian sisters.

With all of them, I experience highly textured, often tragic, visions of our future. Change is painfully slow; progress for us may take generations, as the waves of consciousness and direct confrontation rise, then recede. The small or substantial moves we make, jagged or gentle, subtle or violent, contribute to that process of growth, of revolution. And we are all part of it.

Frequently, the contradictions of my life are harrowing, but I refuse to reject any one facet of myself. I claim *all* my cultures, all my conflicts. They make me what I am; they will shape what I am becoming.

Notes

1 White New Zealanders.

Lynne Spender

Australian by birth, Lynne Spender has returned home after three years in Canada. With an MA in English, she was a teacher for a number of years and is now studying for an MA in Women's Studies at the University of New South Wales as well as undertaking legal studies. She is thirty-five and has two sons aged four and eight. She is a founding member of the Feminist Party of Canada, a member of Women's Electoral Lobby (Australia) and has written Intruders on the Rights of Men: Women's Unpublished Heritage *(Pandora Press, 1983).*

For many years, and prior to my formally joining the women's movement, I saw myself as a fence sitter and tried to rational-Movement I saw myself as a fence sitter and tried to rational-ize that it was really an advantage to be uncommitted, to see all points of view. I grew up in Australia, where as the typical product of a middle class family I had sufficient education to qualify as a teacher but not enough genuine educational experiences to challenge the structures and institutions which modelled my life. I had sufficient conditioning to 'get married', but not enough positive feedback from the 'married state' to expect to live happily ever after. I had enough positive feelings about being female to embark upon child-birth and mothering and even enough enthusiasm to continue my teaching career. I did not, however, remain sufficiently naive to continue mindlessly trying to combine all roles – running a home, teaching, being available as a wife and generally fulfilling the role of superwoman. The seeds of growing discontent and a feeling of injustice were planted and began to germinate.

After two interstate moves, in the wake of my husband's career footsteps and after several times starting at new schools on the bottom rung of the promotional ladder, I was ripe for a radical change.

In the 1970s when I was juggling a teaching 'career' with the responsibilities of home, marriage and child care, I remained fairly insulated from the larger issues of the outside world. The women's movement was little more than a convenient ally in fighting my personal battles at school, at home and among my acquaintances. I read Germaine Greer[1] and also used extracts from *The Feminine Mystique*[2] with senior English students, but to deal with feminism in any frame of reference other than my own individual one seemed unnecessary. In fact, I think I found much of what Germaine Greer had to say rather threatening.

By 1977 with two small children and having withdrawn, disillusioned, from teaching, I found myself at home as a 'housewife'. I know I resented having to write 'housewife' on forms and having to deal with tradespeople and doctors who assumed that I would only understand them if they spoke in monosyllables and who kept their more detailed information for 'the man of the house'. I came through this I think, to have a concept of women as a group and to be aware of the systematic and institutionalized treatment that women received as a categorical and inferior group. Much of my time at this stage was taken up with reading material that my committed feminist sister placed unsubtly under my nose (including Adrienne Rich's *Of Woman Born* which I read during the early stages of labour with my second child).

As a result of my reading and my increasing awareness of the lives of women around me in suburbia, I began to match a fair theoretical understanding of feminism with a general view of Australian society. The picture was not a pleasant one.

In 1978 for want of something better to do and for need of anything at all to do, I agreed to yet another move – again in the male career path – and this time, to Toronto, Canada, where we planned to spend several years. No doubt I was in part motivated by good liberal philosophy that such a move would broaden our horizons, be a wonderful experience for the children, and generally provide the solution to my rapidly developing case of 'the problem without a name'. Thus, with children in tow and all other signs of suburban living sold or placed in good homes (dog, cat and guinea pig), I headed for cold Canada knowing only one name – that of a feminist friend of my sister. I was a little daunted at the prospect of being unable to enter paid work (no permit for me other than that of wife and mother) and I knew I had to establish a life either through my nuclear family or start from scratch on my own. After several contacts with my husbands' colleagues, I decided that my future did not reside in being a social wife. I put my energies into creating a life of my own.

I was often miserable and very isolated with two children to care for, but I was also aware that I had a freedom in Canada that I had never experienced in Australia. No one had preconceived notions or expectations about my behaviour and I was able to explore any new avenues I wished to follow.

I contacted the feminist name I carried on a piece of paper in my wallet and the phone call I made proved to be the proverbial 'turning point' in my life. My first outing with her was to a birthday party for the Women Against Violence Against Women group in Toronto. I turned up in my high heels, discreet makeup, and with a complacent awareness that I was in the privileged position of being able to view the world as a smorgasbord from which I thought I could select whatever I thought was tasty. I was wrong. I left the meeting feeling out of place, shallow, uncommitted and purposeless. I sensed and saw in the focused energy of that group, active women who were using their lives to do something more than merely survive.

The network of women involved in feminism quickly replaced the support network of family and friends that I had left behind in Australia. I moved into the inevitable discussion and consciousness-raising activities that a network of women provides. I began exploring with other women the reality of the ideas and theories I had been reading for years. Again at my sister's instigation, I began writing a book of my own.

I still felt a little ill at ease with the Women Against Violence Against Women group whose intensity and twenty-four hour per day commitment to public political action did not match with my own three hours (at the most) freedom from children. I did, however, move freely and joyously into attending rallies, demonstrations, and International Women's Day marches. For the first time in many years I felt purposeful, as if I was actually doing something, making some effort to change the system which I had previously assumed to be immutable.

The formation of the Feminist Party of Canada in 1979 provided a new and specific area for me to invest energy. Then, as now, I was comfortable arranging committees, discussing and writing up policy statements, bringing together information and making connections between woman's current position and her history as man had recorded it. I started to spend time speaking to women's groups and presenting a feminist philosophy to all with whom I came in contact.

After four years in Canada, feminism was my way of life and the women's movement my natural habitat. My fundamental commitment is to women - socially, politically, economically. Of course, I have to deal with men - and raise two male children - but I do so on the assumption that most men will choose to make use of a system that extends privileges to them at women's expense. I am occasionally pleasantly surprised to find a male who has consciously chosen not to participate in the system. I am never disappointed or distressed by men who choose to use the system. I fully expect it.

Looking back at my fence sitting youth and my transformation to radical feminism I can locate several significant factors when I try to explain the shift. Firstly, my family have played a definite role. A mother and a sister who always supported, always understood and often anticipated my needs were more than incidental in my adoption of feminism as a world view. The confidence that came from knowing that they too considered feminism a positive way of life removed much of the trauma and many of the problems associated with standing out against the generally accepted norms of female behaviour. Secondly, while the ideas of creativity and liberation were always part of my adult theoretical framework it was not until I was able to match those ideas with the experiences I had as a female at work, in marriage, in motherhood, and dealing with a number of supercilious men that the ideas became my reality. Certainly the university education I received was not conducive to looking at the world with any framework other than the traditional male one. When I consider now what I studied as an allegedly 'universal' and representative sample of literature at university and when I further consider how different my world view may have looked if I had read Elizabeth Barrett Browning's *Aurora Leigh* rather than James Joyce's *Portrait of the Artist as a Young Man*, I fume. But I also see that such practices as the selection of materials to be studied at university are part of a well-organized system that works to keep 'uppity women' in their place and to preserve the male-dominated *status quo*.

Contrasting my 'before' and 'after' feminist commitment I see that one of the fundamental changes I underwent was in my attitude towards other women. I had chosen to see women only in relation to my individualized existence and to ignore the common areas of experience that we shared as women. I distinctly remember the illumination that occurred one night at a social event in Canada where the women and men were segregated into different areas, and where I came to recognize that the contempt in which men hold women was not confined to the average Australian male and his beer keg. It was also that night that I realized that the men's conversation – which for years I had felt eager to join on the premise that it was more intellectual and stimulating than that of women – centred around boys' games – politics, sport and dirty jokes – while the women's conversation, from which I had divorced myself, focused on the social arrangements necessary for nothing less than the survival of the species. I have not been seduced since into considering men's values and men's discussions more prestigious than those of women.

There was another moment of awakening too, when I was in Canada trying to encourage blooms in the rarely-exposed-from-snow garden. A voice of authority advised me to remove from my garden a particular plant which I considered attractive, but which he determined to be a 'weed'. I did not want to remove its colourful display from a fairly sparse garden plot and as a result was engaged in a debate about who had decided what was to be a weed and what was to be a plant. I felt a sense of elation about being able to make my own decisions on the basis of my own experience and was not intimidated by the authoritative edict that wanted me to deny something I found positive and have me rename it as negative, and destroy it. The 'weed' stayed. From that time, 'who said?' has become a basic tenet of my philosophy as I re-evaluate the rules which have been presented to me in a male-dominated society. It is now part of my fabric that I do not have to accept that because men have said so, and because they have been saying so for centuries, their word is law.

A major influence in shaping my current values has been the close relationship with my sister and my mother. My sister and I flatted together, taught together, lived near each other, and generally used each other as sounding boards to test the validity of our own experience when it has not fitted with that prescribed by a small town community or by society in general. It was my sister who consistently pushed me to deal with ideas, alternatives and a concept of intellectual inquiry. I can genuinely say that my only intellectual experiences have been in the company of other women (and two, at the most, attentive and listening men). Now I look first to women as friends, companions and *thinkers*. I always expect to find common ground and common experience with women. Of course, I – and they – are sometimes disappointed, but never permanently or completely.

In our society, the idea of conflict among women is blatantly exploited by the men who stand to gain most from divisions between women. It has been men who have structured our social and economic arrangements so that women are obliged to compete with other women for men – and for jobs – and it has been men who have profited from these arrangements. On a personal level men have received immense satisfaction from the idea and the practice of women competing with each other for male attention and male resources; economically, men have been rewarded by appropriating for themselves positions of control over both women and money. They have promoted divisions between women, not only to keep women from perceiving men as 'the enemy' and thus uniting against them, but to lend credibility to the convenient myth that women are petty, jealous and emotional. In spite of the evidence that women have in their own lives that it is men, at their football games and in their politics, who are vindictive, petty and emotional, men have ensured that attention to these qualities has continually been focused on women.

I refuse to play this game. I find it easier to identify the man-made structures and propaganda aimed at producing conflict between women than to put energy into acting out the alleged conflict. To me, this whole area is one where it is not naive to work on the basis of ignoring the problem in the hope that it will go away. I genuinely believe that if enough women refuse to act out conflict with other women and instead put our energies into working co-operatively, then much of the conflict *will* go away. The divisions between 'radical' women and 'conservative' women (all of whom see themselves as primarily concerned with women's options and status) need not be destructive ones. To switch the focus from these divisions and to turn it to the imposed structural arrangements that disadvantage *all* women by disallowing anything other than man-made rules and regulations, may well deprive men of one of their major advantages. It is worth a try!

I am learning to see myself as autonomous – bound only by remnants of the conditioning that almost relegated me to passive acceptance of a second-rate existence. I am fascinated and liberated by what I can only call 'the world of ideas' and I take much delight in challenging each of the limitations which previously dictated my life. I am actively working on my children to encourage them to learn sensitivity to others combined with a sense of their own ability to recognize and act on injustice and inequality wherever they encounter it. I am aware that my input into my children's lives is only one of many influences and that as they get older, peer pressure (and the need to define themselves and their own space) may well remove them completely from my influence. I have concluded that the best contribution I can make to their lives is to live my own in the best way I know – with the conviction of the value of feminism and the validity of women's experience there for them to see. I believe that such a commitment can be communicated.

Assessing the position of women today I am aware of much evidence that suggests that women may have once lived in a society where 'progress' actually meant the improvement of the quality of life for all people, rather than a frenetic scramble to capitalize on technological capabilities regardless of the cost in human terms. I am also aware that for centuries women have protested against the inhumanity and injustice of a system devised by men to satisfy male needs, which includes the need for dominance.

I see myself and the present generation of women as part of a recurring pattern of rebellion against the male-operated mindless machine age and the exploitation of human/natural resources. I also see that if this women's movement does not succeed there may be no further opportunity for any movement at all.

Notes

1 G. Greer, *The Female Eunuch*, London, Paladin, 1971.
2 B. Friedan, *The Feminine Mystique*, Harmondsworth, Penguin, 1973.

Babette Francis

Babette Francis was born in India, but has lived in Australia since 1953, when she married. Her husband is a Queen's Counsel. Prior to marriage she worked in a pharmaceutical firm and as a journalist and sub-editor. She has a Bachelor of Science with Honours in microbiology and chemistry and is a trained breastfeeding counsellor. She has eight children – four boys and four girls – the eldest of whom is twenty-six and the youngest eight years. Babette has published many articles on women's health and lactation and on anti-feminism. She is a founding member of 'Women Who Want to be Women', National and Overseas Co-ordinator of this group, a member of several pro-life groups, and a committee member of the Council for a Free Australia.

The real meaning of 'feminist' is 'a believer in equal rights for women', but since the 1960s 'feminist' has been distorted to mean a 'believer in specific methods of achieving equality', i.e. abortion on demand, government-funded 24-hours-a-day crêches and propaganda for education based on the assumption that sex differences are entirely socially induced rather than innate. As I do not accept these beliefs or methods but consider myself a feminist in the true sense of the word, I use 'women's liberationist' rather than 'feminist' to denote those who do subscribe to these beliefs.

Christianity was the historical event which had the greatest effect on establishing the philosophical basis for the equality of women, and the Christian ethic gives a continuous impetus to efforts to enhance women's status. In contrast, the status of women in Islamic countries is regressing. In Pakistan and Iran current 'Islamic' laws allow women to be lashed or stoned for adultery. In Pakistan women have been barred from playing sport in the 1982 national games and in hockey matches abroad. Among Christian denominations, the Catholic tradition in particular held steadfastly to the principle that women should not have to subject their bodies to contraception, abortion and sterilization to achieve equality with men.

In the twentieth century, the women's movement has had three distinct phases: (i) emancipation: achieving voting rights; (ii) liberation: equal pay and equal opportunity; (iii) recognition and status for uniquely female roles. I consider myself as representative of this third stage. Betty Friedan is in transition between (ii) and (iii) but she calls this 'the second stage', and says in her new book:

> In reaction against the feminine mystique which defined
> women solely in terms of their relation to men as wives,
> mothers and homemakers, we insidiously fell into a
> feminist mystique which denied that core of woman's
> personhood that is fulfilled through love, nature, home.[1]

Friedan is now denigrated as a revisionist by many of her former liberationist colleagues.

I was at Bombay University during the last years of British rule in India. Having already lived through one liberation movement, I tend to analyse women's lib against that background. It is still in its aberration phase, a phase characterized by slavish imitation of what 'the rulers' do. In India when we imitated the English in dress and culture, we achieved nothing. Not until we took a pride in our own culture and demanded to be independent as Indians were we successful.

The blacks in the USA also went through an aberration phase when some tried to 'pass' as white (if their skins were light enough) - their civil rights struggle achieved success only when they held up their heads and said: 'Black is Beautiful.'

Women Who Want to be Women (WWWW) members correspond to that stage of political consciousness because we aim to enhance the status of uniquely female roles and to achieve status and economic justice for traditional female roles and 'caring for persons' vocations.

A true liberation movement places high value on children for children enshrine hopes for a better future. Women's lib places no value on children, nor does it take a pride in women's capacity to be 'different' to men, to bear children and to breastfeed them.

Liberationists don't say 'pregnancy is beautiful' but ask for abortion on demand (never for pregnancy support services). They don't say 'breastfeeding is beautiful', but burn their bras, symbolic of the denial of lactation. They never say 'children are beautiful' or ask for a homemaker's allowance so they can raise their children with dignity, but demand government-funded crêches where others will care for their children.

Women's lib is not immune either to the danger that they will be taken over by Marxists who seek revolution, not reform. In all revolutions it is not only the oppressors who are punished but the innocent are also killed. Women's lib is afflicted with this same kind of excess – the slaughter of millions of unborn children through abortion.

I was a passive feminist until the consciousness-raising that preceded International Women's Year. I took equal rights for granted, did not experience any discrimination and believed that although the main work of men and women was different, the roles were of equal value. I still strongly believe that, but 1975 and in particular the 'Women's Health in a Changing Society' conference in August that year marked my transition from passive feminist to political activist. For the first time I was confronted by a group of women who did not believe the maternal role was beautiful, valuable or 'equal' to the male 'provider' role. Women's liberationists of course deny this – they claim it is not they but 'society' that does not value maternal and homemaking roles. In a financial sense this is true, but why then do liberationists oppose a homemaker's allowance and income-sharing between spouses? They are afraid too many women would be satisfied and would thus be locked into a 'stereotyped' role.

The amount of literature they produced denigrating motherhood appalled me. International Women's Year (IWY) was the year of publications such as *If I Was a Lady*[2] with cartoons depicting a bedraggled, frumpy housewife, broom in hand and hair in curlers, captioned 'What's wrong with her? I don't know, I think it is because she is a mother', and the *Role Your Own Kit*[3] kit with a poster of a nude, pregnant woman captioned: 'A hen is useful to men, she lays eggs between her legs.' These were published by women's liberationists (who thought of themselves as feminists!) and funded by the hapless Australian taxpayer.

Assuming that the publicized 'Women's Health in a Changing Society' conference was genuinely concerned with health, I sent the organizers an abstract of my paper on successful lactation. I was invited to present the paper in Brisbane. At that time my eighth and youngest child, Lisa, was nineteen months old and still happily breastfed. I enjoyed having eight children and was a happy wife and mother with high self-esteem because I considered raising children important work.

The only discrimination I have experienced is not because of my Indian origin but because of being a mother rather than a 'career woman'. At the health conference the emphasis was totally on abortion, contraception and lesbianism; those of us who tried to speak of motherhood and the female role were rubbished or made to feel traitors to the women's cause.

In December 1975 I was appointed to the Victorian Committee on Equal Opportunity in Schools; the other eleven members were either liberationists or bureaucrats from the Education Department, and with the exception of one who had majored in physics, the others had degrees in humanities. My training in the biological sciences caused me to query premises other committee members took for granted, i.e. that sex differences are socially induced rather than innate and that females are a disadvantaged group.

The fact is that neither assumption is correct. Recent neurological and endocrinological research[4] show that sex differences are innate and that male and female brains function differently. Some researchers define the brain as a sex organ that differentiates males from females. Culture and societal conditioning obviously play a part, but both build on what is already biologically inherent.

Nor, in the Australian context, are females a disadvantaged

group. When assessing the status of underprivileged groups such as the blacks in the US or Aborigines in Australia, a number of criteria are used: infant mortality, life expectancy, incidence of disease, alcoholism, violence, suicide, accidental death and injury, involvement with drugs, crime, rates of imprisonment, level of literacy, retention rates at school, success rates in examinations, and employment and income levels. Applying these criteria to males and females, on every count except the last, it is males who emerge as the disadvantaged group.

I also disagreed with the committee's recommendations for 'non-sexist' education, believing it was far more important to recognize sex differences, especially in maths, spatial concepts and literacy, so that appropriate programs could be devised for each sex rather than waste taxpayers' money on gender-neutral education.

When the committee concluded its work in July 1977, I dissented from their recommendations and wrote a comprehensive minority report.[5] Both were printed by the Victorian government and sent to all schools in Victoria, and some copies were sent interstate.

I was contacted by several women who read the minority report and who supported my views. At the time we were active in Women's Action Alliance (WAA), an organization whose aim is to raise the status of women whether they choose to be homemakers or to enter the paid workforce. However, some of us found it increasingly restrictive trying to lobby through WAA because it had no policy on abortion. We felt the abortion issue was crucial to the debate. My scientific training even more than my Catholic upbringing convinced me that human life begins at fertilization, and I could see no justification for destroying one life to 'liberate' another from housework, childbearing or whatever. Adoption is a far more ethical solution for women who do not want their babies.

During 1979, the International Year of the Child, some of us tried to persuade the WAA committee to take a stance opposing abortion, but without success. The precipitating incident that led to the foundation of 'Women Who Want to be Women' (WWWW) was a press release issued by all twelve members of the National Women's Advisory Council (NWAC) unanimously opposing the Lusher motion which had sought to end Australian Federal government funding of abortions. We felt that if the NWAC was truly representative of Australian women, it would have been divided on the issue as Australian women are divided on abortion.

WWWW was founded on the 22 March 1979, the night the Lusher motion was debated in Parliament. Our first activity was to launch a nationwide petition to Parliament seeking the abolition of the NWAC on the basis that it was not democratically elected, was not representative of Australian women and was a sexist and discriminatory imposition as men did not have an unelected council interfering when elected MPs were considering issues of concern to men. In our view, the NWAC in its unanimous support for government funding of abortions, and later in its 'Draft Australia Plan of Action' which recommended 'non-sexist education', was giving our elected Parliamentary representatives a wrong impression of what Australian women wanted. The petition, so far as we know, is a historical 'first' – the first petition presented to the Australian Parliament on a specifically 'women's issue'. It is ironic that a group of homemakers should achieve a 'first' in this arena – and that our opponents objected to our use of this democratic mechanism although they claim they want to encourage women to use the political processes.

As a prelude to the UN Mid-Decade for Women, the NWAC held a series of State conferences and 'elections' in 1979 for delegates to a national conference in March 1980. The conferences were dominated by radical liberationists and were quite unsatisfactory so far as pro-life, pro-family women were concerned. In the end about twenty pro-life, pro-family women versus 100 liberationists were 'elected' to attend the national conference in Canberra. I was one of four Christian women elected from Victoria as against eleven liberationists. The result of the national conference was predictable – the NWAC package with its 'Draft Australian Plan of Action' calling for 'all methods of fertility regulation', 'non-sexist education', and the provision of contraception to minors was passed with some favourite clauses on 'sexual preferences' added.

For the UN World Conference in Copenhagen in July

1980, besides the official representatives from the Women's Affairs, Foreign Affairs departments and the NWAC, the Australian government funded twenty-two women from non-government organizations to attend the Non-Government Organization (NGO) Forum which was run concurrently with the UN conference. WWWW's Victorian co-ordinator, Mrs Valerie Renkema, was among those funded. We also raised funds so that WWWW's Queensland co-ordinator, Mrs Jackie Butler, and I could also go. In Copenhagen we teamed up with another WWWW member touring Europe, two Festival of Light members including Mrs Mab Walsh, organizing Chairwoman of the Women for the Family and Society conference, and a member of the Society for the Protection of the Unborn Child (SPUC) from New Zealand. We also established links with representatives of Texas Eagle Forum and the National Council of Catholic Women from the USA.

Before leaving Australia, Valerie, Jackie, Mab and I obtained press accreditations from the papers and church journals for which we wrote. This gave us unrestricted entry to the UN conference and to all reports, press conferences and interviews. For security reasons, the access of the general public to the UN conference was restricted to the main hall – the other Australian NGO representatives did not have the full access we had, and even the official Australian government delegates were not able to conduct interviews as we did. Members of the NWAC and the Women's Affairs department seemed stunned and annoyed that we had turned up in Copenhagen and with press badges to boot. We found their frustration very entertaining and it showed up the shallowness of the liberationists' claim that they want women to 'go out and take part in decision-making'. Liberationists only want women to be political activists if they have a liberationist ideology. Lobbyists for pro-life and pro-family values are anathema. Mr Ellicott, then Minister for Home Affairs and leader of the Australian delegation, also seemed taken aback to see us there and would not give us a pre-conference comment for our readers back in Australia, although leaders of the Israeli, Indian, Vatican, USA and many other delegations were happy to oblige.

The UN conference dramatically illustrated what WWWW and I have always contended – that women's issues cannot be separated from general political issues and that it is unfair to have unelected advisory bodies on 'women's affairs' as these only emphasize liberationist priorities while the concerns of the majority are overlooked. The UN conference ended in a farce.

Anyone who had examined the agenda prior to the conference could have predicted that it would end up in a bun fight on the Palestinian issue: in an agenda item that was supposed to consider the plight of *all* refugees, there was specific mention only of 'Palestinian refugees inside and outside Israeli occupied territories'. But Australian women were given no prior opportunity by the NWAC to study the agenda – our State and National conferences focused on the ghetto of so-called 'women's issues', abortion, contraception for minors, and lesbianism, all of which were irrelevant at Copenhagen.

It was ironical to hear Dame Beryl Beaurepaire (then Chairwoman of NWAC) deplore the intrusion of 'extraneous political issues' into the UN conference. Many of us consider abortion, contraception for minors and 'sexual preferences' are also 'extraneous political issues'. Moreover, these are issues we are far less enthusiastic about than the security of Israel. Even a caucus of Third World women at the NGO Forum passed resolutions expressing their deep concern at 'the attempts at forcing birth control and family planning on the so-called developing nations by various means including that of tying it to economic aid'.[6]

Jackie Butler and I also travelled to the UK, Canada and America. We met Mrs Phyllis Schlafly, dynamic leader of Eagle Forum, the heroine who led the victorious battle against the ratification of the Equal Rights Amendment to the US Constitution. Phyllis Schlafly is a tremendous inspiration to WWWW – her book *The Power of the Positive Woman*[7] has been sent by us to all Federal and State parliamentarians, State Premiers and Ministers of Education. Phyllis Schlafly is an example of what one woman can accomplish despite a well-organized campaign by women's liberationist groups, the media and even Presidents Ford, Carter and their wives and families, all of whom backed ERA.

In 1980, Phyllis Schlafly was very happy because the Illinois state legislature had just rejected the ERA. During a subsequent visit to the USA and New Zealand in 1981, when I again spoke with her, she was even happier because the Supreme Court had just ruled that Congress did not have to draft women when it drafted men. This was a vital decision for the anti-ERA forces, because they could show that had ERA been in effect, the court could not have exempted women. Phyllis and her supporters continued lobbying legislators in the various unratified states and gave them homebaked bread – 'from the breadmakers to the bread-winners' – as a symbol of the wife and mother role.

The ERA finally lapsed on the 30 June 1982. It was an historic occasion, and WWWW issued a national press release to all sections of the media congratulating the women of America on their victorious fight against an amendment the intent of which was to make gender of as little relevance as eye colour.

By this, our fourth year, WWWW has established informal links with pro-life and pro-family groups not only within Australia but also in countries ranging from the USSR, Denmark and the UK, to the USA, Canada and New Zealand. We publish a newsletter five times a year and produce resource material and papers on sex differences, pro-life and pro-family issues. We co-operate with other like-minded groups. On four occasions during 1981 we have sent detailed submissions to every Federal parliamentarian on a range of topics.

In 1982 we were one of five women's groups invited to pre-budget talks by the Prime Minister. As part of our sub-mission we presented Mr Fraser with a homebaked cake inscribed: 'To the Men in the House from the Women in the Home'. The cake was symbolic of the work of homemakers which is not included in estimates of the Gross Domestic Product.

We have had a significant impact in raising the political consciousness of Christian women, not least of all those in Women's Action Alliance, who in 1981 modified their constitution to give some recognition to the rights of unborn children. The change is not as explicitly pro-life as WWWW would like, but it is a step in the right direction.

Although women's liberationists deplore the fact that young females are taught to regard other females as potential rivals, in a very real sense I have found that it *is* women, not men, who are our political rivals. I like women, but by the same token my opponents also are women. If it were not for these 'other women' and their male followers, the media and political parties would be supportive of WWWW philosophy.

Of more serious moment is the censorship of traditional roles liberationists wish to enforce in literature, textbooks and the media. While censorship of pornography – even pornography combined with violence – is anathema to most liberationists, their determination to exercise the most rigid censorship of the depiction of maternal and traditional roles is almost pathological. It is never clarified whether this brainwashing is to be openly acknowledged or whether children are expected to digest the non-sexist message subliminally.

I like men and find them more intellectually stimulating than women. The man I married is special and is a wonderful husband and father. He has all the qualities I most admire in a human being – he is caring, intelligent, has a sense of humour and is strongly supportive. If all men were like him, there would be no women's liberationists. In reading the life stories of so many prominent liberationists, one becomes aware of the impact alcoholic and violent fathers and/or unfaithful husbands have had on the lives of these embittered women. It is not altogether surprising that they refuse to accept the idea of marriage as a partnership of equals and of 'family' being based on marriage, but define 'family' as any variation – such as two lesbians and a budgerigar!

Of course, I am not satisfied with the current position of women. We have advanced in some ways, not progressed in others – there is not sufficient social status or financial recognition given to the enormous contribution women make to the well-being of nations through their childbearing, childrearing and homemaking roles. However, I would not want to go back in time because there never was the kind of equality WWWW aims for. Men and women are equal but different, not equal and the same. Sex differences are not an oversight by the Almighty, but part of his plan. Pope John Paul II in his encyclical 'on human work' said:

> The true advancement of women requires that labour should be structured in such a way that women do not

have to pay for their advancement by abandoning what is specific to them and at the expense of the family, in which women as mothers have an irreplaceable role.

Notes

1 Excerpt in *New York Times Magazine*, 5 July 1981 (*The Second Stage*).
2 *If I Was a Lady*, National Council of Australia, 1975.
3 *Role Your Own*, Women's Movement Children's Literature Co-op Ltd, Melbourne, 1976.
4 D. McGuiness and K.H. Pribram, 'The origins of sensory bias in the development of gender differences in perception and cognition', in M. Bortner (ed.), *Cognitive Growth and Development*, Brunner/Mazel, 1979. R. Restak, *The Brain: The Last Frontier*, New York, Doubleday, 1979.
5 B. Francis, *Minority Report – Victorian Committee on Equal Opportunity in Schools*, Premier's Department, Melbourne, 1977.
6 *NGO Resolutions: Third World Women*, Forum, 80, Copenhagen, 25 July 1980.
7 P. Schlafly, *The Power of the Positive Woman*, New York, Arlington House Press, 1977.

Sylvia Kinder

*Sylvia Kinder was born in Liverpool, England, and has been
an Australian resident for fourteen years. Aged thirty-three
she is guardian to two younger sisters (eighteen and twenty).
She is tertiary trained, and currently a secondary teacher in
an alternative school in Adelaide having worked previously as
a primary school teacher, psychiatric nurse and as a worker in
a women's studies resource centre. She belongs to a number
of feminist groups and has always been involved in a variety
of organizations such as the teacher unions. She has written a
number of articles on a variety of topics, including one on
the history of the Adelaide women's liberation movement,
published in* Worth Her Salt *(ed. M. Bevege, M. James and
C. Shute, Sydney, Hale & Ironmonger, 1982).*

I am now and have for some time been a dedicated wimin's[1]
liberationist. I use the term wimin's liberationist rather than
the ambiguous 'feminist', which I believe embraces all wimin
with a commitment to wimin, and is used by wimin today of
clearly opposing ideologies.

I grew up in the dark streets of Liverpool, a childhood
spent where bombs left wide gaps between houses, where
people saved paper bags and string, spread their bread spar-
ingly, and stored tea and sugar as if for the next rationing.
As the eldest in the family of five children I learnt early to
set aside childish needs and look after myself both physically
and emotionally. My father's frequent and distressing visits
to the bedroom I shared with my sisters and his strange way

of showing affection, such as holding me between the legs, were, I decided, my problem. Firstly, I accepted his behaviour as inevitable, for no matter how I prayed (I believed in God then) or took care with my behaviour (I firstly blamed myself) his molestations persisted. I was aware that overt attempts to protect myself would attract notice. I knew instinctively that this would do no good but rather create more pain for me – later experiences confirmed this. I was also afraid my rejection would divert his attentions to my younger sisters and so I educated them about the dangers of sexual advances from men. By puberty I had managed to protect myself completely and my father turned his interests to my sister. This proved too much for me and together my sister and I revealed his paedophilia to my mother. She demanded he seek psychiatric help and he supposedly did so. I knew my mother's acceptance of his 'cure' was her fantasy which enabled her to cope in continuing her life with him, which she accepted as inviolable. I became acutely aware of how trapped wimin with children and no economic resources are. The years until I left home at seventeen were tense. My relationship with my mother and siblings was coloured by my refusal to pretend that everything was now fine in the family. My father never changed even after my mother's premature death on New Year's Day 1970. Years later when all his children were safely away he was arrested for sexual relations with a young retarded womon and released with a two year suspended sentence: his many other sexual offences remained undisclosed.

My mother had longed to become a dancer and sent me, poor though we were, to a relative's ballet school when I was six years old. I loved it, receiving validation of my personal worth through success in dancing examinations and competitions. At eleven years of age I transferred to a professional school but at sixteen despite showing talent I was forced to give up the hope of such a career as my family lacked the finances to help me through a full time dancing school.

Dancing was not my only emotional solace. I formed a close attachment to one of my two grandmothers who lived nearby and with whom I spent a considerable amount of time. My other grandmother and aunts who I saw once each year also played an important role for me as nurturers and models. I also sought the company of a few tried and tested males, particularly my grandfathers, one of whom became my ideal of what a man should be: strong, caring, loving towards children, community-minded and emotionally self-sufficient.

With an ordinary education, much determination and lots of optimism at nineteen years of age, a friend and I emigrated to Australia on the £10 assisted passage scheme. I worked in clubs and pubs, on switchboards and behind dusty office files, lazed on surf beaches, dated the 'boys' from Vietnam or those on 'rest and recreation leave'. Amongst all of this a young man from my home town appeared, sensitive, easygoing and who cared for me.

My mother's sudden death and my decision to raise my two youngest sisters changed the direction of my life and brought my latent feminism into clearer focus. At age twenty-three I was the surrogate mother of two children aged seven and ten. Having put much thought into bringing the girls out to Australia I believed it to be a lot to ask of my male lover to be a total father and so I did not ask it. He assumed whatever role and responsibility he was willing to offer.

I changed my occupation to fit in better with raising children and attended teachers' college where I met the wimin's movement. Ideas which I believed were unique and sprang from my own head I discovered I shared with other wimin and could read about in books. My anger over the lack of power people had over their own lives, reinforced by three years psychiatric nursing, drew me towards socialism. I experienced collective working on campus both in mixed groups and with wimin. With wimin collectivism worked better. Wimin are trained to sacrifice their interest for the good of a family, and thus do so more easily for a group who share a common goal. Wimin do not often demand a penalty for donations of their time and energy, but gain instead friendship, support and caring.

Too often wimin come to the wimin's movement bruised and wounded by battles with patriarchal society, perceiving the wimin's movement as the new god who will cure them with a touch, and become angry when it doesn't I believe the wimin's movement to be a space in which you gain encouragement to develop your own healing skills and strengths, where when you reach out for support there will be a hand to comfort and help. It is motley collection of wimin with various pains and personal anguish striving for some joy here and now, whilst working towards the creation of a better life for all. There is no blueprint, no promise of perpetual joy and an end to struggle and misery.

Once I was distressed when sisters, having fought long and hard, suffered a setback and became prophets of doom: 'There's no future for the wimin's movement', and so on. Now I am angry and sad. Sad that they have suffered and lost hope; angry that patriarchy has scored another victory and that some wimin use their disillusionment to validate their own lack of action.

As an activist over eight years, I have been involved in a variety of wimin's groups and services from different perspectives – from paid worker to one of many at a general meeting. In the first few years of involvement I had the care of two primary aged girls, a house in suburbia, a full time teaching job and a long-standing heterosexual relationship. I had always been an energetic worker and as a non smoker, non drug imbiber, low alcohol consumer, balanced (on the whole) eater, regular dancer, and being slim and healthy, I was able to combine within my life: regular wimin's liberation meetings one evening per week, periodic rally organization, selling an anti-imperialist newspaper outside factories, handing out leaflets, occasionally speaking at various places on a number of issues, being an active member of the South Australian International Women's Year Committee for the United Nations and being involved in a teachers' action group. From these experiences I learned about the way men operate in Left groups and the position of wimin in them. I had contact with factory workers and became more aware of the difficulties involved in organizing within and outside labour unions. I became a confident speaker at both small meetings and larger rallies and began to learn how to communicate ideas in different settings. I also met a wide cross section of wimin, from the 'feminists' at the wimin's centre to the housewives in the suburbs where I taught. My work on the International Women's Committee brought me into direct contact with wimin from groups in various churches, the peace movement, aboriginal organizations, various left groups and activists with decades of experience.

I became very aware of the magnitude of the problems facing wimin, the great forces united to maintain patriarchal oppression and the many possible fronts on which to fight. I had become a member of the Women's Studies Resource Centre Collective and when a job became available in 1977, I applied and was successful. I also became involved, although peripherally, in the growing 'feminist bureaucracy.'

The appointment of wimin's advisers in areas such as the Premier's Department, Education, Department of Community Welfare and the establishment of Equal Opportunity Commissions and the various officers to support such persons, soon created a paid feminist administrative group who sought each other out both for political and personal support. The informal network very quickly became an important social grouping. I am convinced of the value of such networks, but also recognize that, being informal, they can establish confusing baseline acceptable behaviour which determines inclusion. The struggles which inevitably take place between wimin striving to effect some changes for wimin in a myriad of ways and from very different positions, can, and do so easily, become overly personalized and distorted. The occurrence of divisions between wimin within the bureaucracies can and does have wider implications than in the broader wimin's movement. This is because of the role of those institutions in supporting, recommending, encouraging and promoting wimin and wimin's projects. Whilst their power is often overestimated, the impact of their decisions can and does have wide reaching effects. However, it is more often the decisions of men further up the hierarchy that ultimately do the damage and bureaucratic feminists often receive more blame than they have earned. 'Career feminism' thus carries certain responsibilities and problems that deter many wimin, myself included.

On the personal level 1977 and 1978 were difficult years, from which I emerged much changed. I was having problems domestically, the elder of my two (now adolescent) sisters, and my male lover were locked in a battle of wills: she struggling to assert her independence, he attempting to maintain untenable positions and I torn between them. Eventually I left him taking the girls with me. The stress did not abate, and so several months later after my lover had made some personal changes I decided to return to him. The elder of my sisters left home at this point.

Throughout 1978 I experienced grief at the separation from my sister and the lack of communication between us. I also felt considerable guilt that I had failed as a 'mother'. Despite improvements in my relationship, I decided not to work so hard at maintaining it. I found myself spending more time socially as well as politically with wimin. I now began to obey my own impulses rather than living out a lifestyle I dictated to myself.

By mid-1978 I was startlingly aware that my feelings for one friend, Pat, were sexual. Overwhelmed and confused I reflected on my heterosexual relationship: warm and mostly caring but somehow lacking. I had decided that what I had was all there was. But here was sheer passionate desire. Should I deny it and live out my life in pleasant mediocrity in a house in the suburbs caring for my remaining teenage sister and male lover, working and being a feminist activist, or should I talk of my feelings and cope with the result of such action in whatever way I could?

So strong were my feelings for Pat that I had to tell her. I had expected her to listen caringly but was overjoyed when she responded to me, if not ardently, at least with increasing warmth. So many aspects of my life fell into place at this point. My intense relationship with two wimin in my teens, my lack of sexual interest in men and my total monogamy for over ten years. I could no longer face the prospect of living out my life with a man I liked and cared for but for whom I felt more compassion than passion. I realized I wanted to have a room and a life of my own and to claim a lesbian feminist identity.

None of this has been as easy to do as to write of it. My lover of ten years and I parted with tension but on good terms. He has met my lover and is aware of the reason for my decision. He has also made many positive changes himself and I believe we did the best for one another. For a year I lived with my sister and another friend and then moved into a small house I am buying. My sister, now seventeen years old, has some difficulty in accepting my lesbianism but on the whole our life together is pleasant. I am happier now than at any time in my life. I do not see lesbianism as the only choice for feminists but am aware that the energy required to maintain a sexual relationship with a man is a great personal drain which can only be readily assessed when the relationship is over. Relating sexually to wimin can also be draining but the experience can be used to enrich the lives of two wimin, who can turn their positive energy gained from each other to further the cause of wimin's liberation. I do not feel that my lesbianism separates me from heterosexual wimin for I have committed my energy to wimin regardless of their sexual preference; but rather, their commitment to a man or men separates them temporarily or permanently from me and other wimin.

To enable me to work effectively as a militant 'feminist' I have developed some tools to assist me. The first of these, to use the words of songwriter Helen Reddy, is to be the 'best friend to myself'. To me this means taking care of my physical and emotional health as a priority. Therefore I consider the implications of my actions for myself as well as others and consider carefully the consequences of actions which may cause me physical or emotional pain. I am also actively involved in developing skills to handle conflict in a positive way and, with groups of wimin, further explore and increase our conflict-resolving ability.

Important tools for fighting patriarchy are: a knowledge of the nature and extent of our oppression, a sense of the history of our struggle, a telling of our pain and hearing other wimin speak of theirs, and the experience of the joy and strength to be found in working with other wimin. To achieve these ends I have been engaged for some years in developing and teaching wimin's studies courses. The courses I have been involved with have several key attributes: they are almost totally free of institutional control, cost little or nothing for the students, are open only to wimin, and involve the students in planning and direction. I believe that by bringing wimin of different ages, backgrounds and opinions together, presenting an honest, but positive view of the current wimin's movement, and dealing effectively with the predictable conflicts that arise, many more wimin are enabled to take up the fight against patriarchy and survive.

Effective groups are an important tool in developing

strengths and strategies for the struggle for wimin's liberation. For many lesbians both inside and outside the wimin's movement, wimin's studies courses focus too much on the problems of heterosexual wimin. It is often difficult to come out as a lesbian in a group that appears to be dominated by heterosexual values. Thus the idea for a lesbian studies course, I believe the first in Australia, developed in my mind. There have now been three of these ten-week courses covering a range of topics from lesbian history and music, to sexuality and theory. Each course is convened by two wimin, one who is familiar with running the course and one learning, thus we can spread and share our skills. I would like to see courses for black and ethnic wimin run along the same principles.

Looking at my life now I am happy with the picture that unfolds: living in a fairly close community of wimin in Adelaide, teaching adolescents in an alternative high school, co-ordinating a wimin's studies course, studying to be a psychotherapist and politically active as a lesbian feminist. Old wounds and pains have been salved and healed. I see my future as engaging with other wimin in the long ongoing struggle to make this world a better place for all wimin, whilst ensuring much joy and happiness for ourselves along the way.

Note

1   I used the word wimin as the plural of women and womon as the singular of woman. The changing of words which define wimin in relationships to men is an important political activity as is also the reclaiming of archaic words with positive meanings for wimin and the creation of new words to express ideas for which existing words are inadequate.

Valerie Riches

Valerie Riches is a British wife and mother, and Secretary of The Responsible Society, concerned with family and youth. Married, she has a daughter who is a medical practitioner and a son who is a bio-chemist. She has done a two year training course in social work and has written a number of newspaper articles.

I enjoy being a woman. I respect, yes respect, my husband. Our love for each other is sealed in a total commitment to our marriage. This does not mean that each of us becomes less of a person or that I sacrifice my individuality to take on my husband's identity. It is a partnership – he does his part, I do mine. We do not compete, we co-operate and our relationship has grown in depth and strength over the years.

I regard motherhood as the most honourable and valuable contribution a woman can make to humanity: there is nothing degrading or exploitative of women in being home-makers. It would be degrading to receive a salary for what can only be given in love. I believe that to deny the physical and emotional differences between man and woman is to deny the very essence of womanhood.

Because of my parents' financial difficulties in times of harsh social conditions, my formal education ended at the age of fourteen. After my children were born, I studied at home and did voluntary work for a family welfare association which eventually led to a two-year training course in social work. The course fitted in well with my family life and I was around the home when my teenage children arrived back from school – an age when a mother needs to be available more than ever before. I found that it is possible to combine motherhood and a career successfully, provided one enjoys robust physical and emotional health and works out an order of priorities: family first and job second. With energy and drive anything is possible, as many other women have shown long before women's liberation arrived on the scene.

Women's liberation matters because it is about a great deal more than equal pay and equal job opportunities and matters of justice. It raises deeper issues concerning the nature of woman and different attitudes to children and motherhood. It raises social issues, the implications of free contraceptives for all – free sex of any variety and at any age – abortion as a right – easy divorce – the rights of prostitutes and lesbians – pornography. My heart sinks when I open the pages of women's liberation papers and magazines. They seem to like dirt and a mechanistic view of life which degrades people, especially their own sex. All this is a far cry from those true feminists of an earlier era who pioneered votes for women and strove for the dignity of women, motherhood, family values and matters of simple justice which would contribute to the welfare of the nation; a benign form of women's liberation which led to equal pay and access to the professions. These feminists saw women as complementary to men, with no need to renounce their femininity by imitating the male role. They did not seek to undermine the value of the maternal and family role of women. Nor did they intend society to be structured in such a way that wives and mothers are now in the position of feeling compelled to work outside the home.

I could have given my heart to a feminist movement concerned with the cultural growth of the characteristics most deeply associated with womanhood: tenderness not aggression, people not things, love not hate, spirituality not materialism. But women's liberation fosters the aggressive values of men.

It is said that popular revolts reflect popular discontent. I do not believe that to be so. The women's liberation movement has been fostered by a clique of women in the media who have the power to shape female opinion. Careers in mind, they often have no children and do not want them. Women's magazines go in for the sexual revolution in a big way; sex is a commodity to be sold and the most important factor in the business is circulation figures. I am staggered by the magnitude of the personal problems of some of the agony aunts who use their columns to sell ideas to unsuspecting women. One famous agony aunt has publicly admitted that her only training for the job was a broken marriage and five and a half years of psychoanalysis. Others have revealed their hatred of parents, their illegitimate babies and abortions, their lesbian activities, and their taste for sexual perversions.

Sigmund Freud asked, 'What does a woman want?' The women's libbers have not worked it out either. As one said 'We will not be able to sort out what we do want from men and what we want to give them until we know that our physical and psychological survival – at home and at work – does not depend on men.' Meanwhile men and women are still creating children who need to be cared for and reared and we are seeing a deterioration of motherhood in terms of quantity and quality; more child battering and children in the care of local authorities.

Women's liberation has lost sight of the importance of motherhood in the lives of human beings. Women are complex beings. The fact that they can actually produce another human being from within their own body perhaps accounts for women's great mystery. The mother is the most important person in every human being's life. Everything about her, her personality, her character, the way she brings up children, have more influence on an individual's future development than all the other influences combined. Maternal love is the primary emotional and psychological need in everyone's life. What a marvellous inheritance and responsibility! But women's liberationists seek to deny it: they would deny their wombs if they could.

With the emergence of the Pill in the early 1960s, *all* women had the freedom to control their fertility. We were told it was 'safe' and 100 per cent 'reliable'. For women's liberation the Pill was the cornerstone of their sexual revolution. It was also the promiscuous man's best friend, removing the final barrier. Sex could be enjoyed without love and without babies.

It was only after a time of trial and reflection that it became known, mainly in medical circles, that the Pill, that powerful steroid which affects every cell in the body, was not so safe or reliable. It is interesting to note that among the most vociferous opponents of the Pill nowadays are some women's libbers who look upon it as a drug produced by men for the convenience of men. Germaine Greer has spoken of the plight of women drugged up to their eyeballs whilst their sexuality is freely available.

Today's number one social priority is 'Stamping Out Pregnancy', as *Family Planning News* once crudely put it. The deaths of some unfortunate women and the ill-health of many is of less importance. So the pregnant woman, once the ideal and symbol of health, a glory of nature, has become a failure of technology. Some sincere people still cling to the belief that a free contraceptive service will do away with the need for abortion. The statistics speak for themselves: more contraception equals more abortion.

There is a great deal of semantic hypocrisy around. None disturbs me more than the chant 'A Woman's Right to Choose' (to kill her baby). The screaming harridans who thus rhythmically chant away their femininity would oppose the punishment of child murderers and, no doubt, demonstrate for the Campaign for Nuclear Disarmament. Women's libbers resort to euphemisms – the baby becomes a 'foetus', and its death warrant is the 'termination of an unwanted pregnancy'. The wilful killing of another human being opens society to a climate of opinion which can then condone the killing of other 'unwanted' human beings. The reason why perverted members of the medical profession and the women they serve get away with the killing of millions of unborn human beings is because the victims are completely helpless to oppose what is being done to them.

Virtually all women's libbers see the family and child-rearing as great sources of oppression. That is why they resent little girls playing with dolls – they might enjoy learning the practicalities of mothering. Extreme women's libbers go further; they would have the traditional family destroyed. It was the aspect of child-care that brought me to my final flashpoint. I was sent a little leaflet published by the Equal Opportunities Commission. It was headed, 'I Want to Work

But What About the Kids?' What an egocentric, infantile demand! No hint here of the hitherto good womanly characteristics of putting first the needs and dignity of children. Is it too much to expect that women, unless there is real financial hardship, should delay their careers in the best interests of their children? Isn't parenthood a career in itself, of such importance that work outside the home could wait until, at least, the child is five years of age? No woman, save the cretinously *avant garde*, thinks the tax-payer should be expected to pay for children to be deprived of their basic needs of time, love, and care, because some selfish women demand the 'right' to work.

But whether we like it or not, the British taxpayer is funding the Equal Opportunities Commission set up in 1975 and costing about £2½ million a year. There was no great demand for this body; no massive demonstrations calling for it. It encourages divisive attitudes and seeks to redefine history and the English language. The word 'man' must be eliminated; words like 'man-power' and 'man-made' are to be dropped in favour of 'workforce' and 'artificial'. No question of 'the best man for the job' - sexist language that! But it becomes dangerous when captive little ones are subject to interference in the classroom and playground to avoid 'sex stereotypical play activity' i.e., no depiction of girls playing with dolls' houses or little boys playing at engine drivers.

In 1963, Betty Friedan wrote *The Feminine Mystique*. Now, in the 1980s, she writes in *The Second Stage*:

> From the daughters, working so hard at their new careers, determined not to be trapped as their mothers were, expecting so much and taking for granted the opportunities we fought for, I've begun to hear undertones of pain and puzzlement, almost a bitterness they hardly dare admit.

Is this a new awakening? Certainly some women's liberationists are beginning to realise that the Pill has not been the answer to the sexual freedom they thought was theirs and that they have been used as female guinea pigs for the pharmaceutical industry. Some are protesting angrily at the denigration and violation of women at the hands of the pornographers. And *Cosmopolitan*, praise be, has bravely thrown up its trend-setting liberated arms in despair at the increasing incidence of herpes genitalia, an incurable, recurrent and highly contagious sexually transmitted disease. Will this manifestation of nature's antagonism to so much sexual abuse actually mean that women must face the fact that there is a destructive side to the sexual revolution?

We have a long way to go before women's liberation sees these links. And even further to go before it accepts that social traditions borne of experience and wisdom over centuries are sometimes necessary for social order, and even, astonishing idea, help women and their children to be happier in the long run.

Margrit Eichler

*Margrit Eichler lectures in Sociology and Women's Studies
at the Ontario Institute for Studies in Education. German by
birth, she is content to remain in Canada. Margrit is forty,
married, with a thirteen year old son. She has her PhD, she
has written many articles, and her book,* The Double Standard: A Feminist Critique of Feminist Social Science *was
published in 1980 by Croom Helm.*

In the fall of 1968, I was a graduate student of sociology at
Duke University in North Carolina, USA. I had recently
married, was pregnant, and was trying to write a proposal for
a dissertation. Linda Fischer, a co-student and friend, mentioned that she regularly met with a group of women in
which issues relating to women were discussed. It sounded
interesting, and two weeks later I went with her. I had joined
a consciousness-raising group in which I continued to participate until I left for Canada in December of 1970.

In the group, we discussed all the issues affecting our lives.
At the time, my greatest worry was how to look after our
child when it would be born, since simply handing it over to
a babysitter seemed heartless as well as prohibitively expen-
sive, with my husband and myself both living on student
fellowships. Since we were both from Germany, neither of us
had a single relative in North America.

When I mentioned that this was a problem for me, it turned
out that two other women in the group were also pregnant,
and also worried about how to care for their children. We

planned (and later put into practice) a baby co-op, in which we would pool our babies once they were born. Every parent with the exception of Patty and her husband David who both had full-time jobs and could, at most, take off one half-day per week, would look after all three babies two half-days per week. This gave us good care for five days a week, at no cost, and a built-in system of babysitting at other occasions on an exchange basis. Patty and David offered to have the children at their home, which meant some babysitting for one of them every day, before they left for work or after they had returned. The baby co-op existed for a year and a half and served everybody's needs well.

In the group, we discussed all the important issues, talking about oppression, liberation, sexism, the origins of women's lower status, housework, our private lives, the position of women in general, and ourselves as persons. It was illuminating, sometimes exhilarating, sometimes upsetting, and sometimes frustrating. It seemed to me that we were asking all the right questions, but that the answers we were coming up with were often too undifferentiated, too sweeping, and in many ways too naive. But at the time no better answers were to be had. It was my fascination with the questions raised and my dissatisfaction with the answers given that made me decide this would be the area in which I would concentrate my own scholarly efforts, once my dissertation was completed.

Meanwhile, our group decided that rather than just talking, we would do something. We eventually settled on writing and publishing non-sexist children's books. None of us had any experience with any aspect of publishing. But we learned, and as of now (1984), Lollipop Power Press is still in operation and has successfully published and distributed a whole series of books.

Eventually, I had to leave the United States because my unrenewable exchange visa had run out after four years. I decided to try and find a job in Canada. My husband was still working on his PhD in Political Science and had to remain in North Carolina, and we decided that our son would stay with him until I had settled in Canada. I got a job at the University of Waterloo, with the understanding that one of the courses I would teach would be in the area of women's studies. Since that time, I have continued to write, research and teach in women's studies. My involvement in the feminist movement, and particularly in feminist scholarship, has been a connecting thread over the past fourteen years, and I anticipate that it will continue to be important for me for the rest of my life. Looking into the past, I find nothing that would have structurally predisposed me to becoming a feminist, except for some personality characteristics. My family is solidly middle-class, slightly conservative, and very religious. My father worked as a chemical engineer and my mother was, and continues to be, a dedicated and perfectionist housewife. My two older sisters provided me with role models of happy housewives, although my eldest sister has in recent years become a career woman as well.

My father, I believe, was secretly sorry that he had only three daughters and no son. When he realized that I wanted to study, he was pleased to learn that at least one of his daughters was interested in pursuing a university education, but this pleasure was somewhat diminished, I believe, by his sentiments about the proper role of women, which centered around being a wife and mother as a full-time occupation. He told me, before my first term started, that he was very willing to pay all my expenses for attending university, but that if it turned out that I met the right man and therefore did not finish my studies, he wanted me to know that he would not consider the money wasted, for he believed in the saying that 'if you educate a man, you educate an individual, but if you educate a woman, you educate a family'. It was a generous statement, and he meant it, but it demonstrates the ambivalence which I encountered about my career involvement: on the one hand, it is something to be proud of, but on the other hand, it is a distinct second choice as compared to marrying and raising a family, and combining the two just is not an option that one would even consider.

I had been a relatively happy child, but an unhappy adolescent. In retrospect, I attribute a lot of this unhappiness to the deep dissatisfaction which I felt with the female role as I experienced it, but I could not identify the reason for my unhappiness at the time. The notable aspect of my life is that I have always had good relationships with girls and women. Indeed, I cannot recall any time in my life when I did not have at least one good female friend.

The two most important aspects of feminism for me are that it provides a framework for interpreting the position of women, as well as that of men and children, and that it holds out the promise for a better future. One spin-off from this is that as an active feminist I feel connected with other people in a joint endeavour. It is uplifting to know that what I am doing is part of a huge collective effort that has already been a positive force in history and is likely to be increasingly important in the future.

In 1971, in my first year at Waterloo, I was working for the first time as well as trying to organize my life so that I could fetch my son, which happened five months later. I was, in effect, a single parent and had to get used to living alone again, since my husband came to Canada three years later. I was also trying to finish my dissertation. I put a mattress in my office, and used to bring my son to sleep there while I worked on my dissertation at night. When I finally did finish it and passed my final examination in 1971, I felt as if a millstone had been removed from around my neck.

Since I taught classes in traditional subjects as well as women's subjects, one of the first things that happened was that I realized even more concretely than before that many of the things I was supposed to teach simply did not apply to women. However, as far as teaching about women was concerned, there were virtually no Canadian materials available at the time. Marylee Stephenson had asked for submissions for papers for a session at the Sociology and Anthropology (CSAA) meetings in 1972. I proposed a paper to her, and we had a few telephone conversations about the session, and about teaching about women in general. We realized that we had exactly the same problems: there was no way of finding out what materials were being developed and how other instructors coped. Effort was being duplicated, since we all dealt with our problems in isolation. We decided to start a Newsletter, and at the CSAA session we announced its beginnings and assembled a mailing list from those present. The first issue of the Canadian Newsletter of Research on Women appeared in May 1972. It grew rapidly, in terms of content, size and circulation, and has since become a major vehicle for disseminating research news concerning women in

Canada, as well as an important international periodical, renamed in 1979 *Resources for Feminist Research.*

By 1975, I had to decide what I actually wanted to do and where I wanted to live. I had immediately liked Canada for its openness in accepting a stranger as an equal participant and decided to stay. Feeling the need for a change, I applied for a job at the Ontario Institute for Studies in Education (OISE). I was hired specifically to teach in the area of women's studies within the context of sociology. The first year was desperately lonely. I felt stereotyped. Having been identified (quite properly) as a feminist before my arrival, people reacted to me according to their preconceived notions of what a feminist is, rather than according to what I said or did. This changed abruptly when the department hired two other women, both of them very strong feminist scholars, namely Dorothy Smith and Mary O'Brien. It meant that we were seen as individuals as well as a group representing a particular perspective, and led to a very supportive environment for feminist studies.

In 1980, I joined the Board of Directors of the Canadian Research Institute for the Advancement of Women (CRIAW), and served as its President in 1981-2. One of the major projects with which I have been involved in CRIAW is the establishment of a computerized Talent Bank of Feminist Researchers, which is about to start operating and will contain the vitae of feminist researchers across Canada. My overall involvement with the feminist movement has focused primarily on scholarship, and on political issues relevant to research, teaching, and dissemination of information. My past and current involvement with women is, however, not just professional: I feel a kinship with other feminists, irrespective of the nature of their involvement.

Of course, there are not just benefits, there are also costs and problems attached. Sometimes I wonder whether it is all worth the effort, particularly when little evidence of change can be seen. There *has* been a lot of change in the last ten years with respect to the position of women in society, as well as with respect to sexism in scholarship, but this is not always visible in the short run. However, since I also get a sense of purpose out of my involvement, such doubts are usually merely a sign of temporary exhaustion.

My marriage has been affected by my personal involvement with feminism, as well as by the feminist movement in
general. If one radically questions all allocations of roles on
the basis of sex, marriage must by necessity take on an
entirely new meaning. Some of the spin-offs are unexpected,
and not always welcome. In this, all of us are pioneers, and
pioneers typically have a rough time carving out new paths as
well as trying out some which turn out to be blind alleys. If
one rejects the old structure - a marriage which is based on
patriarchal notions - this does not imply that one can easily
erect a new structure. As the confinement of the old structure has crumbled, so also has its security and predictability.
It is, at times, rather frightening.

In my early years of teaching, there was a fair amount of
distrust of academic feminists expressed by other feminists,
culminating in allegations that we were using the movement
for our own personal purposes, and coupled with the notion
that sisters should not criticize each other. This is an issue
that I resolved many years ago, at least to my own satisfaction. As far as criticism is concerned, it is the very essence of
scholarship, and without it there cannot be progress in our
knowledge. However, there is a difference in style between
constructive and destructive criticism, and one can aim for
constructive criticism as well as try to accept criticism in
that sense. As far as the supposed gap between academic and
non-academic feminists is concerned, I see it basically as a
false distinction. All of us are part of the movement, and
none of us can even pretend to be able to do all of the
necessary work that needs to be done. I think of the various
activities in terms of a division of labour: many of us must
do many different things, and none of us can do them all
in her own life - so the best we can do is to play one part
which is useful and fitted to our personal abilities and incli-
nations. Disagreements as to which parts are more important
are silly, while disagreements as to particular tactics are just
normal aspects of any collective movement, without which
there would be no growth.

Overall, it seems to me to be impossible to be satisfied
with the position of women today, but nevertheless changes
that have taken place are real. As far as the ultimate goal of
the feminist movement is concerned, I see it less as equality

with men, and more as the creation of a society in which there is no social stratification at all, that is, in which people are equally valued irrespective of their sex, race, age, religion, or occupation. I do not think that we will approximate any such ideal society within the next few hundred years, but at least it is a worthwhile goal to work towards.

Peggy Seeger

Peggy Seeger was born in the United States but now resides in Britain. She is forty-seven and has two sons (twenty-three and nineteen) and a daughter (nine). Peggy is well known for her singing of folk and contemporary songs and is involved in songwriting, music arranging, composing and conducting. Most of her songs about women are on her records: 'Penelope Isn't Waiting Any More' (Rounder 4011) and 'Different Therefore Equal' (Blackthorne 1061).

I was my father's first daughter after four boys. He loved women in every shape and form and he homed in on me with a gentle and all-consuming devotion. This caused me not only to think that women were special but that *I* was unique, a misconception that both helped and hindered me as I grew up. It gave me a great deal of self-confidence but tended to make me emotionally and mentally lazy.

My earliest contact with a real feminist was my mother. She was a good, old-fashioned woman who cooked, sewed, sang to her children . . . but she was also a superb pianist, composer and music teacher. I was aware from a very early age that it was normal for a woman to do work other than that required by house and family. There were times when she was 'not to be interrupted'.

I went to college because it was expected and I couldn't think of anything else to do. It was but an extension of high school and once again I was not asked to correlate facts or come to my own conclusions. I stayed at Radcliffe for two

years and left in 1955 spending the next four years in
Europe, Russia, China, and finally England, where I settled
down with Ewan MacColl, twenty years my senior.

Ewan was a playwright, a brilliant theatrical producer,
singer and actor who had decided that folksong was the key
to a popular cultural movement. His working-class background could not have been more different from mine.
Unemployed from the age of fourteen, he spent the Depression in the Manchester Public Library working his way
systematically from A to Z. He had ability, a huge store of
facts at his fingertips – *and* a good memory. My education
began with our partnership. It was not only a matter of dis-
covering history, language, social movements, but of dis-
covering the working class itself and this was my real introduction to the ideas of politics and militant action.

Ewan was active, involved, emotionally explosive. I was
passive, dreamy and quite terrified of emotional involvement.
The mixture was good and we've stayed together ever since.
My work with Ewan introduced me to the working class of
England and Scotland among whom he had grown up and
to whom his life and work was dedicated. He had what I
call gut politics, as distinguished from my mind politics.

Motherhood was the turning point in my life. For the
first two or three days of my son's life, I was desperate. I
had suspected nothing of the pain, the blood, the utter bone
weariness – nor the frightening aspect of twenty years of
unremitting responsibility. Even though I had home help, my
response to motherhood was one of despair – for two days.
Then my delight and discovery took over and I never looked
back. Motherhood opened up a whole new world to me, a
world in which I was no longer the most important central
figure, and I have never regretted undertaking it.

The children multiplied and life became more complicated.
My life gradually became one of organizing people and things,
juggling family and profession, so that a number of disparate
strands could weave together into a pattern in which I could
exist myself. I find myself in the middle of writing a song
then it flashes into my mind that I haven't cancelled a
child's dentist appointment. Or in the middle of banjo
practice I re-set the bread, or take the car for a service. Bit
by bit, my concentration begins to diffuse. A sucker, am I?

Maybe - but I am proud of my ability to keep this little house of cards from falling down. At this time, I found, however, that my periods of creativity, so difficult to snatch, were very intense. In a way, I was doing what my mother had done. My two loves - family and music - were on parallel paths, boosted by quarts of black coffee. I wrote my songs while driving home on a motorway from a singing date. Eighty miles an hour, in the dark, with my spiral notebook in my lap, writing blind and turning pages - secluded and away from the telephone and the kids.

At that time my work was varied - I collected folksongs, did interviewing with Ewan. When the BBC radio ballad project was in full swing, I not only arranged all the music but I rehearsed the musicians and singers and directed the final recording in the studio, often playing an instrument at the same time. This was before multi-tracking, when sound effects, music, singing, all had to be dovetailed in the studio. This led to further work in making music for documentary films - engrossing and time-consuming work, with very skilled session musicians, most of them men. Looking back on it now, I remember no problems as a woman in my late twenties in working with these men, most of them older and more experienced than I. The camaraderie and good humour of the studio will stay with me as a treasured memory.

I became interested in feminism at the point when I felt swamped by these various pressures. I wanted to be good (i.e. effective) at whatever I undertook. In the *back* of my mind was the hope that I really was 'the good wife', 'the good mother' who didn't leave her four year old daughter gasping with asthma because she had been booked to sing two hundred miles away. In the *front* of my mind was my desire to contribute my talents to making the world a better place while also earning a living. There were many times when back and front did not match at all and I was emotionally schizophrenic. But I chose that life. I chose to over-work. Staying at home was just not enough, and it still isn't.

As 1980 was International Women's Year, we felt that I should write a song for it and I literally dashed off *I'm Gonna Be an Engineer* in four hours. It has since become one of the best known songs in the women's movement - quite incredible, as it is very long and hard to sing. I was asked to sing at a number of women's events and soon discovered I knew nothing about the movement at all. I also found that I lacked most of the resentments that many women have. I had had a supportive father, brother, and now had an encouraging and sharing lover who also could do housework. I had had a series of women helpers in the house. So once again, I was lacking gut experience and I had to arrive at my awareness of most women's problems through observing, thinking about and listening to other women.

I also knew very few songs that were acceptable at these female-oriented events. In folksong, women play the varied roles that they do in life: the songs reflect the mores, the social trends of the times in which they were written. Women are loved and left; they turn into nags; they work as servants in big houses; they don men's apparel and follow their lovers; they marry for money; they marry for no money; they are tricked out of everything but their ability to laugh or cry at themselves. For activist feminists the message is often not direct enough. But the songs are those carried down by working-class women – and men; they are expressed in excellent language; they have good tunes; they speak for the times which are not ours; most important, they are accepted by women who are not already 'in the movement'. Finding myself lacking suitable contemporary, direct action songs for such concerts, I set out to write some. Not having the necessary knowledge in my experience, I sought out battered wives, single mothers, women who had been raped, women on picket lines, and many many others. I interviewed them, listened carefully to their voices of experience and used their words, their tone of expression, even their breathing patterns and cadences. These songs are accepted by women both inside and outside the movement and I put them on an album, 'Different Therefore Equal'. In the process of making it I had discovered how other women live. It was quite a shock.

I now have a reputation as a feminist, a term which has a modern everyday usage (suggesting the exclusion of and often antipathy towards males in general) and a classical definition (advocacy of the claims and rights of women). I am a classical feminist. How can I be otherwise? I have had too many helpful, supportive men friends and family to subscribe to their exclusion in my life. I really *like* the idea of men and I like many men in person. Of course, I have come into contact with many males whose views on and behaviour towards women are repulsive. I have also met a number of women within the movement who regard their more orthodox sisters with surprising disdain and lack of tolerance. Most women have relations with men – live with them, like them, love them, are attracted in some way – and no women's movement can afford to ignore that.

I have conflicting feelings about the women's movement. I am forty-seven with grown children. My work partner is male. I am not a joiner, a group person. I feel out of place, out of step with the predominantly young, single, childless women who seem to make up the activists of the movement. I feel out of date. I don't know the jargon. I'm not well acquainted with the progress of many of the issues. I am often left with a feeling of being an observer. I am very angry about the position of women in our society, about the oppression and violence which we suffer as a sex, but this drives me to work with men as well as with women. I am disturbed by the public image of the movement, that of lesbian, single, childless, white, middle-class, young, man-hating women – the most vocal sections of our activists often give that impression – but I do understand that most fledgling movements must be aggressive when the opposition is so entrenched and strong.

Of all the important issues, I find the nuclear predicament the most urgent. At present I am working with an anti-nuclear group whose membership is predominantly women. One of our main problems has been their lack of self-confidence in presenting the anti-nuclear case in the presence of men. I am appalled at the ease with which they are shot down, trampled on, made to feel inferior by husbands and male acquaintances. They leave meetings confident, armed with facts, seemingly ready for conflict and return shattered the following week. They are virtually told that women cannot, should not, meddle in such affairs as nuclear power. Thinking and reasoning with women friends about such things has been more useful to me than a consciousness-raising session.

The current position of women is far from satisfactory. We

have had the Sexual Discrimination Act, yes . . . but employers are devious and implementing the Act is very difficult.
There are now refuges and sanctuaries . . . but some women
and children live in them for years while the man of the
family dodges court action and defies injunctions. Homosexuals and lesbians find public attitudes are changing . . .
slightly. We have the Equal Opportunities Commission . . .
but the average wage of women compared to that of men is
lower than ten years ago. We still get the less skilled jobs, the
highly sexist education – we are laid off first when jobs get
scarce. That the ERA should not have passed, with its
innocuous, generalized wording, is absolutely incredible!

Our women's movement is still predominantly white and
middle-class. The mass of women have hardly been touched
by *real* changes in attitudes and legislations. We have had a
number of strikes led by women, but it seems to me that the
movement has not capitalized on these to raise general
consciousness. The number of battered, raped, deserted
women is rising dramatically. Women in all walks of life
report increasing hostility from men as they claim the right
to equal wages, equal privilege, equal opportunity, even equal
time in which to talk. And we haven't even touched the
problems of women who do part time work, factory work,
sweat-shop work, home piecework. If there has been any
advance it is that the women's movement now exists in the
public eye, even if it is spoken of sarcastically or humorously.
Men are definitely aware of us. But we must beware of putting too much trust in legislation and written rights – for not
until they are put into action can we say that we really have
them.

I have referred a number of times to having been a unique
case, privileged all my life, never having been poor, unloved,
raped, battered, deserted, bored, irrevocably put down. This
has distanced me from what most people's lives are really
about. For artists, this can be useful as we can then perhaps
be more objective. We can be funnels through which other
people's experiences may be strained, crystallized and re-
shaped into a poem, a statue, a painting, a song.

I have fought for gut experience and gained it through
identification with the people I am close to – yet strangely also
with many people I have never met. The tragi-comic nature

of life itself is a constant wonder to me and I live agonizingly through others. If a film is sad, I weep copiously, to the consternation of companions. Tragic stories in the papers stay with me for days. From being quite introverted, I have become shamelessly communicative, even to the point of talking to perfect strangers on buses and in shops. I fill up with other people and their lives because . . . Why? I want the world to be as good for them as it has been for me, so I therefore have to communicate my own experience, even if it is only in the terms of closing gaps between myself and them. It has made me a useful and constructive person, this way of living – bad tempered at times, impatient and officious – but perhaps only by communicating and forcing the channels between our individual selves to open do we become truly human. Or hu-woman, as some of my sisters would say.

Brinlee Kramer

*Brinlee Kramer is the seventeen year old daughter of the
well-known American feminist Cheris Kramarae. She writes
feminist short stories and poems, and is currently a student
at the University of Illinois.*

I used to feel that I had no choice but to be a feminist. My
mother, for as long as I can remember her, has been an
Unconventional Mother.[1] My first memories of her are of
her sweating over her PhD dissertation, which was all over
the house (other mothers *cleaned* the house). I remember the
proud day she finally got her degree and we got a pizza and
drove to the park for a picnic, my sister and I hanging out the
windows yelling, 'My mom got her PhD!' I remember coming
home after school to a babysitter instead of a mother because
Mom was up at *her* school teaching. And I always remember
her politics; they are a part of her personality. Other people
are generous, cheerful, shy; she is a feminist. It is such an
important part of her that, in growing up around her, it is
inevitable that I should have learned to adjust to (and often
accept) untraditional views.

My formative years were spent right smack in the middle
of the 1970s. In the US, at least, this was the 'Me' Decade, a
time of consciousness-raising groups and scream therapy. As
far as I know, my mother did not indulge in the latter, but
one of the former met in our living-room with frightening
frequency. They were actually a support group, mostly
women, who knew what it was like being a woman at a large

169

university. They sat around the table laden with carob brownies and whole-wheat muffins, drank herb tea, and complained enthusiastically. They frightened me a little. They weren't like the kids at school, or their mothers. But they weren't as overbearing as their bright clothes and effusiveness would indicate, and, fascinated by the food and their enthusiasm, I would hang around the edges of their circle, a small, serious-faced, somewhat confused groupie. And they would talk about all *sorts* of interesting things like feminism and socialism and racism and every kind of 'ism' a little girl could dream of. I would sit there eagerly, unwittingly inhibiting their conversation, drinking in the stories about mean people that were surely more interesting than the scary children's stories I wasn't allowed to read. I giggled with delight as they burned the pants off bosses and co-workers in their absence. I surreptitiously stored up the bad words they used – even their language was liberated. I watched, goggle-eyed, as women broke down in tears.

Although I loved sitting in their meetings, I often got tired of the women who came to them. For one thing, I hardly ever saw my mother, who was working on her dissertation and who started back to school when I was seven, and these women were taking away *my time*. Besides, they were weird. I didn't like their clothes. Other, *normal* women shaved their armpits and spoke quietly. These women wore big, clunky jewelry with little fists on it around their necks. And they were so single-minded it was boring. They never stopped talking about feminism; of course, that was because they had no other chance to talk about it except at my mother's meetings, but I didn't know that then. And every time I saw them, they were angry. So my interest in feminism was part morbid fascination and part real interest in them and what they were saying.

By the time I was nine or so, feminism and sexism and racism had been explained to me, and the women's movement lost a lot of its silliness in my eyes. It was no longer carob brownies and herb tea in my living-room – it was important issues. We were talking about *people* here. We were talking about *me*. When I took my feminist attitude to school with me, I didn't feel the least bit precocious since arguing was so much a part of my background. I was a tomboy – one of the guys. I wouldn't be a nambsy-pambsy *girl*. Yecch. I would *not* be dainty. I would *not* wear skirts. I would *not* play with dolls. I played kick soccer and ran races during recess. In sixth grade I wrestled regularly with a boyfriend and won *every time*. And when my phys. ed. teacher tried to give the girls smaller basketballs than the boys, I brought him an article from *Ms.* magazine that said girls were as strong or stronger than boys till the age of twelve (he read it silently and pointedly ignored me ever after). No man would take advantage of *me*.

I really believed everything I said about the women's movement. It was fun having a role; Jim was a baseball expert, David was a maths genius, Brinlee was a feminist. But I didn't really know anything about it. I didn't know the history of women's suffrage. I didn't know that the fight for the Equal Rights Amendment had begun long before my mother's support group moved into my living-room. I didn't know, or I didn't fully understand, how *wrong* prejudice is. At this point, I was a feminist because of my mother, and solely because of her; unequal pay for equal work was a concept far in my future. I liked being a feminist then because my mother and her friends approved of it so strongly.

My mother, it seemed, became even more radical; or perhaps it only seemed that way as I reached the age at which one is easily embarrassed by one's mother. I became less radical as I entered junior high school. By eighth grade I was just tired of it. I wasn't tired of the idea of equality. I was tired of clitorises and speculums, of finding ourselves. The topics didn't seem to have anything to do with feminism. I see now that it had something to do with knowing yourself and with caring about and for yourself; but at the time, it just seemed silly. I thought the women were all out to embarrass me personally. I simply didn't *want* to know about my genitals, but they seemed so important to the women in the women's movement. So by the time I was thirteen I had stopped talking about the ERA: I didn't understand my mother's groups any more. They had frightened me off. And I am still put off, after a fashion. However, I am a feminist now because, having seen and considered the issues involved, I can't imagine any other way to be. It seems to me to be an inarguable point that men and women are equals, just variations of the same species. I am a feminist now because I am a woman now. Feminism and equality under the law are a lot more important to me now because they concern *me*, not some inconceivable adult Brinlee Kramer far in my future. I am a feminist now not for approval from my mother or attention from my friends, but for my own reasons, for the beliefs I have grown into.

Feminism is a hard thing to define. To some, feminism is the study of everything to do with women (their health, their spirit, their sexuality, their relationships). To some, feminism is purely a political issue - simply the pursuit of equality under the law. And to some, feminism is somewhere in between. Common to all breeds of feminism, however, is respect for women and the acknowledgment of their value as workers, friends, and all the things that women are. But though I have implicitly defined a feminist as someone who respects women, I don't think that just anyone who says (stop me if you've heard this before) 'Of course I believe in equal pay for equal work' is a feminist (especially since anyone who *believes* in equal pay for equal work probably *believes* in Santa Claus). And though my opinions on feminism compare in every important way with my mother's, I wouldn't dare to call myself 'as much' a feminist as she. She suggested, when I was deciding what to say about degrees of feminism, that the difference is often in how verbal a person is about his/her beliefs, and that I do not think of myself as being 'as much' a feminist as she because I am much shyer and quieter than she is; she rarely hesitates to differ when confronted with opposing viewpoints. I don't think this is the difference (between the two of us, anyway), for I can be just as argumentative as she when in the presence of glaring chauvinist stupidity - when people say outrageous things, I am just as outraged. And it's not the degree of one's feelings either - what I feel about feminism, I feel just as strongly as my mother. But, obviously, there is enough of a difference between my mother and me so that I see her as a gung-ho feminist, someone whom I use as an example of ultimate feministness. Why are we so different, though it seems, on paper, that we should be so similar?

I consider myself a feminist. The reason that some people reading this will not believe me is that many of the people reading this will be Feminists. Upper- and lower-case feminism is an idea I came up with while talking about this paper with my mother and father. The problem with differentiating between feminists and Feminists is that it's often a *feeling* one gets. When I see a woman wearing army fatigues and hiking boots, I get a *feeling* that she's a Feminist. When I see a woman wearing a skirt and heels going to an Abortion Coalition meeting, I can almost guarantee that she's a feminist. But it's not just clothes that make the feminist. Two of my mother's Feminist friends are remarkably well dressed, and one of them wears high heels (which confuses my mother). It could be the way they carry themselves; perhaps Feminists take long, strong strides, while feminists walk normally (just kidding). And Feminists don't (usually) have deep voices and hairy chests, so that's not the difference either.

Flo Kennedy wears nail polish and she is a Feminist. I wear nail polish and I am a feminist. Bella Abzug wears women's hats and she is a Feminist. I wear men's hats and I am a feminist. My mother thinks men and women are intrinsically equal and she is a Feminist. I think men and women are intrinsically equal and I am a feminist. The same jokes will make Feminists and feminists laugh. The same political idiocies that go on will make both Feminists and feminists scream and rend their garments. Babies make both Feminists and feminists happy. Contrary to popular belief, neither Feminists nor feminists are man-haters. There *is* a difference between us, but I can't absolutely define that difference.

I like what Feminists say about equal rights and our value as women and people; I often don't like the way they say it. In their desire to challenge the status quo they often take actions that are loud, sudden, and disconcerting not only to antifeminists, but also to those of us involved in, but not making decisions about, women's liberation activities. I would appreciate a little sensitivity from older Feminists, although I understand and agree with what they (we) are saying. I understand they feel angry, because I am angry about the same things, and I sympathize with their need to express their anger. But I often find their publicly expressed anger rude and startling. They frighten me sometimes; I never know what's coming next. When my sister got her first period, we went out to dinner to celebrate (already that's pretty weird). Jana was *seriously* worried that Mom might blow up balloons or break into song with 'Happy Bleeds to You' in the restaurant.

I am a feminist, but I don't think that what I put on my face or feet or body has anything to do with my politics. I am not abasing myself or my womanhood by wearing eyeshadow, for heaven's sake. But my mother thinks that high heels are an integral part of a sexist society. I wear makeup – I love wearing it, and perfume and high heels and skirts. My mother is very basic – she is an Earth Child. She wears what is comfortable. She says fashions encourage women to be more physically vulnerable and to rely on public approval. But I like spending the time on myself. Wearing nice clothes makes me feel like I'm worth silk and wool and natural fibres. Oh well, maybe I'll understand when I'm older.

Besides nit-picking disagreements like those above, my main problem with the feminist movement is that it is so out of my control. As a *young* woman, I am welcome either to accept my elders' wisdom or get out. Ever since my mother's students and consciousness-raising groups filled up my living-room and took up my mother's time, I have felt that it controlled me. I have no control over the women who do things that I think are unnecessarily rude, yet by being a feminist I am associated with them. It has been such an important part of my life, and still is, yet at times I feel asphyxiated by it (perhaps its importance, its ubiquitousness, *is* why). Even though I have come to terms with feminism, I have yet to come to terms with Feminists. As a younger feminist, I face this dilemma: unless I agree with older Feminists, I will have no influence with them; if I agree with them, I will have to deny some of my real feelings.

Notes

1 My mother, Cheris Kramarae, teaches Women's Studies at the University of Illinois, writes books on feminism (she and Paula Treichler are working on a feminist dictionary now), and organizes international conferences on language and gender.

Laura McArthur

Laura McArthur is Canadian, married with three sons and one daughter, aged fifteen to twenty-five. She is President of the Right to Life Association in Toronto.

Who needs the women's movement? Not Canadian women – certainly not the type of movement that has been foisted on women in recent years. The Canadian women's movement seems to be made up of extremist feminists led by a few 'elitists' purporting to speak for all women.

By some twist of logic, the feminists, while directing their most vociferous attacks against the character of men, are at the same time trying to emulate them by denying their womanhood. One can only wonder why any woman would want to give up the particular strengths and advantages enjoyed by women to become a second class male in order to gain some illusory equality on men's terms.

My views about women and men have been formed, not from peering through my kitchen curtains, but rather from years of experience working and mingling with women and men from all walks of life. More recently, I have closely followed the activities of the women's movement and have debated with its members on many occasions.

My innate sense of worth as a woman was reinforced by the women I knew in my youth, and by most women I have met over the years. I was born and raised on a farm in the province of New Brunswick during the depression years, the second youngest in a family of eight girls and one boy. I

175

learned at a very early age just how individual each woman was, and the women I knew, although so different in interests and views, were confident and competent in their chosen fields. As a result it never occurred to me that women should not be in the forefront, in fact I thought we were!

Perhaps that is why, at the age of seventeen when my father died and I had to become self-supporting, it did not seem strange to me that my first job in communications was one normally held by men or that my first supervisor was a woman. When I came to Toronto in my early twenties to pursue my career, I again worked side by side with men, and when I was promoted to supervisor over many of the men I worked with, I encountered neither hostility nor discrimination. I was qualified and I pulled my weight, which earned me the same salary and benefits as my male counterparts. I would not have settled for less.

I can honestly say that I have never been discriminated against solely because I am a woman, however, under the feminists' definition of harassment, I would have to admit to having been harassed because I did hear the odd whistle and encounter the water-cooler flirtations. This, however, did not seem to 'threaten' my womanhood or damage my psyche very much because I later married one of those whistling water-cooler boys.

Although, as with all young couples in those days, we had very little money, my priority for the next few years was staying at home caring for my children, an occupation which proved to be immensely rewarding. After my youngest child entered school eleven years ago I became a full-time volunteer for Right to Life and have been President and Chairman of the Board of the association for the past eight years.

From my youth, surrounded by women, to today, sharing an apartment with my husband and three grown sons (my daughter is married) I have managed to survive without the help of a women's movement, in fact, in recent years I have survived in spite of it.

Although I have not fallen prey to the alleged discriminatory practices of men, I have felt the impact of discrimination as imposed by society. Nowhere has this discrimination been more clearly demonstrated than against families who decide to have several children, and where the mother chooses to stay at home to care for them. Everything in society from housing to entertainment is geared to the two-salaried family. Many women, including myself, who are prepared to give up such luxuries as new cars, holidays, and even the dream of owning a home in order to do what we, as women, feel is most important to us, will not be a part of a women's movement that plays such a major role in down-grading the family unit and motherhood. No leer a man could cast upon a woman could match the degradation and ridicule directed by the feminists at a mother with several small children. No man could ever dream up a more vicious or more personal attack on the very being of a woman than abortion, yet the feminists have been in the vanguard of the abortion-on-demand movement.

The feminists brag about the gains they have made against sexism in the area of textbooks and advertising. Does showing more pictures and advertisements of men washing dishes and changing diapers while Mom is out collecting garbage really denote advances, or does it show just how far the feminists are out of touch with the real world? My 6'5" lumberjack grandfather changed diapers. My very manly father was our favourite babysitter, and I drove a team of stallions plowing fields. So what's new?

Since the feminists claim advances in the area of advertising, I wonder if they realise they are now engaged in reverse discrimination. When is the last time you saw an ad showing more than 1.8 children? I have four children – are the feminists trying to tell me something?

Men, thank God, will continue to be men, and positive women will continue to be proud of their womanhood whether it is as a mother, career woman, or in any other chosen field.

Indeed, exploitation, sexism and discrimination do exist, but they are not unique to women. Both men and women can be vulnerable because of single parenthood, ill health, insufficient job training, handicaps, or advanced age, to name a few. Many of these individuals need help, and in a caring and enlightened society, both men and women should be working together to eradicate such cruel and ugly practices. Unfortunately, the women's movement, by pitting women against men, has exacerbated the problem. It is high time the women's movement paused to take a good look at the destruction it has wrought.

Who needs the women's movement? – not women.

Yvonne Carnahan

*Originally from New Zealand, Yvonne is now an Australian
resident. She was a teacher for twelve years. At thirty-six she
is the National Co-ordinator of the Women's Electoral Lobby
and a member of the Australian Federation of University
Women (Bachelor of Arts and of Education).*

Since early 1979 I have worked as the National Co-ordinator
for the Women's Electoral Lobby (WEL). Until that time I
had little personal contact with feminism – I had attended a
women's liberation meeting on one occasion, but other than
feeling sympathetic to the women's movement I would not
have considered myself a part of it.

The end of my marriage brought the beginning of a new
involvement in women's issues for me. Prior to that time
I was fully involved in teaching, in studying for my first
degree, in running a home and in supporting my husband in
his work. There was little time left for other interests. However, the breakup of my marriage not only left me with the
time to become involved, it also brought a desire to involve
myself in work concerned with women's opportunities and
rights.

As with most marriage breakups, that time in my life was
particularly traumatic. Because of events that occurred I
spent three weeks in a women's refuge and some time after
that felt that because the women's movement had been supportive of me at a time when I needed it I wanted to give
something in return.

179

I was told about the possibility of the position with WEL, applied, and as a consequence was invited to take part in their annual National Conference which was being held only a week later. I went to that conference expecting, as I had been told by an outsider to expect, a screaming rabble of women. Nothing could have been further from the truth. The women were articulate, they were confident, and they were well-informed. Opinions were given from a position of knowledge and research. Little was said which gave the impression of uninformed prejudice, and the women gave each other the courtesy of listening to what each had to say. An atmosphere of intelligence was also combined with tremendous friendliness in the informal gatherings. I came away from that conference thoroughly stimulated and eager to work for a group of women I considered more than worthwhile.

I volunteered to work as interim National Communications Officer, as the position was then called, and in due course was interviewed with others applying for the position. I was then officially appointed. The payment was miniscule (the organisation running only on voluntary contribution), but it was a job I wanted to do.

Although I am working as part of a feminist organisation, I consider that in fact I am working for *people*, both female and male, but doing so through the women's movement. I'm, working for the opportunity for people to be who they are according to their own talents and abilities and interests, as a contrast to fitting in with sex role stereotyping, which I see to be just as stifling for men as it is for women. Opponents of feminism consider that biological differences are the predeterminant of male and female roles. Changes in lifestyles, already evident, indicate that this is not necessarily so. As an example, twelve years ago it would have been virtually impossible for a male to obtain a position as a teacher of infant children - today it is accepted that individual males have nurturing qualities as do individual women. Similarly, women in the past were prevented from attending university, from taking on apprenticeships in areas such as motor mechanics or carpentry, or from being involved in the political sphere, to name only a few areas. Individual women have proven that, given the opportunity, they are able to make the most of abilities which have been labelled 'masculine' although possessed by many women.

In the past, my mother was opposed to 'women's liberation'. Her attitude was that women's liberation meant women would have to become bricklayers, and as she had no wish to become a bricklayer she was therefore opposed to women's liberation. This attitude is not an uncommon one. Many people who are content with the choices open to them at present, who fit easily into what is generalised as the norm, are afraid that increased opportunities would instead mean coercion to fit into a lifestyle which they would not choose of their own volition. This, in fact, is what is happening at present for people who do not fit easily into the generalised norm, but somewhere else on the continuum of human ability.

My concept of the women's movement is that we are looking for the accepted right of people to live their lives in a non-alienating way. I consider, therefore, that a woman has the right to live her life as a radical lesbian separatist, as a Catholic mother of eleven, as the head of a capitalist corporation, or as whatever she chooses to be. My commitment is to help make those choices genuinely possible, and to help people live in peace with their differences. For this to occur, people need support, not condemnation from others.

People frequently learn to be prejudiced from an early age. Most people want to be liked and accepted. They therefore learn the code of behaviour that is acceptable to the group that they want to be part of - whether it be a suburban neighbourhood, a Law Society, or a bike gang. However, wherever there is an 'in-group' there is usually also an implied 'out-group', the members of which are not acceptable because of a variety of reasons. It is in people's interests that they learn these prejudices so that they themselves can be accepted and therefore secure. Those with differences are at least tolerated.

Such conditioning begins almost from birth. Baby girls are dressed in pink, baby boys are dressed in blue. On the surface there seems little harm in this, but it can also be seen as the beginning of a person being programmed into a role which ultimately may not suit that person at all. Boys are taught that tears are a sign of weakness, and girls that toughness is unfeminine. All of this has been said many times before in discussions about sexism, and the argument can even be advanced that such sex role conditioning makes for a functional society. However, it can also create a society which does not function properly because many of its people are unhappy in, or unused to, the roles ascribed to them.

As our society functions at present, the psyches of people are being violated. A few years ago I conducted a survey to try to ascertain whether there was more domestic conflict between partners where the wife was in paid employment, or where she was a homemaker. There was more conflict, and for more nebulous reasons such as 'needing to let off steam', from those who were full-time housewives. One of the women I interviewed was a mother of three, beautifully groomed, and going up the wall with the life she was living. What was confusing to her was that she was doing exactly what she had been taught would bring her happiness, and she accepted, on the surface, the standards her husband set, that she alone was responsible for the house and children. She would dearly have loved to have at least a part-time job, and for her husband to have shared with her the money-making and homemaking roles.

'But what can I do?' she said. 'I'm at heart a family person, I'm not a career woman.' The point is, however, that her husband was also a family person. He enjoyed the pleasures of having a wife and children, but also had the benefit of outside job satisfaction and a certain degree of financial independence. Apart from his strong belief in the different roles for men and women, he had little reason not to share the childcare and workload with her, and agree to her wish to take part-time paid work. He usually returned home from school teaching by 3.30 p.m. It is as if society has played a dirty trick on that woman. She has lived by its rules, she has deferred to what she has been taught is expected of her, and she is miserable.

With rapid technological change it is inevitable that there will be increased unemployment. Politicians today cry out that married women are taking the jobs of unemployed youth. To my mind, however, we have a golden opportunity for the opening up of new possibilities. An increase in job-sharing and part-time work could lead to genuine role-sharing. One partner in a relationship could be in paid employment in the morning while the other partner parents, vice versa in the afternoon, and then both could share leisure time in the evening. This is, of course, difficult in the present wage structure and would be considered financially impractical by most people – but it is an example of the opportunities that could be created if people's minds were opened to the possibilities.

A great deal of what is possible depends upon the relationships between people. My concept of how marriage should be is of two independent people who choose to share a mutual dependency, but not a relationship that is so dependent that either one of them becomes exploited by the other. Each gives to and nurtures the other because of caring for that person, but each is also capable of standing alone. I am not, therefore, opposed to marriage (whether *de jure* or *de facto*), but I am opposed to women being placed in a position of total financial dependence upon their husbands.

My attitudes towards women have probably developed and changed over the years more so than my attitudes towards men. As regards men (I am heterosexual), there are some I enjoy being with, some I don't – but women, especially feminist women, have a strength and vitality I had not in the past known about. It is as if in finding the strength to break away from exploitative situations, as many of them have done, they have become even stronger as people and more alive in their personalities.

In terms of conflict with other women, I see it occurring more between groups who generalise about others they have little contact with than I do between individuals who know each other as people. I consider all of the various groups, whether radical or conservative, to be a part of the women's movement and each in their own way is concerned with women's rights. Some women and women's groups act as a spearhead, forcing public attention on to issues that might otherwise be swept under the carpet and these are the groups that people choose to disassociate themselves from when they say 'I'm not a feminist but...' and then go on to espouse a feminist philosophy. Other groups are supportive of feminism but prefer to work within the system rather than outside it to achieve change. Conflict comes between these two groups because the first would consider the second to be upholding the system by accepting gradual improvement and thereby preventing radical change, and the second would feel that to do other than work within the system is to waste energy and achieve nothing through lack of majority support. The third subsection, the more conservative groups, are considered even more guilty of upholding the system because they concern themselves particularly with the rights of women in the home.

Without an assumed enmity, it's possible that all of these groups could achieve a great deal more for women than they do at present if they associated with each other and joined forces in their areas of concurrence. That is not as impossible as it sounds. Time and again I heard women at the Canberra (Australian) Mid-Decade for Women Conference say to other women from an apparently opposing group, 'If that's what you mean, then I agree with you.' It was probably the first occasion on which many women had discussed issues with others they thought of as being in opposition. My particular vision is of genuine sisterhood – that is, support between women (and people) in their right to be different.

I sometimes wonder if any progress is being made. As an example, for over twelve years Rape Law Reform for the Australian Capital Territory (ACT) has been in the drafting stage, and at the end of twelve years one of the proposals that had been decided upon was that immunity for rape in marriage be extended to *de facto* relationships! For as long as there is still an attitude towards women that permits rape of any kind to be legal, then we still have a long way to go.

On the other hand, people I meet socially, when told I work for a feminist organisation, frequently say something like 'I believe in equal pay but I don't believe in (whatever).' Ten years ago they would also have been arguing against equal pay. It takes people time to become comfortable with an idea they see originally as radical, and with persistence I believe that the women's movement will achieve many of its aims. For one thing, I doubt that the Rape Law Reform for the ACT, when it finally comes through, will allow immunity for any kind of rape, and that will be as a direct result of the efforts of the women's movement.

Connie Purdue

Connie Purdue is in her seventieth year and is a 'woman alone' having been married previously twice. She has two daughters and a son, as well as granddaughters and grandsons. A New Zealander, Connie worked in a variety of jobs as factory and office worker, and was trade union official over a period of twenty-seven years. She retired from paid employment in 1976. She is an executive member of the Auckland National Council of Women, past secretary of the Auckland Equal Pay and Opportunity Council, Co-founder of the National Organization for Women (New Zealand), a life member of the Auckland Clerical Union, and editor of Feminists for Life. *Connie has written many articles for the media and a* History of the Auckland Women's Branch of the New Zealand Labour Party *(1975). She says her fighting spirit comes from a Yugoslav father and a militant mother. In 1975 she was granted an MBE for her work among women and children.*

As the daughter of a Dalmatian, growing up in a small New Zealand town I learnt while young the discriminations of bearing a foreign name, of being Catholic, a member of a poor family, and later, of course, from having been born female. Rebellion came easily to my mother born of an Irish Ulster Protestant father and a Scotch Catholic mother. Proud of her pioneer New Zealand background, she refused during the First World War to register as an 'enemy alien' at the local police station, for at that time wives of foreigners

185

took on their husbands' nationality. Facing the birth of her seventh child, she had to capitulate but I still have her registration form witnessed by the local constable that she did so 'under protest'. She also supported the establishment of the Auckland Family Planning Association which led to her eventual excommunication from the Catholic Church. Now that the Church has other answers to mothers than either 'submit or abstain', both   her life and mine might have been very different.

But perhaps the most decisive factor in shaping my life was the tuberculosis that lamed me as a little girl. I could never be like other girls so I determined to be different.

From the arms of my convent education I leapt at the age of sixteen to become the secretary of the Auckland Branch of the Young Communist League. With my brothers, I was of course one of the hundreds of young unemployed of the late 1920s.

Our eyes were set on the golden glow of the Russian Revolution. But soon all this was interrupted by my departure to a sanatorium with TB lungs, eventually sent home with the dictum not to kiss anyone or ever have children. I did both promptly. A brief spell off from politics for marriage and maternity (the most satisfying part of my life), then to help with my children's education I took up an industrial job and began my career with the trade union movement. By this time I was a national executive member of the New Zealand Communist Party, but in my branch I was always critical, incurring the dreadful label of being 'anti-centralist'. My resignation was accepted in 1956, quite an honour really, as most departures are dubbed 'expulsions'. I tired of the Party using women.

I became secretary in 1969 of the first Auckland Equal Pay and Opportunity Council, and was several times delegate from my union to the Federation of Labour Conferences where I initiated luncheon discussions on women's problems. With a university student, Sue Kedgley, I organized the New Zealand tour of Germaine Greer in 1972 and in the same year with Sue, founded the National Organization of Women in New Zealand. With a broad programme it attracted membership, but many left with me when lesbians and abortion-on-demand supporters took over. With a woman lawyer, I took a deputation to a Labour MP in May 1972 that led to the setting up of the Inquiry into Women's Rights, from which came our Human Rights Commission. Still in employment, by then as Social and Travel Officer for the Auckland Clerical Union (a job I invented for myself), I continued in employment until election as a Labour candidate in 1974 to the Auckland Hospital Board, and later in 1980 to my local Borough Council. For my pro-life opinions I was dropped after four years as a Women's Representative of the New Zealand Labour Party but was appointed by the Government to the Social Development Council in 1978 and to the Board of the Accident Compensation Corporation in 1981. Some Labour people must still have liked me for it was on the nomination of a Labour MP, Mike Moore, that I gained an MBE in 1975 for work among women and children.

Today, I feel myself to be very much part of the growth of the feminist movement of the third stage. As editor of the New Zealand *Feminists for Life* magazine I work with young women who see feminism as truly 'for women' only if it is also pro-family and pro-life. This is a stage slowly being reached by Betty Friedan and others, admitting their faults of emphasizing lesbianism and abortion. I see women still being 'used' and exploited by men for their gain.

The bitterness that divides the women's movement, making we who are pro-family and pro-life now 'the radicals', ignored by the 'establishment' feminist with her support from that vast network established in New Zealand from the United (?) Women's Conventions, is a sadness that distresses me. To work for the right to vote and for equal pay brought ridicule, but not the destructive hatred that divides the feminist movement today.

When we worked for 'equality' we did not mean 'sameness'. Yet women seem to be exchanging their heritage as women for a mess of pottage. To work like a man, renouncing maternity and child-rearing, with the non-working young and the aged placed in government-subsidised institutions, seems to me an exchange of tyranny. All the fun and the glory of being a woman is lost in the grey drabness of unisex clothing, manners and behaviour, and surely is not only nonsense but dangerous nonsense.

We are different from men as I learnt very early. Inhibited as I was by my total ignorance of sexual relationships as a

young woman, it seemed to me that the only explanation of
the gap between women and men at this level was that at the
time of Creation, God was colonizing two planets and got the
pairing mixed. So that somewhere in the galaxy all this time,
there are the men that could have understood us, and they
are just as mismatched as we women are here on this earth.

No one can listen in to on-the-job conversations of men
with men, women with women and not realize that the difference is far more than 'social conditioning'. How can men to
whom sex activity means so much ever understand the ease
with which women can live a satisfactory life of sexual
abstinence yet, at the same time, have the capacity, as many
do, for repeated orgasmic response. Our signals are confused
for a woman cannot understand that when she turns up to
work in a split skirt, more or less topless, men take it as a
'come-on' message when her intention is only to say 'look at
me'. Women have to put up with men either talking down to
'the girls' or with sexual innuendo in social conversation
(and we all know how boring either can be), while all the
time we know that the presence of a woman makes men
uneasy.

But we hoped for too much. Many of the warnings of what
women's liberation would do have come about. Children and
the aged have suffered the most from the wrong turnings
taken by the liberation movement in women's struggle for
equality. We, too, have harmed ourselves in our rejection of
the role of motherhood and homemaker. Being close to the
health scene, I note how maternity beds give way to the
demand for more gynaecological care. Hysterectomies are
the fourth highest in operations, I am told. We have an
increase of abortions in New Zealand at our free public
clinics to an almost on-demand service, yet teenage pregnancies and child-bashing continue. No survey can tell us of
the life-long remorse of the mother so often pressured by
some reluctant father to destroy her child.

The myth that motherhood is a denigration, that the
only fulfilment comes from the exercise of 'the right to
work', will eventually bring about a society where all the
non-workers, aged and young, are shut away in State institutions while the young and the perfect are absorbed into total
producing and consuming. Whether this is seen as a Marxist

or capitalist goal, it is the antithesis of human fulfilment.

Deep divisions rend the women's movement today. The refusal to accept we pro-life feminists as part of that movement, the divisions that often erupt between militant lesbians and radical heterosexuals, the denunciation of Gloria Steinem as a CIA agent, are examples of these divisions. Now we can expect similar bitter attacks on Betty Friedan who steadily departed from her *Feminist Mystique* stance to claim in an interview with *Playgirl* that the National Organization of Women had been infiltrated by government agents who gained control as a 'pseudo-radical' group putting forward the slogan 'Revolution-NOW', creating an anti-man image with lesbianism as a main issue. Since then of course, Betty Friedan has reached her *Second Stage*, telling us we are allowed to love men and babies.

I must explain the influences that brought me to the stand that divides feminism today: that is to be for or against abortion as a woman's right. It was long before my return to the Church but resulted from loyalty to our well-respected Labour leader and Prime Minister, Norman Kirk, whose too-early death brought great loss to the New Zealand Labour Party. He had his own pro-life personal belief and he could see that the strength of the Party lay within the support of the working class which was mainly Catholic, and certainly morally conservative. I came out publicly when the Auckland University students' paper advertised a pro-abortion march, supported by one branch of the Labour Party with the headline, 'How to Get Rid of that 10 lbs of Excess Flesh'. This seemed so inhuman to me I wrote them a furious open letter. The pro-life movement took note and invited me to join. Here I learnt what I never knew even after three pregnancies, all the wonder and beauty of life before birth. The unborn is not a 'blob of jelly', or even 'co-joined sperm', but at 10 weeks able to transmit its heart beat and brain waves. We can see its sex, its limbs and watch its movements, and its daily development. Given this knowledge, I am certain, few mothers would go ahead with their child's destruction. This is the dividing line. We pro-life feminists are totally unacceptable to those who take the other stance. Will we ever accept each other or find some common ground?

Nowhere have the divisions among women been more

exposed than at the first 1975 World Conference of Women which I attended in Mexico. To identify myself and to seek out allies, I made a claim for pro-life feminism, I was immediately hissed and booed by about 5,000 women. I met a few pro-life women and best of all, received invitations to meet women of Mexico City in their own homes. But divisions were many: our Peace and Disarmament meeting could not take place because some para-military group had taken over the room; there could be no agreement on a definition of the word, 'family'; Russian women were represented by male voices of authority who staged a walk-out when representatives of Israel spoke; working-class Japanese alleged their official group were unrepresentative. Working-class women of South America and Mexico City were astounded at the inattention to their real problems of poverty, child-starvation, suppression of dissent by their governments, while these middle-class well-fed women expressed all the dissatisfactions of their affluent societies.

As one who is still involved in women's issues, I often wonder whether we have lost or gained when considering the days of the terrible injustices of the past: the exploitation of factory labour, the sexual oppression of women as domestics, the cruelty and hardships of the life of women as peasants and rural-workers in comparison with today's situation. Pressurized into too-early sex with all its consequent medical and emotional costs, women and girls suffer from sexual exploitation. Easy abortion has led to disastrous answers to the problems of fertility. Certainly, the right to vote, to earn equal pay, to have the right to some areas of equal opportunity and a longer life are victories, but often children have to pay for them. Caring for babies and children and the art of homemaking are skills of great importance which we should use with pride. True enough, however, my political mama warned me as a young homemaker, 'If you've got your housework all done dear it's a sign you're neglecting the movement', leaving me with a feeling of guilty pleasure to be found polishing the brass or doing the flowers!

Surely, the greatest gift we can give our children is a warm, happy, loving home-life, nor does this mean any great self-sacrifice. Try working in a factory pressing plastic plates, or sewing cuffs on shirts all day, and the many opportunities available for a mother at home seem a luxury to dream of.

It's good to see men sharing housework but there's a limit. I see the danger of a total removal of the protective and supporting role of the father. We see in animal herd behavior the risks to the group, in particular, the female, from the isolated non-responsible male. Is the increase of violence towards women part of this change? Now as a Catholic come home, in good health and having now achieved my seventieth year, I have a life rich with many rewards and I am by no means inactive. My material possessions are few, having walked out on two husbands and two homes, the first after twenty-five years, the second much later after a few months. I look back on the experiences of twenty-seven years in employment at many trades, and in many community projects which have been won since I was a young mother with three pre-school children and no money (no time for suburban neurosis). My three interesting and loving children live close, and I watch with joy my granddaughters extending their lives with university education. The friendships of women are dear to me but few have had my background of work and trade union experience. Even then the common link of our womanhood provides a base for rewarding communication and involvement.

My hope is that the strength of women will lead them on through the third stage of feminism to a full partnership with men: winning world peace, strengthening the longest lasting relationship of the family, loving and sharing, and cherishing children.

Gloria Bowles

*Gloria Bowles is Co-ordinator of Women's Studies at the
University of California, Berkeley. Her doctorate was in
comparative literature. Married at twenty-five, divorced at
thirty, she is now forty, and lives 'happily alone'. Gloria
has edited (with Renate Duelli Klein) a book on the development of women's studies as a discipline in its own right
published by Routledge & Kegan Paul in 1983 and is
finishing a book on Louise Bogan the poet.*

For me, feminism is tied up with an acting out of principle
rather than raw self-interest. This means a willingness to take
risks. I undertook the development of a new programme in
women's studies because I believe in it; traditional scholarship has ceased to be interesting to me and I think it primarily
serves those who do it. To act out of principle, we must have
the capacity to ignore the nay-sayers. They are all around us,
afraid of any move that is out of the ordinary or decision
that does not follow a careful path they have laid out to
avoid risk. When I wrote my dissertation in comparative
literature on American women poets, some of my professors
predicted dire consequences for my career. When I turned
down jobs in traditional departments, I was told I was 'nuts'.
When I suggested that the university might actually give us
money to run women's studies, I was told that was not likely.
But things worked out in the end because I listened to my
voice rather than the scared, negative reactions of those
around me.

192

It is quite possible that this determination (stubbornness, some would call it) comes out of my privileged white, middle-class background. I was the first child of three; studies show that those of us who are girls are lucky to be the first-born. Childhood snapshots show me in a nurturing relationship with my brothers. Because my mother had two small boys at home, I had to be relatively independent.

Both my parents were college-educated (my four grand-parents had degrees as well), and they encouraged each of their children every step of the way. In junior high, when there was homework to do, I went straight to my room. My brothers shared a bedroom – I always had a room of my own. My mother served the family; occasionally I set the table but, for the most part, I was not asked to help with the chores. My time was my own. What privilege! And how hard my mother worked!

In college, I got on a boat and went to Paris for my sopho-more year abroad, this before the era of formal exchange programs. At Michigan, I worked on the student paper, the *Michigan Daily*, and became a senior editor. (The privilege again: my parents supported all this independence with their money.) When I was in my third year in college, a French friend gave me Simone de Beauvoir's *The Second Sex*. In graduate school at Michigan, studying male literature, I was none the less vividly engaged by the women of those fictions and poetry. My journal of 1965–6 is full of ideas for essays on women in literature as well as revolutionary statements *à la* de Beauvoir about the freedom and independence of women. In 1965, there was the first draft of 'An Essay on Women', as I tried to integrate all I was reading in graduate school, in a woman's way. This was done secretly, apart from the class work which did not admit such a discussion.

Somehow much of these thoughts got buried, when I fell in love and listened to the voices around me that said 'mar-riage'. I was not confident enough then to even know how to hear my own voice. Now I could be a real woman! The intel-lectual achievements, the awards, were OK; but I was already twenty-five – and I had only a half-life! It was 1967 and I had moved to Berkeley, where there were many other things going on besides the dreams of a domestic life. But I did get married and I did get involved with Dansk dishes and spotless bathrooms. And I *went under*, deep into domesticity and graduate school, buried under mounds of books and exams. But cut off, and consciously so, from the world around me. For I had grown up in a political milieu – my father was a lawyer and active in the Democratic party and eventually a judge in Detroit – and I had lived through envelope licking and raucous rallies and the internecine struggles of party politics. I had seen the toll it took on people (mainly, it robbed them of a 'personal' life) and I wanted no part of it. I decided the only reality was personal relationships and Beauty and Peace. I was, of course, denying enormous parts of myself as I pursued this deathly peace. But after all, wasn't I being a *woman*, as I brought harmony to my surroundings and *gave* to people and studied literature in an ambivalent way?

Not that I was unaware of the conflicts. In fact, I wrote about them constantly. I finally decided that an active and engaged involvement with people and conflict *is* life. Somehow I learned from the experience. The two who had married before they knew themselves, separated. We had both been influenced by some ideal of domestic life. I took my PhD exams and felt a sense of power from getting through that humiliating ordeal. Through it all, these ups and downs, there has always been my work. Those childhood years of a room of my own meant that I had developed a discipline and an *attachment* to work and thought that was essential to my survival.

The scene is a living room: it is a Sunday afternoon and we are gathered for a meeting of the women's caucus. I am struck by the beauty and intelligence of these women whom I had not known before because I was so deeply esconsed in marriage. This was my consciousness-raising group, my way to understanding that years of study had cut me off from my own literary tradition. I changed my dissertation topic, taught a course on women's literature and organized a student group to lobby for a women's studies major. A new beginning. What was most important was that feminism helped me to put back together again the personal and the political. It was a personal and political in an utterly new form – as woman-centered and woman-defined – and it healed the split which had been so damaging to my life and work for ten years.

I think one can make some generalizations about the US women's movement based on my experience, which is not atypical. Firstly, it is no accident that the movement in its origins was primarily white and middle-class. We had the leisure and the education to pursue our questionings. Secondly, the coming to consciousness involves a recognition of the profound impact *on one's own life* of the denigration of women. In my case, stereotypic notions of femininity led me into passive domesticity. And years of acceptance of male literature as the norm had cut me off from my own feelings and my own tradition. And thirdly, the coming to consciousness takes place with other women. *We are not alone.*

I have spent the better part of the last seven years building the women's studies program at Berkeley. I identify as a women's studies person because I find the traditional studies limiting and dull and because I believe in an interdisciplinary woman-centered study that challenges all the male paradigms. Feminism gives my life shape and form. Not that I whisper to myself every minute of the day 'I'm a feminist, I'm a feminist. . .'. But I lead my life in ways I define as feminist. I am responsible for my life. I seek the help and advice of my close friends and family – but I am ultimately responsible for major decisions and their consequences. Because I have a high regard for women, I do everything I can to improve our lives. That generosity extends to everyone, within the limits of my power and resources, who has lived in circumstances less privileged than mine. And I am connected to a whole tradition of feminism, a line that stretches throughout history. I am very proud to be part of that tradition.

It is hardest to write about conflicts between women. We expect competition among women who have not yet discovered feminism. This competition is deeply ingrained in us; it is one of patriarchy's most successful strategies for keeping us apart. Usually it is competition for men. But among women who say they are feminists – well, this conflict is almost unbearable. A good friend of mine got up in the middle of a particularly acrimonious meeting of feminists and said: 'We don't need to worry about men. We'll do it to ourselves.' As a women's studies co-ordinator, this facing up to conflict has been one of the most painful parts of my work. Women are not used to having any power at all and, if there is even a little bit to be had, we fight over it. It happens because we do not deeply and carefully examine our motives; it is hard to admit our own jealousies. Most important, we simply have not yet learned to work together. Popular books which tell us how to succeed, such as *The Managerial Woman* and *Games Your Mother Never Taught You*, say that men learned how to work together by playing games. Football teaches you all the plays and, if you lose a game, there is always another one. Women have to find our own ways to 'play the game' but we are a very long way from knowing how. For me, generosity and using power to empower other women has been a credo. But that is only part of it; it is too naive to assume that everyone believes in co-operation and consensus. I have begun to integrate the knowledge that even women who call themselves feminists have in fact embraced the male ethic of competition. I have been too patient; I bend over backwards for women because I think I understand why they believe as they do. But I am slowly learning to get angry more quickly.

At the start of this essay, I said that for me feminism has something to do with acting out of principle rather than raw self-interest. Yet in retrospect I can see that I have gained a great deal from acting out of principle. It has not always been easy. I was frightened when I thought seriously about ending my marriage; in women's studies, there are constant attacks on the program, both from within and without. Some subtle combination of commitment and pluck and energy has so far pulled me through.

The women's movement, of which women's studies is a part, is about growth and change. It is no accident, then, that many of us find ourselves at an impasse with men. Women of my generation want equal relationships. Because of the movement, we have changed much more than men. We have become critical of this contemporary 'Age of Relationships', when people have more expectations from coupledom than any relationship can possibly bear. Those of us who have had the opportunity to develop ourselves are not desperate. We have work, and financial independence, and close friends. The monogamous relationship, the nuclear family, feel claustrophobic compared to many other possible kinds of family organization.

Women in their mid-thirties are at the cutting edge of some new redefinition of relationships and families. From women students come mixed reports about the younger generation of men. The present crisis in relationships between the sexes will begin to be resolved only when men decide it is in their interest to change, too. Nor is it our responsibility to educate men; they must take the initiative.

Again, my experience is typical of my generation. I had a long 'committed' relationship after my marriage. Since 1981 I have been living alone. It is hard to give myself permission to live independently (for are we not supposed to be nurturing females?) even though I need this solitude now for my writing. My present struggle is related to this giving-myself-permission to have my own space and time and quiet so that I can do my work. I regard this as part of the process of my life, which is made easier because I know there are many other women who have similar struggles.

All of this is, then, part of a great movement for social change. Women's studies grew out of the women's movement and remains responsible to it. The women's community keeps women's studies honest and dynamic; academic women's studies, in turn, has much to give the community. I think it is important that there are degrees in women's studies and that, through our large lecture courses, many students are exposed to the ideas of the movement. Yet we must be constantly vigilant, renewing our ties to each other, since it is easy for academicians to become isolated and for community activists to feel hostile towards the work of intellectuals. It is precisely this kind of interaction which makes our lives feel so *integrated*. No more split between public and private, between 'life' and 'work'. It is not the perfect harmony and peace we envisioned as we grew up in the suburbs of the midwest but something more subtle, more complicated, more tumultuous. And much harder than we had ever imagined.

Joanna Bogle

Joanna Bogle is English, but currently travelling because of her husband's job. She has no children, is twenty-nine, and works as a journalist, which she has done since leaving school. She is a Roman Catholic, does church work and writes for the Church newspaper. Formerly a local borough councillor in Wallington, she is active in a number of pressure groups and is often involved in campaigns to save old buildings from demolition. She is active also in the Society for the Protection of Unborn Children. Joanna contributes to major British newspapers on women's topics and is a regular writer for the Daily Mail *and the* Daily Telegraph. *A pamphlet called 'The Positive Women' was published in 1976.*

The youth rebellion of the 1960s caught my parents unawares. For my generation denim jeans, guitars, smoking 'pot' and denouncing everything one's parents loved and honoured became not so much signs of rebellion as positive social duties. Being a teenager in the Britain of the 1960s meant being pummelled by a series of slogans. At best, these were a dreary collection of clichés: 'Peace', 'Equality', 'Social Justice', vague creeds of internationalism. At worst, they were more vicious: the spitting and screaming at pop concerts, the brutal squashing of another person's point of view by preventing him from speaking, the systematic denouncing of the values of home and family.

As the decade receded, I discovered that alternatives were still waiting for me: a forgotten inheritance of beautiful and lasting truths, a Christian faith needing to be explored and honoured, an intellectual freedom to discuss radical ideas, an England wanting my love and service. Meanwhile, however, the slogans of the 1960s had become the government doctrine of the 1970s, enthroned by means of legislation, and nowhere more noticeably than *via* the women's movement.

Why do I feel so extraordinarily antagonistic towards 'women's libbers'? I have been told that I should acknowledge their contribution as the people who won for me the right to pursue a career in journalism. But I cannot accept their version of events which sees them as victor in battles that I am not sure were ever really fought in the way that they describe or won by the means they boast about. I frankly see them as a peculiar and rather frightening mixture of government bureaucrats and irritable, angry middle-aged ladies, who are gleefully spoiling and demoralising my generation, and who have very nearly taken from us the joy and fulfilment of womanhood.

My generation feels it has been exploited. We have been told to sneer at our country's history, at our cultural inheritance, at our homes and families, at our hopes and dreams and sentimental feelings. We have been taught that certain facts – historical, biological, economic – are not to be discussed except within tight guidelines. When the fruits of this curious paranoia are seen to be confusion and misery we are told that it is simply because we have not applied the guidelines with sufficient ruthlessness. 'Women's liberation' to me is not something new or refreshing or exciting. It is a government department – the Equal Opportunities Commission (EOC) – reaching out its interfering tentacles into daily life.

The Commission was established by the Sex Discrimination Act of 1975 basically to: (a) work towards the elimination of discrimination, (b) to promote the equality of opportunity between men and women generally and (c) to keep under review the working of this Act and the Equal Pay Act 1970.

Note that first section – 'the elimination of discrimination'. It gives the power-hungry everything they seek, because it is a term so wide that it can include practically anything. It has given us the playground snooper. One official report published by the EOC recommended members of staff in each school be appointed to keep an eye on 'sex-stereotypical play activity' (i.e. girls with dolls and boys with train sets).

'Ending Sex Stereotyping in Schools' is the splendid jargon-laden title of one of the latest publications sponsored by the Commission, and its sub-title is even better: 'A source-book for school-based teacher workshops'. Book purging is regarded as vital: phrases to be eliminated include 'when man invented the wheel' and 'the farmer and his wife'. Both, it explains, are inherently 'sexist'. It has to be, for instance, 'a farm couple'. The notion of normal married love is not to be propagated – teachers, we are told, must check that 'multiple-parent families (divorced, remarried) are portrayed, and the portrayal does not suggest that such family conditions are automatically damaging to the children'. Nor must little ones be allowed to discover for themselves the joys of our nation's heritage of books and plays, paintings and portrayals of men and women down the centuries, because certain books are strictly unacceptable due to their 'sexist' assumptions and use of language.

History must be carefully vetted lest women emerge as too feminine. Another EOC document, 'Does your school provide Equal Educational Opportunities?', urges that where necessary history should be invented, e.g. female pirates and Red Indian chiefs, in order to achieve what the Commissioners regard as the right balance! There is a 'checklist for analysing children's literature' with ten questions to be answered by a teacher carefully scanning the books which might be read by the children under her control: 'Are girls and boys, men and women, consistently represented in equal balance?' 'Is inclusionary language used?' For example 'police officer' instead of 'policeman'. A student indulging in 'sexist' litera-ture must face 'counselling', a word which in today's sad England is fast acquiring nasty connotations of re-programming and mental corrective sessions.

The EOC in no way represents Britain's females: we didn't clamour for it, weren't consulted about it, aren't allowed to elect its members, have no control over its activities, and judging from the letter columns in the newspapers, are increasingly beginning to call for its abolition.

We *know* that it contributes nothing to women's freedom and dignity to have teachers going through school text-books pencilling out masculine pronouns or words such as 'man-power'. We know it is silly and embarrassing to have children taught that men and women are, except for a few trifling differences of shape, the same and interchangeable.

So why are we having this thoroughly obnoxious and senseless propaganda pushed on us all the time? Perhaps the clue lies in that hardcore group of 'women's libbers' who form the nucleus of the movement. I have met some of them, debated on radio and television with them, heard their stories, tried to understand the emotional messes into which they have got themselves. They are a series of sad women, who merit our warm sympathy, whose lot in life has not been a happy one and who, needing help and inspiration, receive instead the adulation and attention of the modern media.

These women are the campaigners for 'abortion on demand' who themselves have had abortions and now take out their unhappiness and guilt on others; the anti-marriage faction who loathe their own husbands and seek to make the rest of us despise ours; the bogus lesbians who seek in each other's arms the love and friendship they should have received from their own families but for one sad reason or another were denied.

I have experienced bitter conflicts with members of the women's liberation movement. I can see why people get annoyed with me: they argue that I have no knowledge of just how horrible men can be, that I have never endured discrimination, harassment, or insults because of my sex, and belong to a privileged generation. I freely admit that in many ways I have been fortunate. I come from a happy and secure family and the men in my life could never be regarded as ogres: my father, affectionate, dedicated, cheerful and loyal, and my brother from childhood to the present day one of my closest companions. When I married, it was to a man of humour and steadfastness with whom the prospect of sharing the rest of my life was at once reassuring and exciting. My father and brother taught me to expect to find men of decency and I have done so. As a result, I find the women's liberation clichés about male chauvinism slightly absurd. Of course, from time to time I have felt unjustly treated by men. But I have endured equal suffering at the hands of women.

The slogans of the women's liberationists remind me of the recruiting rhetoric during the First World War. The women's lib holocaust has been of minds and marriages rather than of lives – excepting those unborn babies aborted out of existence – but its tragedy will leave a similar gap in the life of our nation. As the social tragedies multiply, the arguments of the women's liberationists sound increasingly tired and the propaganda unconvincing. On abortion, for instance, we have been told endlessly that destruction of a baby in the womb is 'a woman's right', that most women want this right and that if only government funds will pay for such destruction a true sense of liberation and fulfilment among women will be apparent. But what has happened? We have seen the abortion figures rise with sickening regularity every year. We know a baby is not just part of a woman's body: we are perfectly well aware of what lovemaking involves and know just how crucial is the role of the father in the creation of a new child.

When a baby is sucked out of the womb by a suction pump, or cut out carefully piece by piece, it is a nurse's task to lay out all the pieces carefully, in order that no part is left inside to fester and cause illness. When the abortion is over the patient is sent away – in the new 'day care units' she doesn't even get an overnight stay to sleep off the effects of the operation. She takes a bus or taxi home again and she's expected to take up her place promptly in this sexless, gender-free society which has found no place for her little 'unwanted' baby which she has happened to conceive at a time inconvenient for herself and others.

It is a lie to say abortion doesn't harm women, when we know of septic abortion cases in the National Health hospitals, to say nothing of the suicide and nervous-breakdown tragedies that occur during the weeks and months of post-abortion misery. It is a lie to say most British women want abortion-on-demand when thousands of them have thronged the streets of London, Manchester, Liverpool and Glasgow demanding that the law be tightened up and legal protection given to our unborn children. It is a lie to suggest that you can create a newer, happier society by scooping babies out of their mothers' wombs and burning them in hospital incinerators.

And what about divorce? The women's liberationists tell us that marriage is expendable. In fact, most of them don't even believe in it as an institution. Yet for women like me, the experience of committing myself to a life-partner, a man of love and care and integrity, has been the most heart-warming of life's experiences. We want none of the sexual immorality which has been rammed down our throats since adolescence. We are sickened by the slot-machines for contra-ceptives in our colleges and universities, the filthy 'advice' offered by columnists in teenage magazines who push sex at us all the time, telling us how to engage in 'oral sex'.

No, we don't want women's liberation. From a generation which has seen rocketing divorce rates, widespread venereal disease, and a sickening increase of crimes of violence includ-ing rape, comes a plea for a restoration of the dignity and femininity of womanhood. We long to be able to offer our own daughters a vision of hope: a view of womanhood which is exciting and life-enhancing, which takes pride in the unique privilege of motherhood, which recognises a woman's irreplace-able role in the upbringing of her children and which glories in the difference between masculine and feminine.

In the centuries of women's achievement, no woman has ever left a mark on history like the one who said: 'Behold the handmaid of the Lord – be it done unto me according to His Word.' Perhaps that image, of submission to Almighty God and joyful union with him in a sense of vocation, in courage-ously facing the future and all the challenges that lie ahead – perhaps this is what real liberation is all about.

Dale Spender

Dale Spender is an Australian and has been resident in the United Kingdom for the last eight years. She is unmarried, childfree, and has worked previously as a school teacher and university lecturer. At forty, she is 'well qualified in male terms' and her doctorate was published as Man Made Language *(London, Routledge & Kegan Paul, 1980). She is currently working as writer, researcher, editor and broadcaster. She is editor of* Women's Studies International Forum *and has published widely on feminist issues. Her most recent books is* Women of Ideas, and What Men Have Done to Them *(London, Routledge & Kegan Paul, 1982).*

During my adolescence I toyed with the idea of being a lawyer - perhaps through some desire to combine an acting career with security because my knowledge of the law was derived in the main from watching Perry Mason on television. But a law degree took a long time, you couldn't go to parties *and* study and of course, you wouldn't get married if you had such a demanding job. Teaching was a good job for a girl. You could always go back to it after you had the children, the school holidays were the same - and you would get married.

I got two scholarships to university - a teacher's college one which brought with it an allowance and a commonwealth one which did not. I took the teachers' college scholarship and the relative economic independence even though it carried with it a 'bond' - five years service or a fine.

I managed the parties, scraped through my degree and remember not one challenging moment in four years. It was not only that there was absolutely no substance to any course, but that ideas were positively discouraged and treated as distasteful if not harmful. I went teaching and after three years, I married. I was twenty-five and it seemed an assertion of independence, of adulthood. Later when I read of the lives of Olive Schreiner, Charlotte Perkins Gilman and Crystal Eastman who all fell ill in the months between deciding to get married and fulfilling the obligation, I felt an immense sense of relief; I had almost never been sick but I was very ill for almost six months in the year prior to my marriage.

My sister and I had a flat – we were a good pair. The only thing we ever fought about was who should empty the garbage because I never would. I could see the justice of her complaint but couldn't change. So I got married for my own kitchen and an end to the garbage debate (it was, after all, a man's job). I didn't like the kitchen and I missed the garbage discussions. I missed my sister as well.

I tried lampshade making, building a bigger, better house, doing another university degree (after my husband went to bed, because it wasn't fair to ignore him and spend time with my books when he was home watching television). I even began to take teaching seriously, partly through the example and assistance of a man I admired (who didn't use the cane in a school where that was sacrilege) and I became head of the English department.

But it was a strange existence. It was hectic, so hectic in fact that it protected me from having to reflect on anything. I ran a house (and even reached the stage where I would be ironing shirts at 4.00 a.m.), was active in numerous professional organisations, did a university degree (two, to be precise), and kept up a very close relationship with my mother and sister. Yet there were those 4.00 a.m. moments of despair. Of looking forward to busyness as the only possibility till the day I died.

Then a new job – lecturer in a university. New conflicts too. Couldn't 'pretend' any more that I was only working until I had a baby. An abortion when I did get pregnant (pill scare – suspected clot). One very threatened husband, not working, going back to university, economically dependent – a student in the place where I taught. Reversal of roles in some ways but not others. I still came home to tidy up the house and get the dinner; and when at weekends some people came and he was seen washing up – wasn't I lucky that he helped so much. Injustice, injustice, injustice! Only woman on an all male staff – someone to make the tea one of them said. But by now Germaine Greer (you saved my life), and Kate Millet, and Elaine Morgan, and Betty Friedan and the glimpse of something else.

Not that I took them on straight away; my resistance to these explanations was quite high. A friend tried to explain women's oppression to me. But I had never been oppressed or discriminated against in my life. I was just unhappy. Everyone (husband included) said that I just had a personality disorder.

I tried hard to make the image of model wife come true. Today when I hear those echoes I cannot respond with anger, only pain that we go through it, generation after generation of us, trying to adjust, to prove our worth in the terms men have decreed. We live our schizophrenic existence of playing to the pipes of men and knowing they lead only to our despair . . . but what else to do?

Was there any significant event that turned me towards feminism? The only one I can remember is the orgasm night! A buck's party – and all the men off celebrating and an almost pathetic rebellion among the women who decided not to stay home. The bravado that we would not be home first and put up with their drunkenness; the discussion about whether they would be drunk enough to demand sexual intercourse or too drunk to know. A feeling of shared relief if they were too drunk. The horrendous tales related of drunken obnoxious men (were we unrepresentative? I think not). The conversation shifting to orgasm and the brave woman who said that at least tonight she would not have to fake it. The stillness and the query; do you do that too? The dawning recognition as one after the other disclosed the frequency of the fake orgasm. The astonishment and the merriment as questions were asked about 'what do you do' and notes compared. The shared sense of relief, and mirth, and confusion – why? What was the explanation?

And then never again after that night was it mentioned –

embarrassment afterwards. We are caught into the orgasm, afraid to be unenthusiastic about sexual intercourse in our sex packaged and consumerised society. Sexuality, the way it has been defined and constructed in our society, holds no interest for me; it repels me.

After that night I became more confident and less guilty, but it was not one 'click' and the whole world changed. At the same time more reading of feminism; more involvement in women's groups. It was at this stage that I made the simple but momentous discovery that I *liked* women! I found I preferred their company! Gone were the days of feeling that an evening with women was a substitute.

Unfortunately, in terms of my marriage, it showed! At that stage I had difficulty explaining what was happening: in retrospect I can see that I was 'transferring my allegiance' and those who had known me for some time probably found this strange, and disturbing. I tried at first to 'disguise' my changed beliefs and behaviour. I remember coming home feeling good, laughing, rethinking whole areas of my life, and then quickly sobering up inside the front door. It was all right to go out with women and to come home complaining, to intimate that it was an evening wasted and you wished you had not gone: it was not all right to come home bubbling, joyous and excited.

It was a puzzle to me then that my new found joy and excitement should have been taken as evidence that I was a nasty person, a proper bitch. For years I had been on the brink of depression, had felt miserable and guilt ridden because I was *unable* to be happy and content with all the 'goodies' I had been allocated as a woman. Surely there were times when I had been poor company? Why then, when I was literally glowing at times with the assurance and satisfaction of my new found feminist explanations, when I was surely better company, was I met with such hostility?

Why was it that last month, when I was so unhappy, I was at least acceptable, neurotic but nice: yet this month, when I went springing round the place, animated, enthused and purposeful, I was still neurotic (of course) but nasty? One of the most deeply felt understandings of my life has been the recognition that when I was miserable, I was dependent: when I felt guilty, I apologised, was deferential. In my miserable state I had constantly been in need of counsel, constantly requiring reprimands, constantly without confidence – and that was nice – in a male dominated society! When I became confident, when I started blaming society and not myself, I was not nearly so manageable: and that was nasty! I know now the significance of the American slogan 'Uppity Women Unite'.

I just wanted some growing space. I just wanted to find out more about the *me* who had for so long been dormant and was now finding expression with my new friends. But my new friends were all 'women's libbers'.

Then there was London, and the women's movement – full time! It was in London that I became increasingly conscious that we know so little as women that is useful to us. Everything we learn, from home, the media, education, every way in which we become human in our society is permeated with negative notions about women. We are wrong, we are other, we are less than the norm.

In a more theoretical way I began to appreciate that while women are known as the deficient category, the deficiency lies not in the women, but in the ways of knowing. I saw that the great god 'research methodology' was made by men – and suited men! If the questions I wanted to ask were not admissible it was because men would not admit them. If the research I wanted to do was not appropriate it was because it was not comfortable for men.

I started to be amused by notions of male authority and objectivity and to see that it was little more than men's good opinion of themselves. One of the fundamentals that keeps patriarchy going is the faith of the whole society that men know more, and that what they know is better. I came to realise that the world looked very different when such faith was abandoned. I framed then, for all future reference, Virginia Woolf's words of wisdom – that for centuries women have been serving as looking glasses for men, reflecting them at twice their natural size. When we stop, when we become 'disloyal' (Adrienne Rich's word), and reflect them at the size they invariably warrant, when we see 'willy waggling' rather than phallic power, their capacity for living (which also means their capacity for aggression) diminishes accordingly. A mean and petulant antagonist is easier to deal with than a grand enemy.

While my marriage deteriorated around me I could not suppress my feelings of growing and glowing. It was a contradiction I had to try and resolve and a daily problem that wouldn't go away. It is not so straightforward as 'once I was blind but now I can see'. My confidence was regularly punctured by doubts, and my assurance undermined by fears. Living alone was a prospect that could quickly send me running for cover. I had never aspired to spinsterhood and I had been initiated into those beliefs that women alone were lonely, that women without children were embittered, that women without men were incomplete. These fears helped to circumscribe my behaviour and keep me in my place on the premises that the devil you know is better than the one you don't. I don't know how it ended: I can't decide whether it was sudden or slow. I do know there were moments of blind panic, when I asked myself was I making the greatest mistake of my life.

I think it is essential that we construct life-enhancing knowledge about women – and men – and I think it is important that we begin with ourselves, making the personal political, piecing together the fragments of what we know in the most meaningful, humane, rigorous way. We cannot afford to replicate the mistakes of men, making some people less than human, denying them a voice, labelling them as unstable or stupid when they do not flatter us to make us feel good. And we must be prepared to acknowledge that human beings can change.

We must seriously try to describe and explain the world we live in. Our problem is where to begin.

Should I turn to religion where so frequently women are held to blame, where their existence is penance, the injunction being to go forth and multiply in pain and sorrow as the price for not being among the powerful? Should I take evolution, and the survival of the fittest as my framework for explaining the human condition? Or Marxism and capitalism, two sides of the same economistic coin that glorifies male achievement and reduces human and life-enhancing values to the periphery, in the interest of technological conquest. Or perhaps Freud, who provides the twentieth century version of women's fall from grace, an amalgam of theological misogynistic prejudice given the gloss of scientific truth? Freud, who used women's experience of their lives as evidence of fantasy, who constructed a mythical complex out of women's accounts of incest.

History glories in men's wars, conquests and exploitations. Successful peace movements are non-events; confrontation is primary and co-operation absent; men are men and women are non-existent! There is no history, no heritage of what women have done to give life, preserve, manage, enhance, sustain, support, maintain, mend, patch, repair. Men's laws, men's literature, men's values: the bravery of the eve before the battle, the comradeship of those under threat, the glory of the victory – which means 'defeat' for the 'other': but no echoes of women on the eve before the birth, no mention of the sisterhood of many of those life and death struggles, no echoes of the joy of that particular success and magic when life begins, not ends.

When the only ways of knowing the world are pervaded with this value system, then I reject them all. When there is only a male dictatorship which decrees that males are dominant, I am a member of the resistance – the women's movement. When there is a male god, I am a heretic and I join those many, many women of earlier women's movements who have insisted that it is our responsibility to be outsiders when social systems are malevolent, that we must disobey unjust laws and be disloyal to tyrants.

We have not been reared with the knowledge that whenever there has been male power there has been female resistance and that for generation after generation women have tried to assert the feasibility of a human society in which procreation, nurturance, warmth, security and creativity are fostered. Today we are doing not something new, but something old, when we strive to promote consciousness of preservation. Ecology is the sister of feminism, the extension from the private to the public realm. It is where the profits of power and dominance are replaced by the profits of living, conserving, co-operating, where the values at the core of the women's liberation movement find their expression.

For me, the women's movement is only partly about equality, for I do not seek to be equal in a terrible system and I certainly think the legal equality of women can be accommodated without any great changes to the system. I want women to be equal in the sense that I want women's values, insights, experiences to be *equally* represented in the way we construct meanings and organise social systems. I don't want women to be in the position of providing an 'alternative' when men's plans go wrong. I want male values to be accountable, I want them scrutinised by a critical audience.

Why should we not be in a position to say to men 'Give us three good reasons for this war or recession that you want: give us three good reasons for being violent at home or abroad, for exploiting these resources or developing that particular weapon, for investing in pornography or keeping women poor.' And when there are no satisfactory reasons forthcoming why should we not be in the position of being able to say: 'we are not convinced; it will not be done.' *Our* resources are needed for patriarchy to continue: it might be that the only way we can achieve our equal representation is to withdraw our labour from patriarchy and make the presence of our power felt.

My entry to the women's movement has led to feelings of vulnerability, despair, and shock. That cannot be denied. For identifying with women, instead of men, means taking on, in part, the notion of one's powerlessness, victimisation, and lack of resources. In my own head, for example, I was much less exposed to the danger of rape when I believed that the women who were raped contributed to it in some way, for after all, there was no way *I* would provoke or initiate such an attack. Recognising now that *all* women are potentially rape victims, that most rapists are known to their victims, that the object of rape is dominance, I no longer have that (false) security that it won't happen to me. But to portray the women's movement as simply a means of coming to terms with many of the horrors of women's existence is to deny much of the joy.

My current involvement with women is considerable. The man I live with, I know well: my brother and father are friends more often than foes. But there are days, weeks, months when I am not in the company of men. I am prepared to engage in discussions with anyone, but not confrontations, and few are the men who ask genuine questions. They rule themselves out of my life, I do not rule them out. I have only one life and neither the time nor the will to *react* to a belligerent man who thrusts himself into my space and demands explanations, accountability from his subordinate. I laugh and leave. When his goal is to put me in my place I will not even respond in the terms he sets down, for that simply confirms the prejudices with which he began. It takes two to make a conqueror and a conquered: when men play conqueror, I withdraw my resources and leave them with emptiness. But I am mindful all the while that I am privileged: when the conqueror is one's husband or employer, the option to withdraw one's labour isn't always there on an individual basis.

As a white westerner I know that I use more than my share of the world's resources, that I am privileged, that there are millions who are starving or being brutalised. I know that I profit directly from racism, war, exploitation, and that I cannot abdicate from that responsibility. Everywhere I look within my society I see avarice and waste, profligacy and poverty, dehumanisation and destruction. I have seen conscription and Vietnam, nostalgia and the Falklands, no finances available for want, but unlimited amounts for war. I am part of that society. I cannot walk away: my life cannot be laundered.

I live in a society which practises a savage monetarist morality at home, builds arsenals, trades in destruction and styles itself 'defender of the free world'. There has to be resistance and I want to use my resources to challenge that system which reinforces and fosters such gross inequalities.

I don't think I have any tensions based on allegiances to different women's groups. I find no conflict between nationalities, sexual preference or colour. I am aware that I stand in relation to many black and third world women as men stand in relation to me and that there are differences which must be respected, explored and validated. They are not divisions or conflicts. We are all in the end subordinate to men; we share our oppression, our relative poverty (for according to the UN Statistics women own less than 1% of the world's resources), our availability, our biological capacity. We are all 'other'.

I am more likely to be tense with women who have gained power and influence by throwing in their lot with male values for rewards in male terms. It's not that I disapprove or feel self-righteous. I recognise that we must survive and for the majority of us this necessitates 'trading' with men who own and control resources. It's not that I am against women occupying positions of power and influence: there can be absolutely no doubt that one woman in a particular place can make a dramatic difference in terms of jobs, welfare payments, and protection. It is that I don't have any faith in joining the system: in changing from *within* as a means of changing society. And many women who are in influential positions want a confirmation that I feel unable to give. For many of them it is tough enough, anyway, just dealing with the way they see themselves reflected by men. They don't need my puritanism to contend with.

Men, men! This agonising among feminists about whether we are being fair to men. To me this is one issue which is simple and straightforward: it is their power, their dominance – and the resultant 'corruption' – that I object to, not their souls. I find their 'willy worship' tedious and their brutality incomprehensible, and I know they were not born that way and that they can change. But it isn't *my* responsibility to change them. To me, making women responsible for men's consciousness is just an extension of the scapegoat syndrome, an insidious advancement on making women responsible for male sexuality. If I'm told it's *men* I have to change I just see that as another patriarchal plot for robbing women of even more resources.

Obviously some men begin to understand the ramifications of male power in the same way as I begin to understand the ramifications of white dominance. They listen, they learn to 'follow' the maps of others rather than insisting on taking their route. But just as there are no prizes for whites who act reasonably, neither are there pats on the back for men who choose *not* to use all the resources at their command against women.

These men would agree that it is difficult to abdicate from control, from being in charge of meanings, to have to validate experience which is not their own. I don't think I have met any men who even begin to know what women are talking about unless they have lived with (and stayed with) feminists, and have allowed understandings about women's consciousness to become part of their fabric.

There is nothing to be gained by conflict with other women. Either it is quickly resolved, or one withdraws. For me that's a political decision. Every time women put energy into conflict with other women, patriarchy wins. When you explain what's happening in this way, it isn't difficult to withdraw. It takes patriarchal values to stay, fight *against* women, and win! The structure, the models, the values, they all coerce us to conflict situations. Politics dictate that some of us withdraw, take the conflict with us and let the others get on with important jobs – jobs that are hardly being done while we spend time and energy on resentment and recriminations.

I feel committed to a cause which is not only worthwhile, but essential. I have many good friends, work that sustains me, a mother and sister who are my very source. I know that there is much I do not know, but that prefaces everything and is for me a form of security. Life is a process of discovery and growth and I will spend all my years finding out.

Part three
Conclusion

We are women all
and we dance the celebration.
All that is strong and soft
beats in the frenzy
of the dance.
Unasked, almost unwanted,
it pulses out,
the heat and friction
of our lives.

Robyn Rowland (from 'Celebration', *Filigree in Blood*, Longman Cheshire, Melbourne 1982)

The preceding chapters have raised interesting and contradictory viewpoints. This conclusion will focus on three main areas: the issues which emerged as contentious; the experiences of the women and how these might explain their differences; and the similarities between them. For the purposes of the conclusion, contributors will be referred to as feminists or antifeminists according to whether they belong to pro-life/pro-family groups which are classified by the women's movement at present as antifeminist, or if they name themselves as antifeminist. But as indicated later, the dividing line is not always so distinct.

A wild patience has taken me this far.

    . . .

Anger and tenderness: my selves.
And now I can believe they breathe in me
as angels, not polarities.
Anger and tenderness: the spider's genius
to spin and weave in the same action
from her own body, anywhere –
even from a broken web.

Adrienne Rich, from 'Integrity'
(*A Wild Patience has taken me this far*, Norton, 1981)

1 Issues of contention

Surprisingly, the majority of writers call themselves 'feminists'. The conservative or antifeminist women see themselves as part of the movement for equal rights for women and see 'women's libbers' as the 'extremists'. A number of the feminists, however, regret the passing of the term 'Women's Liberation Movement' which denoted a more activist and socialist-based movement, and the emergence of 'feminism', which is often interpreted, as Barbara Ehrenreich (1981) comments, as 'lifestyle' feminism. Antifeminists argue that sex differences are innately biologically determined, and feminists that they are caused primarily by social conditioning. Francis argues that women *must* be different by virtue of their childbearing capacity. But Carnahan quotes the changes women and men have already made in their lives as evidence for the conditioning argument. Mitchell's view, however, is that at birth we enter the socially constructed categories of 'man' and 'woman', with biology as the reference point and implemented by conditioning.

The issue is important because it determines the position taken on the concept of equality by the two groups. Antifeminists stress that they want equality, and some, that it already exists politically and judicially. They want to be equal but *different*, and see feminists as wanting to be equal but the *same* as men, even to the point of 'denying their own wombs'. They do not consider the feminist argument that in Western society when a group is 'different', it is ascribed a 'less than' or outgroup status: women become 'different' and 'less important' than men. Their viewpoint leads the antifeminists scornfully to reject the implementation of similar education for girls and boys and of non-sexist language, which is ridiculed without reference to the concepts behind its use: a belief in the power of language to construct social experience.

Francis discusses the three stages of the women's movement as: emancipation; liberation (equal pay and opportunity); and recognition for 'uniquely female roles'. Feminists would disagree with the word 'uniquely' here because it excludes men from childrearing; while Curthoys sees 'role-sharing' as the only way to give women equality in the family. It leads Zillah Eisenstein (1981) to argue that antifeminists in fact want 'preferential treatment' for being women.

The concept of oppression is also contentious. Antifeminists see it as irrelevant and non-existent. Bogle lists the decent men she has known and says: 'As a result, I find the women's liberationist clichés about male chauvinism slightly absurd.' Cotter too writes: 'This widely circulated view of women as an oppressed class...simply wasn't true, certainly not for the women I knew.' Francis also contends that the only discrimination she has experienced is in her role as mother – and then from 'women's libbers'. It is clear that the antifeminists have no strong sense of being part of an oppressed social group, 'woman', which Mitchell discusses as part of a feminist consciousness.

The antifeminists see their success as due to individual merit. Landolt says she became a lawyer 'prior to the recent feminist wave which "legitimized" women in the legal profession', and Bogle refuses to accept that the women's movement helped her break into journalism. The assumption here is that if a woman is unhappy or has failed to 'make it' there is something wrong with her and not with society. The feminist consciousness perceives women *as a group* discriminated against by men *as a group*. They have either experienced that oppression or understood others' experience of it. This perspective has given the feminists a realisation of the need for co-operative group action for change. But it also threatens the *status quo*. As Spender (D.) comments: 'When I started blaming society and not myself, I was not nearly so manageable.'

Within this antifeminist belief of individual solutions, lies the concept of 'choice'. They believe that women should have the choice between a job or motherhood. If they do, antifeminists claim that most will choose the latter. Feminists contend that 'choice' is not a reality for most women because of discriminatory social structures, and Mitchell points out that it is class-limited, available only to the privileged, and even then difficult to exercise. Carnahan notes that people are currently coerced to fit a 'norm' which may not suit them and what they need is real choice, 'to live their lives in a non-alienating way'. Friedan in *The Second Stage* also comments on 'choice':

> What worries me today is 'choices' women have supposedly won, which are not real. How can a woman freely 'choose' to have a child when her paycheck is needed for the rent or mortgage, when her job isn't geared to taking care of a child, when there is no national policy for parental leave, and no assurance that her job will be waiting for her if she takes time off to have a child. (1981, p. 23)

Relationships with men form an area of misunderstanding and confusion for women. Antifeminists argue that feminists hate men and marriage (Francis). Most of them have had positive experiences with fathers and husbands, who are often described as 'wonderful' and 'loving'. Fesl's husband for example is supportive and she sees women's liberation as intolerant of men. They appear not to have experienced brutal husbands or those who tried to stop them from exercising any of the 'choices' they make about their lives. Francis writes: 'I like men and find them more intellectually stimulating than women.' However, there is a tendency also to see men as less moral and worthy. Cotter describes men as 'slightly inferior' and Purdue says that they 'use' women. At the same time Purdue fears the removal of the protector role from men, and the 'risks to the group, in particular the female, from the isolated non-responsible male'. This emerges in a number of antifeminist chapters: men need the moral guidance of women and family, otherwise they are a threat. Thus, women who represent a threat to the family put other women at risk. There are therefore two groups of men:

decent, loving husbands and fathers, and those unmarried, childless and irresponsible men. There is no mention of the married, but cruel and unloving husband. The antifeminist black women, Fesl and Sykes, however, clearly understand the violence of white men, if not black.

When the antifeminist talks of feminists as 'sad' women with unhappy lives, she does so in a tone which implies that it is the *woman's* fault — that she chose badly or worked the marriage wrongly. It also invalidates the experience of many women — that it is *men's* behaviour, unfairness and social-isation that is the problem. Antifeminists leave the impression that their loving and wonderful husbands are somehow a reflection of *their* greater worth as women.

For feminists too men are a 'problem'. Curthoys criticises the anti-male, anti-child aspects which have emerged as representative of the women's movement. Most of the femin-ists express their desire to have relationships with men but not at the cost of their selfhood and only on an equal basis, which many men deny them. As Spender (L.) writes: 'Most men will choose to make use of a system that extends privi-leges to them at women's expense.' Bowles and Spender (D.) talk about the fear and panic experienced in breaking their marriage relationship and the difficulty of exercising this choice. It is frightening to try and build equality into a marriage that often began with different and unequal ground rules. Eichler writes: 'As the confinement of the old structure has crumbled, so also has its security and predictability.'

Curthoys asks why the anti-male attitude did grow, and why it developed into an anti-male-with-children stand for some. French, Kinder and Scutt supply in part an answer to this. Kinder's experience of entrapment under her father's unwanted attention gives an insight into the real difficulties of life with incestuous men. Scutt's experience of the rape laws raises again the issue of men's violence against women, and is reinforced by French's moving account of women in pre- and post-war Germany. All three chapters illuminate the reality of women as victims, and bring the cruel side of men's power into focus.

Scutt comments that far from being 'man-haters', the problem for the women's liberation movement is that we care about men too much.' This makes women incapable of being brutal enough to withdraw their support in order to exercise some power. Basically, women want to be able to live and work with men, but are appalled by their cruelty. Spender (D.) exclaims — 'Men, men! This agonising among feminists about whether we are being fair to men', — and sees their dominance and violence as objectionable, 'not their souls'.

Men's attitudes to sexuality also offend antifeminists and feminists alike. Riches sees the Pill and the sexual revolution as leading to more problems for women than they previously had and many feminists would agree. However, Riches sees feminists as colluding with that revolution. Both Purdue and Spender (D.) however, advocate celibacy as a potential life-style and Spender comments that sexuality as our society defines it 'repels me'.

There is general agreement among feminists that men need to change and that women are stuck with relating to them as 'our lovers, husbands and friends, as well as our employers and employees. They are the fathers of our children, as well as, sometimes, our gaolers' (Stott). But, comments Spender (D.), 'it isn't *my* responsibility to change them. Just as there are no prizes for whites who act reasonably, neither are there pats on the back for men who choose *not* to use all the resources at their command against women.' And herein lies the answer for feminists. The men who are acceptable as lovers, friends and colleagues, are those who understand (or try to) the feminist perspective, accept that they are part of the group which has an unfair share of power, and live in a way which does not exploit that potentially greater power over women. Marriage, then, is created by 'two independent people who choose to share a mutual dependency, but not a relationship that is so dependent that either one becomes exploited by the other' (Carnahan). French's two visions of manhood — the destructive machismo, and the sharing and life-affirming man — represent the contradictions women have to live with and the real risks they face in trusting men. As the antifeminist Francis comments with respect to her husband: 'if all men were like him there would be no women's liberationists.'

With respect to relationships with other women, some antifeminists stressed that they had always had close women friends whom they valued; others had not. Their antagonism to 'women's libbers', however, is virulent. They see them as a threat to home and family and to their identity as women and mothers. Ironically, Francis comments: 'I have found that it *is* women, not men, who are our political rivals. ... If it were not for these '"other women" and their male followers, the media and political parties would be supportive of WWWW philosophy.' In comparison, feminists all write of the 'joy' and really fulfilling experience of that first occasion when they 'made the simple but momentous discovery that I *liked* women' (Spender, D.). As Mitchell points out, most women spend their lives 'in relation to men', but the women's movement changed that by giving women back their friendships. Kinder's chapter is an example of the caring and loving concern of one woman for all women.

In terms of power conflicts between women, Bowles feels that 'we have not yet learned to work together', whereas men learn this when young by playing team games. Bardwick (1979), in her book on transition, discusses the difficulty for women of learning to trust each other after being reared to see other women as competitors for men. For many feminists, however, the new woman-identification means less conflict, and Kinder's experience is that women actually work better together because they are trained to think of others.

A major conflict between feminists and antifeminists arises over motherhood, children, the family and work. Antifeminists argue that motherhood is a high status job but feminists have devalued it and denigrated homemakers because they are not paid. They see feminists as forcing women into the job market, and Cotter says that they ignore the fact that most of the jobs women do are menial and lowly paid. Feminists, however, argue that it is society which has devalued motherhood. Mitchell says it is incorrect to say women are being forced into the workforce, as they have *always* worked, e.g. in mines and factories. The exceptions, she says, are those women in a small privileged section of the middle class who want to hang on to their privilege. Feminists also argue that in terms of economic reality, most women need to work.

Substantial numbers of families in the US, especially in the lower income levels, rely on the woman's pay for 40 per cent of their total income.[1] Betty Friedan cites evidence that 45 per cent of the mothers of children under six who work do so now because of economic necessity, compared with 10 per cent in 1960.[2] The Ford Foundation estimates that in 1990, only one out of four mothers will be at home full time. Inflation is a major problem. In Australia in 1980, over three fifths of the total labour force were married women, working for both social and economic reasons.[3] But alongside the increase of mothers in the workforce, there has been *no* comparable increase in government aid to those mothers in terms of parental leave to care for sick children or high quality freely available child-care. Feminists argue that society thus puts value on women as workers but not as mothers.

Francis and 'Women Who Want to be Women' strongly argue for payment for homemakers and contend that feminists do not support them. However, the feminists Anna Coote and Beatrix Campbell discuss as one example, the Child Benefit in Britain, which the women's movement lobbied for and which 'represented a tax-free, non means-tested, cash benefit paid directly to the mother' (1982, p. 97). Moreover, feminists recognise the work involved in homemaking. Higgins comments that homemakers work 100 hours a week and there is also the 'emotional "work" involved in catering to the sexual and emotional needs of the man, mediating relationships between children and the father...' (1973, p. 5). Part of the reason why support has often been nebulous is that antifeminists differ on the issue. Landolt and Francis for example strongly argue for it, while Riches sees it as degrading to be paid for services 'given in love'. The salary would come from taxpayers' money, which many antifeminists like Bogle and Francis object to being used for equal opportunity activities and non-sexist textbooks. Working women may object, however, to their taxes being paid to women who stay at home. Income splitting and increased family allowances have also appeared in the debate, but the issues have not been discussed clearly or openly enough by feminists and antifeminists in order to clarify their positions.

A second aspect in the family debate is that 'women's lib places no value on children' (Francis), and therefore on motherhood. Antifeminists quote previous tracts of the women's movement to support this viewpoint, which often did reject motherhood. Some still do. It was/is motivated by the negative value ascribed to the role, which antifeminists see as coming from feminists and feminists see as created by society. Feminists like Sue Higgins have argued that motherhood is *'experienced* as inferior by women' (1973, p. 7, her stress).

Friedan has stated that 'our failure was our blind spot about the family' (1981, p. 203) and feels that the women's movement went through an extreme reaction against motherhood and family. To an extent Curthoys would agree, stating that although it has its drawbacks, the family can also fulfil the real needs of people for 'security, commitment and continuity'. Her answer to the difficulties of family life lies in role-sharing. She, like Friedan, also attacks the Right for its limited definition of 'family', which will 'destroy the new equality which gives the family the strength to resist dehumanizing forces which are emerging' (Friedan, 1981, p. 40).

Mitchell too discusses the joys and difficulties of parenting, but she argues that the women's movement has always fought to 'improve the conditions of motherhood'. She sees the idyllic concept of motherhood which the antifeminists present as false and class-based. The Right, she says, rarely fight for the black poor woman to have *her* motherhood highly respected: 'Motherhood is always highly regarded in our society in theory, but the conditions in which most women have to realise the ideal are often atrocious.'

Barbara Wishart, an Australian lesbian mother, has recently talked about her child conceived through artificial insemination by donor. She comments that many women face a conflict over the feeling that motherhood *'is* negative, *is* oppressive, and *does* confine most women', and yet there is still 'something *positive* or *worthwhile* or even *wonderful* about being a mother' (1982, p. 27). She draws a distinction between the institution of motherhood and the potential each woman has for creating her own definition of the experience. However, the issue clearly remains a difficult one for feminists, many of whom want to have children, but not within the tight and limiting confines represented by the antifeminists.

Antifeminists present motherhood in idealised terms of loving husband and sufficient income. Francis, Cotter, Landolt and Holt have large families. They disagree with child-care, indicating that mothers should instead be paid to care for their children. Landolt comments: 'It seemed to me that anyone could be a lawyer but I was the only one who could be the mother of my children.' The stressing of the importance of this job and their unique ability to do it, indicates a need to show they are indispensable, to ensure as it were, job security and their power base within the family.

Perhaps the most divisive issue which does emerge is focused on abortion. Antifeminists are strongly anti-abortion, and do not comment on whether this includes rape and incest cases; Francis comments that adoption is the answer to unwanted pregnancy; however this ignores the feelings of the mother. And this is the crux of this issue. Their orientation in the abortion debate differs because feminist concern is mainly for the woman, and antifeminists are concerned for the 'unborn child'. It is noteworthy that all the antifeminists mentioned the issue, but few of the feminists did, and it may be that the women's movement is underestimating the importance of the abortion debate. Landolt points out that it split the movement in Canada, alienating many women like her, and Purdue comments that: 'This is the dividing line.' She argues that men are to blame, because they pressure women to have abortions. Landolt also sees women as conned on the issue by men: 'I believe that the feminists have fallen into a male trap. They are attempting to adapt women to a wombless male society, instead of adapting society to meet the needs of women.' The feminist Barbara Ehrenreich has also seen the issue as double-edged, because freer abortion rights may in fact be 'further undercutting male responsibility towards women and children' (1981, p. 99).

Many feminists would agree that society is male-dominated, but would add that 'the needs of women' include control of their reproductive capacity. Feminists are thus pro-choice, not pro-abortion. There is then no conflict with Francis when she says that Third World women are against enforced sterilisation and abortion. Of course they are – *choice* is the issue. But it needs to be debated further, particularly when

Sykes's comments are considered. In Australia, a liberalising of the laws represented a new freedom for white women, but a greater risk of forced sterilisation and abortion for black women. Sykes stresses the lack of understanding, or an unwillingness to understand this perspective, on the part of white women.

It is noteworthy that although a number of feminists mentioned race and class as relevant issues, antifeminists did not. Rather they stressed religion. The two Aboriginal women clarified their objections to the white women's movement: that basically it is racist. Both Sykes and Fesl note that the movement does not address the problems of black women and Sykes's example of the abortion issue exemplifies this. Fesl writes that as an 'oppressive agent of women in our society, sexism runs but second to Australian racism which we have imposed upon us not only by white men but by white women'.

Sykes and Fesl are concerned that feminism and an awareness of sexist issues might split the black community, endangering its survival: 'there is no room for a sexist division in our society' (Fesl). Contrary to this, however, Te Awekotuku writes: 'I believe sexism to be the primary offence against humanity' giving in support the example of men's brutality to all women.

The complexity of cultural difference is clear in Fesl's discussion of arranged marriages. This is a difficult issue and would create conflict for even non-racist feminists, and for many black women whose voices might not be heard. Neither Fesl nor Sykes appear personally to have experienced an arranged marriage. Cultural differences between women can, however, only be resolved by respecting those differences and by listening to women speak of their own culture.

Curthoys, Seeger, Spender (D.) and Mitchell address the question of oppression caused by race and ethnic group. Spender (D.), with Te Awekotuku, sees sexism as the prime oppression and comments: 'I am aware that I stand in relation to many black and Third World women as men stand in relation to me', but 'we are all in the end subordinate to men.' However, Curthoys warns that 'the notion of "women's oppression" tends to obscure the reality of those cases of female privilege and male underprivilege arising from class or ethnic group'.

Mitchell accepts that for black women the current oppression is racism, but feels that it is dangerous to let that lead black women to the conclusion that 'sexual oppression isn't going on as well'. Te Awekotuku talks of the re-emergence of Maori culture in New Zealand in recent years and sounds an ominous warning when she comments: 'as the refurbished tradition develops, a potent and ironic misogyny appears.' Almost in echo of Spender's comments on men, Te Awekotuku says: 'racism is the responsibility of the racist — and *they*, not I, should work it out.'

The feminist contributors have also stressed the issue of class, and are concerned about what value the women's movement has had for working-class women. Seeger feels that they are mostly untouched by it. Curthoys says that they have gained some strength and support from it, but that they have been put off by the apparent rejection of motherhood. However, feminism has led many middle-class women to have contact with, and thus to understand, the realities of working-class women's lives.

The issues of race and class generally are not discussed by the antifeminists. They do, however, draw considerably on religion. Holt's contribution relies on biblical authority and Francis concludes with a quotation from a Pope. Many feminists reject orthodox religion as misogynistic, based on inequality, and see it as a method of controlling women's lives. Spender (D.) deplores a state of being, 'where existence is penance'.

Finally, Kramer's paper delineates strongly the experiences of young women in today's society. Friedan has recently written of her concern over the 'daughters', and their question: 'But you people who fought for those things had your families. You already had your men and children. What are we supposed to do?' (1981, p. 16) Kramer makes it clear that the difficulty for the new generation is that they are living in a different society to that from which many of the current leaders of the women's movement emerged. Young women need to clarify feminism for themselves and its relevance for them *now* — not what it meant in the 1960s. But the control of the direction of the women's movement is not in their hands.

In a recent article in the *Sydney Morning Herald*, titled 'In the 80s the Daughters of Germaine and de Beauvoir want a whole lot more', two young reporters wrote about being a young woman today.[4] Liz Doyle (24) writes: 'I don't consider myself a feminist although I agree with the movement's objective and cannot deny its influence on my life.' She then goes on, like Kramer, to indicate that she understands power structures and the way women are discriminated against in the workforce: 'their own needs are different (from men's) but not unresolvable or beyond compromise.'

Amanda Buckley (25) also recognises that 'earlier women cleared the way for equal pay, equality of opportunity, and for the right to be taken seriously as workers'. But she too, with Kramer, feels that older feminists look down on their younger sisters because they did not come 'up the ranks the hard way...they see us as "soft" and despise the way we dress and the way we relate to men'. Her group, she says, came to feminism through intellectual means rather than through difficult marriages and discrimination in their jobs.

Kramer draws interesting distinctions in trying to define Feminists and feminists: 'I like what Feminists say about equal rights and our value as women and people; I often don't like the way they say it.' The issue of the clothes they wear draws comment from all three women, and they scorn the stand that 'feminine' clothes make women more physically vulnerable. They feel 'the worst days of sexism are over' and that independence has taken over from the need for security in their lives (Buckley).

Many feminists will shake their heads and sigh over the idealism of the young, but one message is clear. Not enough dialogue (which includes *listening* from *both* sides) is going on with younger women in the movement. Buckley sums up when she says: 'We can learn a great deal from older women, but they don't understand that our fights are not the same as theirs.'

2 Why the differences?

How is it that two women like Scutt and Landolt could have similar experiences in the legal system, yet be opposed? What indicators emerged to give some understanding of what makes women feminist or antifeminist?

One important issue is 'the personal is political' and its relevance. For feminists, a personal experience or set of experiences of injustice and discrimination often created an identification with the group 'women', which was seen to be oppressed. Carnahan, for example, had a marriage breakup which resulted in her staying in a women's refuge. The kindness and support received there, led her to want to give support to other women. Spender (L.) talks of the 'feeling of injustice at being expected to be a superwoman'. Treated like a 'housewife' after leaving work she came 'to have a concept of women as a group'. Her experience, in other words, matched with what the women's movement was saying.

Spender (D.) describes the awareness not as a 'click', but as a process, whereas others experienced the 'click' when experience matched theory, or like Stott 'just growed' into feminism.

Where they had not actually experienced discrimination, feminists had made the effort to find out what other women's experiences were like. Seeger realised that her life was not like that of most women. She writes: 'I was lacking gut experience and I had to arrive at my awareness of most women's problems through observing, thinking about and listening to other women. ... I discovered how other women lived. It was quite a shock!'

The antifeminists stress that they have never experienced discrimination as women. But there seems an unwillingness on their part to consider, and empathise with, the experiences of women other than those in their social group. They do not feel part of an oppressed social group. As Holt writes: 'I could not imagine any woman with my background having such goals', as the feminists. It is threatening and upsetting to many people to step outside their own world experience or social class, because often the 'just-world' hypothesis can no longer operate for them: the belief that the world is just and if you have a problem then it must be your fault.

Antifeminists often cite Friedan now as a feminist who recanted, misunderstanding her desire to grip the difficult and changing issues of feminism — though there are many points in her book which feminists will, rightly, rage over! However, antifeminists too have a problem with one of their leaders, Anita Bryant, the fundamentalist preacher, singer, anti-gay and anti-liberationist leader, now divorced from her husband. She says:

> The answers don't seem quite so simple now. . . . I guess
> I can better understand the gays' and the feminists'
> anger and frustration. . . . There are some valid reasons
> why militant feminists are doing what they're doing. . . .
> Having experienced a form of male chauvinism among
> Christians that was devastating, I can see how women
> are controlled in a very ungodly, un-Christ-like way. . .
> most men are insensitive to women's needs. We have
> been so conditioned and taught. (1980, p. 68)[1]

The change in Anita Bryant is not total. She did not, in this interview, support the ERA. It does, though, indicate the power of the *personal* experience of oppression. But for women who have been lucky, the personal as political may fall down. Women need to understand their own experience, but also to validate, understand and empathise with other women's experience which may be totally different to theirs. Without that, no concept of women as an oppressed group is possible.

There is a difference in the average level of education between feminists and antifeminists here, though no strong deductions can be made from this. However, it may be that education gives the individual a greater chance to learn about experiences which are different to their own. For example, those who have not studied in those much-denigrated women's studies courses, may not have met in their own experience issues like the genital mutilation of young girls, or the results of wife-battering, incest or rape, or the more subtle forms of discrimination, in, for example, language. The antifeminists are severe on non-sexist language. But they reject it by trivialising it, rather than debating the feminist stand that language is part of a power base for males and helps to construct our social reality.

A further difference between feminists and antifeminists may lie in the source of their sense of personal power and self-esteem. If a woman's power base lies in her role as mother in the family, she needs to defend that position from threat. If she has other sources of power, for example in work, her identity is different. It is not surprising then that self-esteem, self-identity, a sense of personal control and of being important and needed in her role, is necessary to *all* women and they will defend the source of those feelings. Ehrenreich has commented: 'It is almost as if the economic stresses of the seventies split women into two camps: those who went *out* to fight for some measure of economic security...and those who stayed at home to hold on to what they had' (1981, p. 99). The antifeminist leaders, however, do spend considerable time 'out' rather than at home.

Another differentiating aspect may be the political positions of the feminists and antifeminists. Toch says that people with doubts about the existing social system are more likely to be sensitive to social injustice and are ready for change. Many feminists came originally from socialism or labour politics and many antifeminists appear conservative or right-wing.

Feminists are also woman-identified, i.e. they have a primary feeling of 'things-in-common' with other women. Antifeminists have allegiances to their class or race. This may change, however, for those antifeminists who are beginning to experience networking and group power. Cotter understands that individuals are powerless, but 'as a group there was a lot we could do'. This new awareness will be a strength for antifeminists.

Finally, two experiences which seem to have had an impact on the contributors appear to be: their first meeting with a feminist group, and their experiences of men and marriage. Francis comments that she became a 'political activist' (antifeminist) due to her first experience at a women's conference where she was jeered at. She comments: 'liberationists only want women to be political activists if they have liberationist ideology.' Fesl too was turned off by her first contact with a women's liberation group, whom she felt to be intolerant.

Carnahan and Spender (L.) were two feminists who experienced that first meeting differently. For Carnahan it was a meeting of courteous, intelligent and friendly women. Spender's group led her to reassess her priorities in life and her sense of who she was.

Most of the antifeminists and feminists had supportive mothers, fathers, or both, and the antifeminists have loving husbands. Feminists have often experienced the other side of men, though: their brutality, unfairness or insensitivity, e.g. Mitchell and Curthoys from men of the New Left; Kinder in her father; French, during and after the war; Spender, Bowles, and Carnahan in their husbands, and Stott in her employers. These experiences with men encourage women to reassess what they have been led to believe their relationships with men will be, what they are in reality, and what they should be.

3 Similarities between feminists and antifeminists

The line between feminist and antifeminist is not always as clear as expected. Purdue, for example, though a pro-life proponent, has always worked hard for women in the workforce and values many of the platforms of the women's movement. She feels she is a feminist. Sykes and Fesl reject feminism, but they would not be grouped with the antifeminists because their fight is with racism and therefore potentially with *all* white women. The feminists themselves give differing viewpoints and Seeger classifies herself as a 'classical feminist' because she is not anti-male. Spender (D.) spends most of her time with women, yet Stott and Seeger do not believe in excluding males from gatherings. So although the women here have been roughly grouped together as feminists and antifeminists, in reality we cannot so easily dichotomise them. Some similarities, often surprising, have arisen between these two groups.

All of the women had supportive fathers, or strong or supportive mothers. To Purdue's mother 'rebellion came easy' and Cotter's grandmother reared thirteen children in the wilderness of early colonial Australia. They were often made to feel 'special' or were given the expectation that men and women were equal. Seeger comments, however, that there is a danger in this: 'self-confidence made me emotionally lazy and mentally lazy.' The risk is there that if we assume the world is fair to all, mental laziness will cut out the reality of others' experience. Stott, also aware of this, says that having both a supportive husband and supportive father might have led her 'to become one of those silly women who see no need for equal pay and equal opportunity legislation'.

These women are strong, with a sure sense of self, though at times it has been difficult developing it. They believe they can have some impact on the world. Carnahan comments that feminists have 'strength and vitality' gained from breaking away from exploitative situations, becoming 'even stronger as people'. Some antifeminists have raised large families, which is demanding work. They will not be dictated to. Landolt says: 'I could not see any reasons why I should submerge and hide my interests and abilities simply because of what others thought or society dictated.'

All the women are pro-family, pro-children and pro-women, but differ in their definitions, and ways of achieving the related ends. They all believe in choices for women but differ in the choices they think women will make. They all want the role and status of mother redefined and upgraded, and are concerned about the future of motherhood. All believe in equal pay and equal opportunity.

Finally, all agree that 'women's' values are superior and should be cultivated. They loathe the dominance of violent, aggressive male values, and stress the life-force of women; their strong, caring, conservationist elements. Spender (D.) writes: 'I want women to be equal in the sense that I want women's values, insights, experiences to be *equally* represented in the way we construct meanings and organise social systems.' The black women speak of the strength of women and their bonds in black culture, which white women are searching to regain. Te Awekotuku writes in warmth and energy that 'women are stronger, braver and more resourceful' than men.

4 Conclusion

One of the problems in improving relationships between feminists and antifeminists lies in the lack of contact between them and the stereotypes each holds of the other. Eichler discusses the unpleasantness of being stereotyped: 'people reacted to me according to their preconceived notions of what a feminist is, rather than according to what I said or did.'

Carnahan sees this happening between pro and anti forces and comments that conflict occurs 'more between groups who generalise about others they have little contact with'. They could achieve some joint goals if they 'joined forces in their areas of concurrence'. And lest this seem too idealistic, in 1979 when Barbara Deckard wrote the second edition of her book *The Women's Movement,* a coalition of feminist groups and traditional homemakers 'who have never previously been involved with and sometimes have opposed feminist concerns' were fighting to have the Displaced Homemakers legislation passed at the national level as it had been in three states of the US. It was under consideration in seventeen others. It ensured financial and emotional support for divorced or widowed women who after many married years might find themselves 'displaced'.

Jill Tweedie (1982), however, warns of the danger of women on the Right, who, she says, 'provide men with excuses to turn deaf ears' and 'bring up children in the old destructive pattern'.[1] They also make 'the task of men who understand what feminists are on about much more difficult by posing the unspoken question: "if I don't care, why

should you?" ' These problems, of course, cannot be overlooked by feminists. Neither can the use of fear and guilt
in the rhetoric of some antifeminists be wiped aside, for it
creates an insecurity and anxiety in some women and alien-
ates them from the movement on false pretences. Mitchell
comments that antifeminists are not part of the movement
because they are against change and aim to preserve the
status quo. And this is the basic difference between feminists
and antifeminists.

However, the women's movement needs also to continue
to provide what Eichler calls 'constructive' self-criticism.
Antifeminists talk of the inability of feminists to tolerate a
differing view, which may hold some truth. The time has
come when the women's movement can accommodate
change without becoming weak and it will have to, to accommodate the new experiences of young women. Spender (D.)
writes that 'we must be prepared to acknowledge that human
beings can change'. She also cautions that 'we cannot afford
to replicate the mistakes of men, making some people less
than human, denying them a voice, labelling them as unstable
or stupid when they do not flatter us to make us feel good'.

There can be a value in opposition to a social movement.
Carolyn Sherif notes that it can 'strengthen solidarity within
the movement, heightening members' feelings of identity and
determination' (1976, p. 383). Chasteen says it also helps to
determine the strategies, leadership and organisation of the
movement (1976, p. 156). Dialogue with the opposition,
then, can be a useful enterprise.

Both Mitchell and Kinder indirectly warn feminists about
the unnecessary need to defend feminism as the way to the
pinnacle of happiness. Kinder notes that 'there is no blueprint, no promise of perpetual joy and an end to struggle
and misery'. Mitchell also says of 'liberation', that 'nobody
guaranteed that it was going to make you feel happier...
"liberation" is simply a pre-condition for greater fulfillment'.

Women's liberation is often misrepresented. It could be
too that the movement has failed to get its message across
clearly enough. Dialogue is essential. Antifeminists may work
to undermine all the positive changes women have made. But
if they support antifeminist men, they may lose more than
they bargained for, and find, like Anita Bryant, that they

give men the ammunition they need to fire at *all* women —
including homemakers. They might find that the education
they so crave for their daughters is no longer available for
women, who are naturally mothers and need no further
education; that they might be refused jobs they want because
a lower qualified man wants one; or find their divorced
daughter is unable to obtain credit because we have gone
back to the good old days when men supported women —
except their daughter's husband turns out not to be 'decent'
and leaves her with three kids and no credit.

In 1982 a Supreme Court decision was made in the US
that 'military wives who have followed their husbands from
post to post, never able to accumulate their own seniority
or pension rights, are not entitled to any share of their
husband's pensions in the case of divorce' (Friedan, 1981,
p. 330). In the state of Tasmania, Australia, in 1982, an in-
coming conservative state government did away with
maternity leave in the public service, because they 'couldn't
afford it'. The Ford Foundation estimates that by 1990,
only one in every four mothers will be at home. Who guaran-
tees that an antifeminist's daughter will not be one of the
three, needing to work to support her family and needing
equal opportunity legislation to ensure her job?

It is surely preferable that, while ensuring the best deal
for women within the family, we ensure the best deal for
them in society as a whole — for who knows what choices
the daughters will want, and what want will send them in
their chosen direction. As Stott says, for her granddaughters
she wants 'the right to choose what their life shall be'.

Notes

1 Issues of contention
  1 M. Castells, *The Economic Crisis and American Society*, Oxford, Basil Blackwell, 1980.
  2 B. Friedan, *The Second Stage*, New York, Summit Books, 1981.
  3 K. Hargreaves, *Women at Work*, Ringwood, Australia, Penguin, 1982.
  4 Article in the *Sydney Morning Herald*, 'Good Weekend' section, 17 July 1982, pp. 29–30.

2 Why the differences?
  1 C. Jahr, 'Anita Bryant's startling reversal', *Ladies Home Journal*, 1980, 97 (12), pp. 62–8.

4 Conclusion
  1 J. Tweedie, 'Beating the Queen Bees', article in the *Guardian*, reprinted in *The Age*, Melbourne, Australia, 'Accent' pages, 27 August 1982.

Bibliography

Albury, R. (1982), 'Beyond the slogans in the struggle for fertility control', *Third Women and Labour Conference Papers*, 1, p. 227.

Andelin, H. (1975), *Fascinating Womanhood*, New York, Bantam.

Banks, O. (1981), *Faces of Feminism*, Oxford, Martin Robertson.

Bardwick, J. (1979), *In Transition. How Feminism, Sexual Liberation and the Search for Self-Fulfillment Have Altered America*, New York, Holt, Rinehart & Winston.

Castells, M. (1980), *The Economic crisis and American society*. Oxford, Basil Blackwell.

Chasteen, E. (1976), in R. Laver (ed.) *Social movements and social change*, South Illinois University Press.

Coote, A. and Campbell, B. (1982), *Sweet Freedom. The Struggle for Women's Liberation*, London, Picador.

Crawford, A. (1980), *Thunder on the Right. The 'New Right' and the Politics of Resentment*, New York, Pantheon.

Deckard, B. (1979), *The Women's Movement: Political, Socio-Economic and Psychological Issues*, 2nd edn, New York, Harper & Row.

Decter, M. (1973), *The New Chastity and Other Arguments Against Women's Liberation*, London, Wildwood House.

Ehrenreich, B. (1981), 'The Women's Movements. Feminist and anti-feminist', *Radical America*, 15, pp. 93-101.

Eisenstein, Z. (1981), *The Radical Future of Liberal Feminism*, New York, Longman.

Eisenstein, Z. (1982), 'The sexual politics of the New Right: understanding the "Crisis of Liberalism" for the 1980's', *Signs: A Journal of Women in Culture and Society*, 7 (3), pp. 567-88.

Firestone, S. (1972), *The Dialectic of Sex. A Case for Feminist Revolution*, London, Paladin.

Freeman, J. (1973), 'The Origins of the Women's Liberation Movement', *American Journal of Sociology*, (4), pp. 792-811.

Freeman, J. (ed.) (1979), *Women: A Feminist Perspective*, 2nd edn, Palo Alto, California, Mayfield.

239

Friedan, B. (1976), *It Changed My Life. Writings in the Women's Movement*, New York, Random House.

Friedan, B. (1981), *The Second Stage*, New York, Summit Books.

Gerlach, L. and Hine, V. (1970), *People, Power, Change: Movements of Social Transformation*, Indianapolis, Bobbs Merrill.

Gilder, G. (1973), *Sexual Suicide*, New York, Quadrangle Books.

Gordon, L. and Hunter, A. (1977–8), 'Sex, family and the New Right. Anti-feminism as a political force', *Radical America*, 2, pp. 9–26.

Hargreaves, K. (1982), *Women at Work*, Ringwood, Australia, Penguin.

Heberle, R. (1951), *Social Movements. An Introduction to Political Sociology*, New York, Appleton-Century-Crofts.

Higgins, S. (1973), 'Women in the Family: social science and the female role', *Refractory Girl*, 5–8, Winter, pp. 5–9.

Laver, R. (ed.) (1976), *Social Movements and Social Change*, Southern Illinois University Press.

Lindsay, B. (1979), 'Minority women in America: Black American, Native American, Chicana, and Asian American women', in E. Snyder (ed.), *The Study of Women: Enlarging Perspectives of Social Reality*, New York, Harper & Row.

Lipsett, S. and Raab, E. (1970), *The Politics of Unreason: Right-Wing Extremism in America, 1790–1970*, New York, Harper & Row.

Mitchell, J. (1966), 'Woman: The longest revolution', *New Left Review*, 40.

Morgan, M. (1974), *The Total Woman*, Old Tappan, New Jersey, Revell.

Morgan, R. (ed.) (1970), *Sisterhood is Powerful. An Anthology of Writings from the Women's Liberation Movement*, New York, Vintage Books.

Myrdal, A. and Klein, V. (1956), *Women's Two Roles*, London, Routledge & Kegan Paul.

Petchesky, R.P. (1981), 'Antiabortion, antifeminism, and the rise of the New Right', *Feminist Studies*, 7 (2), pp. 206–46.

Pieri, S., Risk, M. and Sgro, A. (1982), 'Italian migrant women, participation, and the women's movement', in M. Bevege, M. James and C. Shute (eds), *Worth Her Salt. Women at Work in Australia*, Sydney, Hale & Ironmonger, p. 389.

Prior, T. (1982), 'My forty-five years in industry', in *Worth Her Salt*, (as above), p. 123.

Rich, A. (1980), *On Lies, Secrets & Silence, Selected Prose. 1966–1978*, London, Virago.

Rich, A. (1980), *On Lies, Secrets & Silence, Selected Prose, 1966–1978*, Only Women Press.

Schlafly, P. (1977), *The Power of the Positive Woman*, New York, Arlington House Press.

Sherif, C.W. (1976), *Orientation in Social Psychology*, New York, Harper & Row.

Simms, M. (1978), 'Writing the history of Australian Women', *Labour History*, 34, pp. 93–101.

Simms, M. (1981), 'The Australian Feminist Experience', in N. Grieve and P. Grimshaw (eds), *Australian Women. Feminist Perspectives*,

Melbourne, Australia, Oxford University Press, 1981.

Simons, M. (1979), 'Racism and Feminism: A Schism in the Sister-hood', *Feminist Studies*, 5 (2), pp. 385–401.

Snyder, D. and Tilly, C. (1972), 'Hardship and collective violence in France, 1830–1950', *American Sociological Review*, 37, pp. 520–32.

Snyder, E. (ed.) (1979), *The Study of Women: Enlarging Perspectives of Social Reality*, New York, Harper & Row.

Spender, D. (1982), *Women of Ideas and What Men Have Done To Them*, London, Routledge & Kegan Paul.

Staines, G., Tavris, C. and Jayaratne, T.E. (1974), 'The Queen Bee Syndrome', *Psychology Today*, 7, pp. 55–60.

Stassinopoulos, A. (1973), *The Female Woman*, London, Davis-Poynter.

Terrelonge Stone, P. (1979), 'Feminist consciousness & Black Women', in J. Freeman (ed.), *Women: A Feminist Perspective*, 2nd edn, California, Mayfield.

Toch, H. (1966), *The Social Psychology of Social Movements*, London, Methuen.

Vilar, E. (1972), *The Manipulated Man*, New York, Farrar, Straus & Giroux.

Webley, I. (1981), 'The Feminine Politics: "Women Who Want To Be Women" ', *Women's News Service*, 19 March, pp. 1–3.

Wishart, B. (1982), 'Motherhood within patriarchy: A Radical Feminist Perspective', *Third Women and Labour Party Conference Papers*, vol. 1, pp. 23–31.

Index